the

Disintegration

of the

Constitution

the Disintegration of the Constitution

from an average American's perspective

LOUIS SROTE

Published in the United States of America

ISBN: 978-1-73109-701-9
1. Political Science / American Government / General
2. History / United States / General
13.07.22

Acknowledgments

I would like to thank you, the reader, for spending your hard earned money and taking time out of your busy schedule to learn more about the corruption and unbelievable waste that exists at the hands of our government. I am certain that you will find this book informative as well as enlightening. By the end you will have a better understanding of what our Founding Fathers envisioned for our government and why their ideas are just as important today as they were over 200 years ago. Their intent was to build a country with a solid foundation free from tyranny. This republic would be complete with solid principles, liberty for all, minimal government, and most importantly common sense, all of which are lacking in Washington today. It is these ideals, among others, that helped me achieve success in my life. But they did not come instinctually; they were instilled in me at a young age by my parents Jim and Sarah. They taught me that honesty, integrity, a strong work ethic, a solid character, and self-reliance are all traits that help build a well-rounded individual. For providing me with a wonderful base from which to grow I thank them both, and will be forever in their debt. Without their guidance and unconditional love I would have never turned into the upstanding citizen I am today. In fact my parents were responsible for raising two well-adjusted children. My brother Robert Srote, author of the book *Wildfire:*

The Legislation that Ignited the Great Recession, is the hardest working man I know. He is a certified architect with an MBA, published author, mayoral candidate, business owner, father of two wonderful children, Jordan and Zoey, and a loving husband to his beautiful wife Colleen. He is the epitome of what hard work, determination, and perseverance provide. Never one to settle for good enough he always strives for more, as is evident by his many accomplishments. It is his zest for life and ambitious attitude that served as the inspiration for my book, and for that I owe him my deepest gratitude. Finally I would like to thank my beautiful wife Teri. Without her encouragement and support I may have never finished this project. She stood by me through thick and thin and has been my constant companion. For always being there and believing in me I thank her from the bottom of my heart. She is the love of my life and I do not know what I would do without her. I am very fortunate to have these wonderful people surrounding me. Not a day goes by that I do not appreciate everything they do. No one could ask for better parents, a better brother, or a better wife. I am a lucky man indeed.

Table of Contents

Introduction

My career began humbly as a Graphic Artist over seventeen years ago. During my tenure with the same company I was promoted four times, up through the level of Director. But as the economy tumbled, and the industry in which I was employed struggled financially, I became yet another casualty of the Great Recession. Not one to focus on the negative I pulled myself up, dusted myself off, and began the daunting task of searching for a job in a downed economy. After months of pouring through tons of applications, and applying for an untold number of jobs, I was able to successfully procure employment. My career is a perfect example of what can be accomplished by employing one simple philosophy, "If you apply yourself you can achieve anything." I have experienced, firsthand, what perseverance, hard work, and determination provide. With a no excuses attitude and a strong belief in self-reliance, my values have helped mold me into the successful executive I am today. It is also these values that compelled me to write about our government's propensity for social engineering in the modern era. I explain how their enormous role in society is antithetical to the ideals on which this country was founded, proving that government handouts do nothing more than repress the spirit to prosper. Through my exhaustive research I uncover how those in Washington have wasted your money to the point of bankrupting the country. I use my ethical standards and principles to outline a common sense approach to weaning America off government's addictive policies and placing our nation back on the path to fiscal responsibility.

The Disintegration of the Constitution chronicles government expansion, from an average American's perspective, and explains how this growth correlates to the erosion of our Constitutional freedoms. The Founding Fathers' intentions for government are examined to better understand what it was they originally desired, allowing you to better comprehend the meaning behind the Constitution. You will see how the beginning of our nation came to fruition and will walk through a brief history of events as they occurred. Causes that led to the Revolutionary War and our separation from King George III are paralleled with the travesty that is taking place today regarding government oversight and control. Many topical issues are explored, such as the government bailouts and stimulus, taxes, health care reform, entitlements, media bias, gun control, and our trillion-dollar debt and deficit. All are examined in great detail, exposing corruption, collusion, deceit, wasteful spending, and fraud at all levels. You will learn how the government has grown beyond its means and become unsustainable, and if left unchecked will lead to the destruction of our economy as we know it. I explain what must be done to rein in government and get our country back on the right track, including drafting a clear and concise Amendment to the Constitution that details exactly how to contain government now and in the future.

A Brief History

Imagine what it would have been like to live in America in the late 1700s, a time of great turmoil and triumph for the original thirteen colonies. We went to war with Great Britain in 1775 to gain our independence, officially declared our separation from the monarchy in 1776 with the signing of the Declaration of Independence*, ratified the Articles of Confederation* in 1781 to create a new government, won the Revolutionary War and signed the Treaty of Paris in 1783, then spent the summer of 1787 generating the Constitution of the United States* to form a better, more complete government. I will cover these important events as succinctly as possible, providing you with a brief overview of each phase of our independence as it occurred. It is important to understand the historical context surrounding the formation of our country, its government, and the troubles facing the colonists as they separated from the monarchy. Knowing this will allow you to better appreciate the intent the Founding Fathers had for our nation as they drafted the Constitution, and how it applies just as much today as it did back then, over 224 years ago.

Freeing ourselves from the tyranny of the British government is one of the greatest underdog stories of all time, a veritable David and Goliath tale of determination and perseverance. The Revolutionary War exemplified

Full text located in Appendix.

the true meaning of the American spirit. Simply put, if you apply yourself you can achieve anything. Nowhere is that more prevalent than in this great country. Our Founding Fathers knew the potential of the human spirit and wanted a country free from the rule of a king so it could be fully realized. They wanted a government that was for the people, made up of the people, and most importantly, run by the people. Most colonists under British rule, including the Founding Fathers, believed they were entitled to the full democratic rights of Englishmen. While Britain believed the American colonies were not entitled to those rights and could be used and exploited in whatever fashion best suited the king. These conflicting views are what most historians believe made war inevitable between the two countries. However there are many factors that actually contributed to Americans' dissent and ultimate retaliation against the British. Let us explore these and see what it was that ultimately led us to war, and what became of the colonists in their quest for independence.

The French and Indian War[1] was a conflict that took place between two long-time rivals—the English and the French. England and the American colonies fought the French and Indians in North America for control of the Mississippi River, Ohio River Valley, and Canada. The French were expanding their territory and building forts further into British-claimed territory. This concerned Virginia's Governor Robert Dinwiddie because of the proximity of the forts to claims of land that were owned by Virginians. He saw this as a possible threat to Virginia's sovereignty and sent George Washington to deliver a message to the French, asking them to leave the area; he was also asked to assess the French's strength and their intentions.

Washington reached Fort Le Boeuf and delivered the governor's letter, which was quickly rebuked by the French. Washington returned to Virginia and informed the governor of the French's response. Governor Dinwiddie now understood the French's intent clearly and ordered the construction of Fort Prince George in an effort to quell their advance.

In the spring of 1754, as work was underway on the new fort, a large French force arrived and commanded the British to surrender the area. After the British retreated, the French demolished the fort and built Fort Duquesne. Fort Duquesne[II] was believed to be a strategic post for controlling the Ohio Country because of its location at the junction of the Allegheny and Monongahela rivers in what is now downtown

Pittsburgh, Pennsylvania. Prior to the French troops overtaking Fort Prince George, newly promoted Lieutenant Colonel Washington and his regiment departed Virginia to defend the fort while it was being built. During his travels he came upon a French scouting party and ordered his troops to fire, killing twelve and wounding twenty-two Frenchmen. After this skirmish, he ordered the building of Fort Necessity in a large clearing known as the Great Meadows. In early summer, the French counterattacked Washington and forced him to surrender his fort and allowed him and his men to return home unarmed.

At the beginning of the war, during the first couple of years, the British had a very difficult time with the French and lost many battles. However, their luck began to change in 1756 when Britain applied more resources to the battle, under the direction of Britain's new Secretary of State William Pitt. As they slowly began recapturing forts, momentum shifted in their favor and in 1759 they won the Battle of the Plains of Abraham. Winning this battle was a significant step toward superiority as it allowed them to occupy the city of Quebec. A year later they captured Montreal and completed the capture of Canada, effectively bringing the war in North America to a close. The war officially ended with the signing of the first Treaty of Paris on February 10, 1763, also known as the Treaty of 1763. The French relinquished all of their holdings in North America and regained control of the Islands of Guadeloupe and Martinique. The cost of the war was high and would have a resounding effect on the relationship between American colonists and the British.

By the end of the war there were 10,000 British troops stationed in North America, and Britain was in debt to the tune of £140 million (224 million dollars). [III] Great Britain felt the large number of troops was needed to defend the colonies against continuing attacks by the Indians. They tried to extinguish the violence by creating the Proclamation of 1763, which basically stated that the colonists could not encroach upon or purchase any Indian land out west. It even went as far as creating a boundary along the Appalachian Mountains.

The colonists did not like the fact that the government was interfering and limiting their potential to economic growth through westward expansion. Furthermore, they felt there was no real way to enforce this proclamation and limit their movement into the great frontier. This was one of the first major moves against the colonists that began the sour relationship with Britain. Another item that compounded that sentiment was the Revenue Act, [III] also referred to as the Sugar Act, passed in 1764. It actually lowered taxes on molasses but created strong methods of enforcement to ensure those taxes were being adhered to, something that did not exist prior to the implementation of this act.

The colonists believed the methods used to enforce the Sugar Act encroached on their fundamental rights. Britain also implemented new taxes on the importation of other items such as silk, wines, and potash. These new taxes and the methods of enforcement outraged the colonists. So much so that they used whatever means necessary to avoid both, often with colonial officials' involvement, including smuggling items into the country to avoid being taxed.

As discontent with Great Britain grew, the first acts of resistance and political dissent started to manifest. The best example of this was a speech by James Otis, which he read when he appeared in court to express the colonists' extreme dissatisfaction with the way customs officials were allowed to break into any building they felt housed smuggled goods regardless of proof. The written order that allowed British officials to do this was called writs of assistance, and was created to monitor and curtail smuggled goods by any means necessary. Otis asked that these writs be repealed because he believed they violated their rights. Otis lost his case, but it was now clear that the colonists were growing more and more displeased with Britain's rule by iron fist.

Rising tensions between the colonists and the British were enflamed more when Britain imposed the Quartering Act of 1765. [IV] This act forced the colonies to house British soldiers in American barracks and public houses when other accommodations could not be provided. If soldiers outnumbered the housing available, colonists would have to quarter them in inns, livery stables, ale houses, victualing houses, the houses of sellers of wine, and houses of persons selling of rum, brandy, strong water, cider or metheglin, and if numbers required in uninhabited houses, outhouses, barns, or other buildings.

The colonies were also required to pay the cost of housing and feeding of these troops. The primary reason this did not sit well with colonists was because they saw firsthand how the British forcibly quartered their soldiers in colonists' private dwellings during the French and Indian war and they were afraid this new act would allow them to do it again. They also believed Britain was imposing a law that made this behavior legal and forced the colonies to pay for it. The colonists were so opposed to this act that during the creation of the Bill of Rights the Framers specifically prohibited government from doing this in the Third Amendment to the Constitution.

Unfortunately for the colonists, the British were not receiving enough money from the Revenue Act to cover the expense of defending the colonies. As is big government's tendency when they cannot balance their budget, they resort to taxing citizens to cover their deficit, and in 1765 the British did just that with the passing of the Stamp Act. [v] This latest piece of legislation taxed all documents printed or used within the colonies. The colonial unrest against Britain grew even stronger because they felt they were being taxed unfairly without any representation. They considered this a direct violation of their rights according to the British Constitution and believed they should not be taxed without providing consent. Consent they felt could only come from their colonial legislatures, officials they elected but were not represented in British Parliament. This lack of representation ended up being a huge issue for the colonists and another major factor that led to the revolt against Britain. They were so outraged that petitions were taken and assemblies were held protesting the tax. Patrick Henry, one of the Founding Fathers and governor of Virginia (post British independence), introduced a resolution to Britain, which stated, in part:

> The general assembly of the colony, together with his majesty or his substitute have in their representative capacity the only exclusive right and power to levy taxes and impositions on the inhabitants of this colony and that every attempt to vest such a power in any person or persons whatsoever other than the general assembly aforesaid is illegal, unconstitutional, and unjust, and has a manifest tendency to destroy British, as well as American freedom. [v]

In New York City, the Stamp Act Congress held the first significant joint colonial response to the legislation petitioning the English Parliament and the king. Demonstrations and protests sometimes became violent and destructive as more and more colonists became involved. This had become the first widespread colonial resistance to an act passed by British Parliament.

The dissent of the colonists reached a tipping point and spread throughout the colonies like a contagious disease. Rioting and protests broke out against anyone enforcing the Stamp Act. Behind much of the chaos a group emerged known as the *Sons of Liberty*. [VI] They were made up mostly of middle-class workers, such as traders, lawyers, printers, and local politicians. They devoted themselves to defending the liberties of the colonies, but all the while they professed their loyalty to the king because they felt, in the end, Parliament would repeal the tax.

Their primary goal, however, was to ensure their rights regardless of their professed loyalties to the British crown. One of the first major acts of aggression took place on August 14, 1765 [VI] against Andrew Oliver, a distributor of stamps for Massachusetts. His effigy was burned as it hung from a tree on Newbury Street in Boston. The crowd that gathered was so large that the local authorities would not remove the display for fear of their lives. Later that evening, when Andrew refused to resign, the Sons of Liberty proceeded to burn down his office building. They then moved onto his house where they threw stones and beheaded the effigy.

The British Militia, Justices, and Sheriffs all kept a low profile during the incident. It was now clear who was in charge of Boston. Violence, however, was not their only means of persuasion. Many of their members were printers and publishers and used newsprint to disseminate their message throughout the colonies. Almost every newspaper carried daily reports on their activities, their intent being to embolden citizens by providing an account of their successes. Word of their dissent traveled fast and it was not long before the Sons of Liberty existed in every colony.

When the Stamp Act was finally enacted on November 1, 1765, most newspapers continued publishing without the required stamp. The Sons of Liberty's message had permeated the colonists so much so that most of the militia and the authorities had become members of the group. Because of the magnitude of their infiltration there was no way for Britain to enforce the Stamp Act. Any royal troops loyal to the crown were highly outnumbered. Due to the overwhelming opposition, the Stamp Act was eventually repealed on March 17, 1766. [VII]

As time passed, it appeared the Crown was absolutely hell-bent on treating the colonists as second-class citizens. They completely ignored the colonists' opposition to the Stamp Act and were oblivious to their thoughts regarding taxation. How else could one justify the implementation of yet another tax via the Townshend Acts in 1767?

Charles Townshend, Chancellor of the Exchequer, wanted to strengthen the British Parliament and convinced them to pass new taxes on lead, paint, glass, paper, and tea. He even suspended the New York legislature until they agreed to quarter soldiers. The colonists responded swiftly by boycotting all imported British goods, and within a year importation dropped by thirty-eight percent. [VIII] These acts were, later, partially repealed in March of 1770 because of growing opposition.

However, the damage had already been done and the colonists had finally had enough. Colonial protests grew and attacks on officials increased more frequently with each passing day. Soon it became clear that assistance from Britain would be needed to squash the uprising. Lord Hillsborough, secretary of state for the colonies, dispatched thousands of troops to Boston to help restore order. When they arrived they were stationed throughout the city, acting as a force for civility.

Daily contact between the troops and citizens served to worsen relations with Britain further. As unrest grew, small clashes and skirmishes with the troops escalated. On March 5, 1770, five colonists were killed by British redcoats in what became known as the Boston Massacre. Taunting from the crowd, specifically the hurling of snowballs, caused one of the British soldiers to be knocked to the ground. When he arose he yelled, "Damn you. Fire!" After an initial pause, the British soldiers opened fire on the crowd, killing rope maker Samuel Gray, Mariner James Caldwell, and Sailor Crispus Attucks. Two others would later die of their wounds— seventeen-year-old Samuel Maverick and Irish immigrant Patrick Carr.

A local artist, Henry Pelham, witnessed the event and created a drawing illustrating the fight between the colonists and British soldiers. Boston Engraver Paul Revere copied Pelham's illustration and distributed it throughout the colonies. As this illustration circulated, resentment with the British grew to a fever pitch.

The British military squad that fired on the colonists, including Captain Preston, were arrested and charged with manslaughter. The soldiers were given a fair trial to ensure there would be no retaliation from the British. John Adams, Founding Father and second president of the United States, willingly and successfully defended the captain during their trial. He stated that if the soldiers were endangered by the mob, they had a right to fight back. The jury agreed with him and acquitted six of the eight soldiers. The remaining two were found guilty and sentenced to have their thumbs branded.

Just as protests began to wane over recent taxes, British Parliament passed yet another tax in 1773 with the creation of the Tea Act. This allowed the East India Company to export tea directly to the colonies at a cheaper rate, rather than first being sold wholesale through auctions in London and then re-exported to the colonies. The East India Company was one of Britain's most substantial commercial institutions and was faced with extreme financial difficulties due to the lack of sales and overstock of tea that had accumulated in Britain. No one was purchasing their tea due to its high price, which was driven up by exorbitant taxes; instead, they were purchasing much cheaper, smuggled Dutch tea.

It was thought by Parliament that if East India could sell directly to the colonies at a cheaper price than its competition, then they would be able to offload their surplus and help the company recover from lagging sales. The Tea Act also kept in place the Townshend duty, which British officials did not want to eliminate. Some members of Parliament, however, did want this tax removed because they felt the colonists would not approve. So they attempted to hide the tax by having it paid for, first, in London before the goods were exported. This, however, did not work and as soon as the colonists got wind of the tax they immediately protested. Even though the tea was being sold cheaper, they did not like the fact that a tax existed that was implemented against their wishes.

As the ships containing the tea crossed the Atlantic Ocean, colonists organized and met to discuss plans on what to do when the ships arrived. These protests spread to each of the ports throughout the colonies and in every case but one, the tea was sent back to England or the protestors forced the local merchants selling the tea to resign. In Boston, the remaining ship held fast and demanded the tea be offloaded, due mostly to local Governor Hutchinson's vested interest in the cargo. Samuel Adams, another Founding Father, called for a meeting, of which thousands attended, and passed a resolution urging the captain of the ship to send the tea back. While they were awaiting his response, two more ships carrying tea arrived. As the deadlines for the captain's response approached, about 7,000 people had gathered at the meeting. It was at this time Adams received another report stating the governor's refusal to let the ships leave. Adams then stated, "This meeting can do nothing further to save the country." [IX] Later that evening a group of men boarded the three vessels and threw every crate of tea overboard. Britain was upset, to say the least, and felt this act could not go unpunished. So they closed the port of Boston and began putting in place other laws, known as the Coercive Acts.

The colonists referred to these new acts as the Intolerable Acts, simply because the legislation that was introduced restricted some of their rights. Not only was the port of Boston closed until such time that the colonists reimbursed the East India Company for all the tea that was destroyed, the royal governor also took over the Massachusetts government, sheriffs, and juries by appointing officials loyal to the Crown. This act, known as the Massachusetts Government Act, also severely affected the town's ability to meet by limiting them to only one meeting a year, unless otherwise called by the governor.

Britain persisted further and passed the Quartering Act, which allowed British-appointed governors to assign soldiers to vacant buildings if other suitable accommodations were not provided, rather than colonial legislatures—as was the case in the past. Colonial legislatures had not cooperated previously and, therefore, did not adhere to the guidelines set forth in the first Quartering Act. This new act allowed Britain more control assuring their demands were met rather than discarded as before. These latest acts incensed the colonists; they viewed them as a direct violation of their rights and a threat to their liberties. Richard Henry Lee, one of the signers of the Declaration of Independence, described the acts as, "A most wicked system for destroying the liberty of America." [X] These acts were the spark that lit the fuse that propelled the colonies into revolt.

The First Continental Congress was called September 5, 1774, [XI] as a direct result of the Coercive Acts implemented by British Parliament. Delegates from twelve of the thirteen colonies met in Carpenters' Hall in Philadelphia, Pennsylvania, to discuss a response to Britain's Intolerable Acts. Of the various options they discussed, one included a complete boycott of British trade until the Coercive Acts were fully repealed. Among the other items of discussion were creating and publishing a list of grievances and rights, petitioning the king for compensation of those grievances and the need for a second Continental Congress if their petition to the king proved unsuccessful. The colonies proceeded with their plan and on December 1, 1774, the boycott of British imports commenced. They were so successful that imports dropped ninety-seven percent in 1775, compared with the previous year. [XI] The members of the Continental Congress also agreed to halt all exports to Britain if it did not repeal the Coercive Acts by September 10, 1775. [XI] Their petition to the king was ignored by the monarchy and so convened the Second Continental Congress on May 10, 1775. By this time the Revolutionary War had already begun with battles in Lexington and Concord so this Congress' primary function was to organize the war effort and discuss plans for defending the colonies by forming the first Continental Army.

There had not been a shot fired upon the British army prior to the battles in Lexington and Concord. However, Britain was well aware of the colonists growing dissent and the fact that they were stockpiling arms in preparation for battle. They were determined to seize these arms and prevent a colonial militia from organizing. So British-appointed Massachusetts Governor Thomas Gage developed a secret plan to send a band of British troops out to collect the armory in Concord and disband the rebel army. The colonists were leery of Britain's expanded presence in the port of Boston from the onset of their arrival after the Boston Tea Party. This unease forced various patriots to place the British troops under constant surveillance.

As word spread of Britain's planned move on the rebels, the Sons of Liberty sprang into action. Paul Revere and William Dawes were immediately dispatched to ride to Lexington and warn John Hancock and Samuel Adams of the coming threat. In the event of their capture, a predetermined signal was setup to warn the colonists in Charlestown of the movement of the British troops, "one if by land, two if by sea." [XII] One lantern would be lit in the steeple of the Old North Church if the army moved by land, and two would be lit if they moved by water.

On the evening of April 18, 1775, the British troops began their advance toward Lexington. Revere and Dawes rode through the night, warning the colonists of the British advancement. They arrived in Lexington around midnight where they delivered the news to Hancock and Adams. When the British troops arrived in Lexington the next morning, they found themselves face to face with about seventy minutemen, [XIII] a name given to members of the militia because they could be ready at a moment's notice. As both sides stood bewildered, wondering what to do next, a shot rang out as if from nowhere, and with that the Revolutionary War officially began. It is not known which side fired first, but several American minutemen were killed or wounded while the remaining hastily retreated. From Lexington, the British troops marched on toward Concord. When they arrived, the odds were much different. Some estimates state the British were outnumbered by as much as three to one. The famous ride of Paul Revere, known as the Midnight Ride, afforded the colonists enough advance notice to gather a large group of militiamen, so many, in fact, that they were able to repel the British forces near Concord, which forced them to retreat back to Boston.

At the beginning of the war, King George III got word of the rebellion and dismissed it as rumor, never believing that the colonists would actually attack the British army. However, as time passed and word of more battles spread, it became clear that Britain would have no choice but to prepare for war. The colonists tried unsuccessfully to reconcile with the king by sending the Olive Branch Petition, hoping he would step in and repair their relationship. When the king refused to accept their petition, America solidified its departure with Britain by creating the Declaration of Independence. This document was drafted by Thomas Jefferson, another Founding Father, and was a formal explanation on why America wanted to separate from Great Britain. It justified this separation by listing colonial grievances against the king and asserting certain natural rights. It further explains how the Continental Congress, comprised of representatives from the original thirteen colonies, voted on July 2 to declare their independence. It summarized a philosophy of individual liberty held by the colonists, certain "self-evident truths." [XIV] The birth of our nation is celebrated on the day this amazing piece of literature was approved by the colonies—July 4, 1776.

The war lasted seven years and constituted many different battles on many different fronts. The capture of Ticonderoga, Battle of Bunker Hill, attack on Canada, the siege of Boston, the battles of New York, Valcour Bay, Trenton, Princeton, Brandywine, Germantown, Orinsky, Bennington, Seratoga, Monmouth, the massacre at Wyoming, the capture of Stonypoint, the siege of Charleston, the battles of Camden, King Mountain, Cowpens, Guilford Court House, Hopkins Hill, Eutaw Springs, and Yorktown all made for a long, exhaustive war. There were many casualties throughout the war and the long, hard battles tested the very resolve of the American militias and army. The winter in Valley Forge was a true testament to the Americans' undying patriotism. In the beginning their conditions were very rough; limited supplies and housing left men vulnerable to the elements, and as many as five thousand were hospitalized. [xv] Conditions improved with time and by the end of their stay the American army was much better trained to face off against the British troops. Regardless of their training they knew it would be difficult, if not impossible, to be victorious. The American army was outnumbered, outranked, and outgunned. It was clear that they were going to need outside help of some sort. In the fall of 1776 the Continental Congress sent Benjamin Franklin to Paris to negotiate with the French for assistance in the war. It took some time but eventually France conceded their support. With the help of the French, America was victorious and the Revolutionary War came to an end in 1783 with the signing of the Treaty of Paris.

During the Revolutionary War in 1777, a group of statesmen from each of the thirteen colonies gathered to create a government for their proposed nation. They realized they needed a plan that would secure their freedom after declaring their independence from the King. The Articles of Confederation would be their first attempt. In essence, this was the first Constitution to the United States. It spelled out how the national government would operate taking into consideration the states' wariness of strong central government. Within this document each state retained its "sovereignty, freedom, and independence." [xvi] There was no president, executive branch, judiciary, or tax base defined anywhere within the articles. Instead, a committee of delegates was setup with representatives from each state to become the national legislature. They were responsible for conducting foreign affairs, declaring war, maintaining armed forces, and other functions. The Articles denied Congress the ability to collect taxes, regulate interstate commerce, and enforce laws. Interesting, to say the least, considering how differently the Constitution's legislation was outlined. The Articles of Confederation was adopted on March 1, 1781.

It did not take long for the Congress of the Confederation (they were no longer referred to as the Continental Congress at this point) to realize the limitations of the Articles of Confederation, considering there was no tax base to pay off state and national debts incurred from the war and the limitations presented by not having any executive powers to create laws. Everything was handled at the state level. So whenever Congress needed money they had to requisition the states. This, however, never really worked and the states rarely complied. The Articles functioned so poorly at creating a working government that the new union almost imploded as quickly as it began. Its money became worthless because Congress did not have any revenue to pay back its debt; something economists are predicting will happen with our current 16 trillion-dollar debt if it is not brought under control soon. The US Army's troops were deserting or threatening mutiny because they had not yet been paid. All this chaos transpired mainly because Congress needed the cooperation of nine states, sometimes all thirteen, to pass any real legislation, and that was when they could get their representatives to show up. Realizing the extreme limitations of the current structure, Congress convened in Philadelphia with representatives from twelve of the thirteen states for the sole purpose of amending the Articles of Confederation. It soon became clear, however, that a complete rewrite was necessary, and with that the United States Constitution was born.

Creating a document that would be the very foundation of a newly sovereign nation was no simple task. A document that would protect its citizens from internal and external conflict, ensure the government remain just, and would be of benefit to its citizens rather than that of a king, then and for all future generations. It was daunting to say the least, and one that would require many meetings between some very brilliant men, known more commonly as the Framers or creators of the Constitution. Representatives from most of the states met to discuss and debate the issues over the summer of 1787. The chief points debated among them were how much power to allow the central government, how many representatives in Congress to allow each state, and how the representatives should be elected. [xvii] As with its predecessor, the Constitution was and is the supreme law of the United States for the federal government, the states, and all who live within this country.

The portion that made this document so different from the Articles of Confederation was how it created and explained in detail the three new branches of government—executive, legislative, and judicial—as well as giving one branch, Congress, the power to lay and collect taxes. The powers assigned to each branch gave each a specific set of duties, but it did not allow one to be more powerful than the other. This was done, intentionally, to keep the government in check and allow all proposed legislation to be fully vetted before becoming law.

You always hear the media speaking about how one side or the other will not compromise on issues and how terrible it is that they cannot come to an agreement. In my opinion this is not as bad as the media is portraying it to be. Our Founding Fathers understood that compromise could lead to an overaggressive government, and thus designed these branches accordingly. They wanted the process to be somewhat stagnant so that government would never take away the people's rights with just the stroke of a pen. They wanted debate and disagreements so that all views were understood before any laws were passed. The three branches of government created under the new Constitution were the executive branch, which is led by the President; the legislative contains Congress, which appropriates funds; and the judicial, which is headed by the Supreme Court—the final authority on any contested law. This new government was eventually accepted by the Union and on September 17, 1787, the Constitution was completed. It took a while for the new government to take hold. There were some states, Maryland and New York, which initially did not agree with the structure as it was created, and thought instead that the Articles of Confederation should have just been amended. Because of issues such as these it took about a year before it became fully ratified by eleven of the thirteen states, only nine of which were needed. On September 13, 1788, Congress certified the new Constitution and began governing on March 4, 1789. [XVIII]

The revolution against the British was a culmination of many things, but it primarily centered around one specific belief—that the rights of the colonists were being infringed upon because new taxes and restrictions were being implemented without their consent, or as they referred to it, "taxation without representation." Britons and the colonists both agreed that all British subjects should not be taxed without the approval of their elected officials. Since colonists did not elect members of Parliament, they felt they could not be taxed by that governing body, but rather, only through their local, elected officials. The king, however, strongly disagreed and believed that he could do whatever he wished with the colonies because they were merely an extension of Great Britain.

This very same viewpoint seems to be held by our modern government regarding spending and the subsequent growth of government. Their mentality being such that they feel they can spend whatever they wish without being held accountable. When government spending outpaces revenue, just raise taxes. At least that appears to always be their response when the debt rises insurmountably as a direct result of their massive spending and new government bureaucracies, i.e. the Affordable Care Act (new health care law). Forget about being responsible with our money and operating within their means. It is as if they feel they should not be held responsible for the growing debt. While they may not outwardly state this, their actions speak differently. Almost every president in modern history has dug us further and further into debt without any real plans for eliminating it. Bill Clinton was the only president who actually ran a surplus, although most of this was attributed to the Silicon Valley Tech boom in the mid-nineties and pulling money from Social Security. Sure, some presidents have cut taxes and spending here and there, but never by any substantial amount. So is this what our Founding Fathers envisioned when they wrote the Constitution, a government run amok and free from accountability? Before we can answer that question we must first take a look at who these gentlemen were.

The list of Founding Fathers varies depending on which source you reference. Some state that all involved with the American Revolution, creation and signing of the Declaration of Independence, and the Framers of the Constitution of the United States should be considered Founding Fathers. While this does make sense, the problem with using this narrative is the list of those individuals is enormous and would require an entire volume of books to explain each person's viewpoint. According to Joseph Ellis of the Encyclopedia Britannica, only the most prominent statesman of America's revolutionary generation responsible for the successful war for colonial independence from Great Britain, the liberal ideas celebrated in the Declaration of Independence, and the republican form of government defined in the United States Constitution should be considered. [XIX] His *gallery of greats* includes ten specific people: John Adams, Samuel Adams, Benjamin Franklin, Alexander Hamilton, Patrick Henry, Thomas Jefferson, James Madison, John Marshall, George Mason, and George Washington. But according to American historian

Richard B. Morris, in his 1973 book *Seven Who Shaped Our Destiny: The Founding Fathers as Revolutionaries*, identified the following seven people: [xx] Benjamin Franklin, George Washington, John Adams, Thomas Jefferson, John Jay, James Madison, and Alexander Hamilton. For the subject matter relevant to this book, I will be focusing on John Adams, Benjamin Franklin, Alexander Hamilton, Thomas Jefferson, James Madison, and George Washington.

John Adams

John Adams was a political philosopher, diplomat, and American statesman. He was born in the Massachusetts Bay Colony and spent most of his adult life as a Harvard educated lawyer and public figure in Boston. He became associated with the patriot cause early on and was a delegate to the First and Second Continental Congresses. Under George Washington, he served as vice president for two terms where his ideals and beliefs helped solidify his own election when he ran for, and became, the second President of the United States, from 1797–1801.

Adams played a leading role in persuading Congress to declare its independence from Britain, and he helped Thomas Jefferson with drafting the Declaration of Independence. He was very influential with the representatives from the colonies regarding his ideas on government, so much so that he penned a pamphlet called "Thoughts of Government," which was used to assist states when they began writing their own constitutions. Adams advised that the form of government should be chosen to attain the desired ends, which are the happiness and virtue of the greatest number of people. "There is no good government but what is republican. That the only valuable part of the British constitution is so; because the very definition of a republic is "an empire of laws, and not of men." [xxi] Just from that quote alone we can glean that Adams' confidence in government was minimal at best. He believed that in a free republic a government must be divided equally so that no one branch had absolute power. It was these beliefs that were actually incorporated into the structure of the branches defined within the United States Constitution.

Benjamin Franklin

Benjamin Franklin was an exceptional person with many talents and interests. Throughout his life he held many jobs—he was a printer, author, politician, postmaster, scientist, inventor, statesmen, and diplomat. As a scientist he studied physics and posted theories on electricity that were discovered during his many experiments; we are all too familiar with the story of him proposing to fly a kite during a lightning storm. Some of his more remarkable inventions were the lightning rod, bifocals, and the Franklin stove, to name a few. He also formed the first lending library and fire department. His inventions and discoveries made him very popular in France where news of his electrical experiments was wide spread.

Benjamin Franklin was a prominent figure in early American history and helped fuel the Americans' distrust in the British. He was a strong opponent of the Stamp Act and his testimony before the House of Commons was instrumental in getting it repealed. During his stay in London he intercepted some letters that proved the British were trying to crack down on the rights of Bostonians. Upon discovering the news he immediately mailed them to America where they were used to enflame American dissent against the monarchy.

Because of his stature and diplomatic contributions to the state, the Pennsylvania Assembly unanimously chose Franklin as their delegate to the Second Continental Congress. He was also chosen to be on the committee that helped draft the Declaration of Independence. During its signing, John Hancock commented that we must all hang together, to which Franklin replied, "Yes, we must, indeed, all hang together, or most assuredly we shall all hang separately." [XXII] In 1777 he was dispatched to France and became the ambassador for our nation. While in France he conducted the affairs of our country very successfully, including the negotiation of the Treaty of Paris in 1783. He was the only Founding Father whose signature appeared on all four of the major documents used in the founding of our nation, the Declaration of Independence, Treaty of Paris, Treaty of Alliance, and the U.S. Constitution. Benjamin Franklin was definitely a wise man, wise beyond his years.

Alexander Hamilton

Alexander Hamilton was an economist, political philosopher, and a military tactician. Hamilton's resentment for the British government was evident by his involvement in many different rebellious movements. He was the leader of the American nationalists that were calling for a new Constitution and he defended the American Congress' stance against the monarchy by releasing responses to pro-British pamphlets that circulated New York. In one such response he stated,

> … that they are enemies to the rights of mankind is manifest, because they wish to see one part of their species enslaved by another. That they have an invincible aversion to common sense is apparent in many respects: They endeavor to persuade us, that the absolute sovereignty of parliament does not imply our absolute slavery. [XXIII]

His disdain for the king's treatment of the colonies as a subplot of Britain was obvious. The colonists were being treated as second-class citizens without any of the representation their supposed British brethren enjoyed. Hamilton's defense of colonial American rights continued throughout the Revolutionary War. During his preparation for the war he immersed himself in military maneuvers and artillery tactics. In March of 1776 he joined the New York Artillery and later became George Washington's senior military assistant. His military expertise was instrumental in winning the war against the British. His ability to organize and train troops was innate, and he fought local authorities to ensure proper munitions were provided to his soldiers.

Hamilton's credentials did not stop there; just like most of the Founding Fathers, he was a man of many talents. Along with being a military strategist, he was one of America's first constitutional lawyers. He also penned most of the Federalist Papers, which have been used as a primary source for Constitutional interpretation to this day. The Federalist Papers are a series of articles advocating for the ratification of the first Constitution and explain the philosophy and motivation behind the new system of government. Serving in George Washington's presidential administration, Hamilton wrote most of his economic policies, establishing a national bank, funding of state debts by the federal government, tariffs, and peacetime relations with Britain.

Alexander Hamilton's Federalist beliefs, however, were very pro-federal, or pro-government, when it came to his interpretation of the Constitution. When the powers between national and state governments collided, he consistently took the side of greater federal power (sounds a little like our modern government). One major example of this, which was opposed strongly by some of the Founders, dealt with his authorization of a national bank. After the Revolutionary War, America needed a system to pay back the nation's debt incurred during the war. The paper money that existed was worthless and there was no foreign credit available. So Hamilton believed a national bank was needed to resolve this problem. Thomas Jefferson and John Adams both believed Hamilton was dangerously aristocratic and believed his proposition was in direct conflict with the powers granted by the Constitution. It took some convincing by Hamilton, but President George Washington eventually sided with his assessment regarding the "necessary and proper clause" of the Constitution (which allowed the Federal government to pass laws not expressly provided for in the Constitution) and signed a bill to create a national bank into law. This set a precedent, which allowed for future bouts of government expansion based on this clause.

So you see the extension of federal government into the private sector is not just a modern phenomenon. It existed in part, even as far back as 1819. The major difference though is early government was always leery of expanding into the private sector, given their recent memories of living under a monarchy. Whereas modern government, long removed from such memories, fully believes it is in our best interest to socially engineer society. They create bureaucracies that are not needed, such as the Department of Education, and then expect us to pay for them by raising taxes. We already pay taxes at the local and state levels to support public schools. Why then are we also using more tax dollars to fund an entire bureaucracy specifically designed to provide more assistance to schools? There is no need for a department that, on a basic level, takes tax dollars and repurposes them to schools it believes require assistance. This is nothing more than redundant waste created by an inefficient system, especially when you consider how poorly our nation's test scores rank with those of other countries and how our scores have not improved in decades. Throwing more money at the problem is not improving test results either. So allowing this department's budget to grow every year is obviously not the solution. Any way you look at it, this is unwarranted government expansion, and just one example of why our nation is so deep in debt.

Thomas Jefferson

Thomas Jefferson was a farmer, avid reader, politician, architect, writer, and inventor. He had a library that consisted of 6,700 books, which he later sold to the Library of Congress in 1815. His literary prowess and sheer breadth of knowledge served him well as the primary author of the Declaration of Independence. From 1779-1781 he served as the wartime governor of Virginia, but only for one term because his tenure became unpopular by most of the folks in that region. For about five and a half years Jefferson lived abroad and served as both a commissioner and as the US Minister to France, succeeding Benjamin Franklin. When he returned home, he served under George Washington as the first United States Secretary of State, a position he used to advise against the creation of a national bank. Since he favored states' rights, he believed heavily in limited government and protection from government authority. Under John Adams, he served as Vice President from 1797-1801, after which he ran for and became the third President of the United States in 1801, serving under the federalist platform until 1809. When he assumed the presidency, he slashed Army and Navy expenditures, cut the budget, eliminated the tax on whiskey that was unpopular in the West, yet reduced the national debt by a third. [XXIV] Let me get this straight; he cut taxes and expenditures and reduced the debt? You mean raising taxes and expanding government is not the only way to balance a budget? Imagine that, a president who understood what it means to be fiscally responsible.

As president, he negotiated the purchase of the Louisiana Territory from Napoleon and commissioned the Lewis and Clark expedition to explore the new frontier. After his Presidency, Jefferson centered his focus on founding a new institution of higher learning, one that did not contain any religious influences, so students could specialize in areas that were not offered at other campuses. The separation of church and state was important to Jefferson and a virtue he held dear. But he was a strong advocate for individual religious freedoms as well. His vision of a new learning facility was realized in 1819 with the founding of the University of Virginia. Jefferson was also responsible for the architectural planning of the university's grounds. Throughout his life, Jefferson remained involved in public affairs. He was a distinguished figure who believed that each man had *certain inalienable rights* defining liberty by stating, "Rightful liberty is unobstructed action according to our will within limits drawn around us by the equal rights of others…" A proper government, for Jefferson, was one that not only prohibits individuals in society from infringing on the liberty of other individuals, but also restrains itself from diminishing individual liberty. [XXV] In a letter to William S. Smith, Jefferson wrote, "And what country can preserve its liberties, if the rulers are not warned from time to time, that this people preserve the spirit of resistance? Let them take arms." [XXV] He was a firm believer that government, over time, would become corrupt and, therefore, must be righted. So much so that he even stated, "The natural progress of things is for liberty to yield and government to gain ground." [XXVI] It appears we can add clairvoyant to Thomas Jefferson's résumé as well.

James Madison

James Madison was one of the most influential Founding Fathers, mainly because he is regarded as the "Father of the Constitution," or its primary author. Although he strongly disagreed with this, stating that the document was not "the off-spring of a single brain," but "the work of many heads and many hands," [XXVII] he is responsible for writing over a third of the Federalist Papers with assistance from Alexander Hamilton and John Jay. Madison was a politician and political philosopher that believed the new republic needed checks and balances to protect individual rights from the tyranny of the majority. [XXVIII] Not only was Madison the primary author of the Constitution, he also created the first Ten Amendments as well, known as the Bill of Rights. Initially, James did not believe a bill of rights was necessary because he believed the Constitution itself was sufficient. Stating that the Constitution listed the powers of government and specifically pertained to its operation, and anything not contained within was, thereby, automatically given to the people and the states. Alexander Hamilton also feared listing specific rights, believing they would somehow be interpreted as the only rights individuals were allowed. However, anti-federalists were demanding a separate bill of rights in exchange for their support for ratification.

Anti-federalists were those that believed a new constitution was not needed, mainly because they thought a stronger government threatened the states sovereignty and were extremely worried that appointing a president could lead to an eventual monarchy. They believed the Articles of Confederation formed a sufficient government and, thereby, directly opposed ratifying a new Constitution. Even with the balance of powers that existed within the Constitution, they feared it would only be a matter of time before a president would be viewed as a king. Given their perspective and what they had just been through by declaring the independence from Britain, I can understand their concern.

Even though Madison was the primary author of the Constitution, he was extremely opposed to forming a national government. He spent most of his time in Congress working on ways to limit the federal government's powers. He believed Hamilton and Washington were conspiring to create "a real modern, European type of government with a bureaucracy, a standing army, and a powerful independent executive." [xxix] Given the vast differences of opinion regarding government's role, it is amazing this document ever came to fruition. In 1801, James Madison became the Secretary of State in the Jefferson Administration and was integral in convincing Congress to purchase the Louisiana Territory in 1803. They broke from party policy to acquire this land because they felt it was to their advantage that Britain not obtain it during one of the many wars between Britain and France. Napoleon came to realize that it was nearly impossible to defend this huge expanse of land and thought it best to sell it to America rather than go broke trying to defend it. In 1808, due in part to the success of Jefferson's Presidency, James Madison was selected as the Democratic-Republican Party's presidential candidate and easily defeated his Federalist opponent. In 1809 he became the fourth President of the United States where he served for two terms until 1817.

George Washington

Last but certainly not least, George Washington was by far one of the most pragmatic and dominant Founding Fathers. He was considered by many a natural-born leader, as he demonstrated on the battlefield with his leadership and military prowess, which helped propel our country to victory over Britain in the Revolutionary War. He was nominated commander and chief of the Continental Army by John Adams because of his strong patriotism and prior military experience in the French and Indian war. Washington was a humble tobacco farmer who felt undeserving of the title but accepted the recommendation nonetheless. Most members of the Second Continental Congress believed there was no better person to command the new army and agreed completely with Adam's assessment and recommendation.

Their judgment regarding Washington's qualifications proved correct when he employed a strategy during the Revolutionary War that ultimately led to America's victory over the British. He stated, "We should on all Occasions avoid a general Action, or put anything to the Risque, unless compelled by a necessity, into which we ought never to be drawn." [xxx] After the war, Washington resigned as commander in chief and retired to his plantation in Mount Vernon. His retirement was short-lived, however; he soon realized that the country under the Articles of Confederation was not functioning properly and something had to be done to rectify the situation. He also believed that the Articles hampered the war effort, so it was inevitable that he would become involved with the creation of a new constitution.

During the Constitutional Convention in Philadelphia in 1787 George Washington participated in the voting of the new articles but offered little toward the debates. His influence after the convention convinced many to vote for ratification and in the fall of 1787 the new constitution of the United States was ratified by all thirteen colonies. In 1789 the Electoral College unanimously elected Washington the first President of the United States. His tenure during his first term was considered so successful that he was reelected for a second. During his presidency he was considered an excellent judge of character and talent, and delegated important tasks in an efficient and effective manor. He preferred to remain somewhat independent and did not become a member of any political party during his term for fear of undermining republicanism. Washington handled foreign affairs in a similar manner, remaining neutral between France and Britain during the French Revolutionary War. Although, some may argue that he sided more with the British because of the signing of the Jay Treaty, which normalized relations with Britain by cleaning up some of the mess remaining from the Revolutionary War after the signing of the Treaty of Paris. It also removed any remaining British forces from western forts, and resolved any outstanding financial debts left over from the Revolution.

George Washington served as president from 1789–1797 and after two terms decided to head back into retirement as he had grown weary of the whole political process. During his farewell address he stressed the importance of the Constitution, the evil of political parties, and the proper virtues of a republican people. He warned against foreign influence in domestic affairs and vice versa. He also warned against "permanent alliances with any portion of the foreign world," saying the United States must concentrate primarily on American interests. He counseled friendship and commerce with all nations, but warned against involvement in European wars and entering into long-term *entangling* alliances. [xxxi]

Our current government should definitely take Washington's advice regarding foreign meddling. America is way too involved in some countries' domestic affairs even when there is no direct threat to the United States, such as the current war in Libya. Not to mention the 50,000 plus troops still stationed in Germany even after the fall of Hitler and Russian Communism. America's primary goal should be to protect its citizens from any foreign threat no matter the expense, but it should not become involved in foreign struggles that do not pertain to the U.S. It is not our job to police the entire world. We simply cannot afford it— monetarily or philosophically.

All of the aforementioned Founding Fathers were in some way responsible for freeing our country from the monarchy. There were two key issues that inevitably caused them to revolt against the Crown. They felt strongly that they were being taxed without proper representation and they believed the king was intruding on their rights as citizens. The Founding Fathers believed Britain's government was, essentially, too powerful and had free reign to do as they wished with the colonies.

After everything they experienced with Britain, the colonists felt their only recourse was to declare their independence and create a government that was in line with their standards. They spent a great deal of time creating a Constitution that limited government's power; they wanted to be certain their rights could not be infringed upon ever again. Remember James Madison, co-creator of the Federalist papers and primary author of the Constitution, worried about creating a Bill of Rights. He feared it would limit citizens to those rights alone, stripping them of all others. He originally believed that if specific rights were not implicitly stated within the Constitution it was inferred that they were given to the people, barring any need for an actual list of rights. Furthermore, he was extremely opposed to forming a national government and spent most of his time working on ways to limit the federal government's powers.

The remaining Founding Fathers were for limited, controlled government as well, although it could be argued that Hamilton and Washington were a little more liberal on the matter. John Adams' pamphlet, *Thoughts on Government,* clearly outlined a government void of absolute power, creating three branches designed to offset each other to ensure balance between the governing bodies. Benjamin Franklin's Albany Plan was created to give the colonists more power within parliament, even though it was later rejected by both sides. Even Alexander Hamilton's views on government were modest by today's standards, as is illustrated in the Federalist Papers he authored. One such example is in Federalist 51 where he explains the checks and balances that need to exist between the different branches of government, essentially agreeing with John Adam's assessment. "TO WHAT expedient, then, shall we finally resort, for maintaining in practice the necessary partition of power among the several departments, as laid down in the Constitution? The only answer that can be given is, that as all these exterior provisions are found to be inadequate, the defect must be supplied, by so contriving the interior structure of the government as that its several constituent parts may, by their mutual relations, be the means of keeping each other in their proper places." Thomas Jefferson was very skeptical of government as well. When he stated, "The natural progress of things is for liberty to yield and government to gain ground," he understood that because of its very nature, over time government would grow and by doing so would cause liberty (freedom) to give way.

James Madison vehemently opposed big government and spent most of his time in Congress working on ways to limit government's power. George Washington's views on foreign affairs were antithetical to those of today's policy makers. So, has our Founding Fathers' vision for government been adhered to? I would say, "Absolutely not." It is very easy to determine, based on their positions, that their vision has not been maintained. Our modern government's role in society has grown way beyond that of the Founders' original intent. Frankly they have become so irresponsible with their spending and growth that they have placed our country on the path to ruin. So, what must be done to reduce the size of government? What should be done to ensure government remains just and returns to its intended role? How do we control its expansion and eliminate wasteful spending? Answers to all these questions will be given in the following chapters. I will explain how government has grown beyond its means and become unsustainable, and if left unchecked will lead to the destruction of our economy as we know it. I will also explore what must be done to rein in government and get our country back on the right track, including drafting a clear and concise Amendment to the Constitution that details exactly how to contain government now and in the future. You will be shocked to learn how much our Constitutional freedoms have eroded over the years and how inefficient and ineffective government has become at managing your tax dollars. I will expose just how much the Constitution, and our Founding Fathers vision for limited government, has all but disintegrated right before our very eyes.

Freedom of Speech and the Press

The first amendment to the Bill of Rights provides us with the freedom of religion, speech, assembly, and press. It reads: *Congress shall make no law respecting an establishment of religion, or prohibiting the free exercise thereof; or abridging the freedom of speech, or of the press; or the right of the people peaceably to assemble, and to petition the Government for a redress of grievances.* This amendment is arguably one of the most important amendments within the United States Constitution because it establishes some very important rights that are fundamental to the American way of life. Without these rights our society would be very different indeed. Imagine what would transpire if the press was not embedded with the White House or if it were not able to speak openly about policies the government pursued that are detrimental to our well-being. What would happen if we were not able to voice our opinion regarding said policies using our freedom of speech and assembly? The Founders understood that without freedom of religion, press, and speech, society would eventually devolve into an authoritarian state. Ruling in such a manner that would strip most freedoms and liberties from its citizens, just as it occurred to the colonists under the British Crown. But are these freedoms currently being exercised in a manner that is beneficial to society? In that respect I believe there are questions that should be raised regarding each of these rights. Does freedom of speech grant us the ability to say whatever we want wherever we want without fear of retribution? If so, at what point does it become verbal assault? What about freedom of the press? Are most media outlets true government watchdogs as our Founders envisioned? Are they reporting the news objectively and providing you with informative, unbiased coverage of Washington's policies? Or are they using a viewpoint so slanted they should be considered state-run media?

The subject of free speech and the items it encompasses are vast—from art, video game content, printed media, movies, and pornography to the actual spoken word. My focus will concentrate primarily on the spoken word, more specifically, the spoken words of a particular religious extremist group—Westboro Baptist Church. This *church* is a tiny family from Topeka, Kansas, led by Reverend Fred Phelps, which believes military deaths and natural disasters are punishment from God for America's tolerance of homosexuality. They have made national news for protesting military funerals, carrying signs and chanting hateful words aimed at soldiers who fought and died for our country. Phelp's church is somehow linking the death of a soldier to God's anger toward our country's acceptance of the gay lifestyle. This sounds completely logical to me, if you exist in some kind of warped reality. Some of the vile speech that has emanated from this church during its protests: "Thank God for Dead Soldiers, God Hates Your Tears, God Hates Fags, Fags Die God Laughs, and Thank God for IEDs." There are so many things wrong with their message I find it completely reprehensible. Whatever happened to live and let live? No matter how you feel regarding homosexuality, no one can justify how those of Westboro Baptist choose to deliver their message. A funeral is a time of grieving and paying respects, not a time to disrespect the deceased and his family. The irony here is this church is picketing soldiers that died to uphold the very freedoms that allow these morons to protest in this manner.

During the spring of 2006 in Westminster, Maryland, Albert Snyder laid his son to rest—twenty-year-old Marine Lance Corporal Matthew Snyder. Matthew was an unfortunate casualty of the Iraq war. Gathered at Matthew's funeral were his family, friends, and the ever-vile Westboro Baptist Church. They showed up in typical fashion, protesting with defamatory signs and hateful rants, picketing just as they had previously done at 600 other funerals. Not wanting to leave any hateful stone unturned, they also posted disparaging remarks about Matthew and his family on the church's website. They stated his mother had raised him as the devil and taught him "to defy his creator, to divorce and commit adultery." Matthew's father Albert filed a lawsuit against Fred Phelps seeking damages for defamation, invasion of privacy, and intentional infliction of emotional distress, saying the group turned the event into a *circus.*[I] A federal jury awarded the Snyder family $10.9 million [II] in punitive and compensatory damages. The Westboro Baptist Church appealed the decision, where it fell before the Fourth United States Circuit Court of Appeals. A three-judge panel overturned the original verdict and ruled the Phelps family's criticism was covered under the First Amendment. To add insult to injury they ordered Albert Snyder to pay the church $16,510 [III] in court costs.

This story was covered heavily on the O'Reilly Factor on Fox News. Mr. O'Reilly believed that forcing Mr. Snyder to pay court costs was extreme, so he offered to cover the costs pending appeal. The case ended up going before the Supreme Court, where it was upheld 8-1. The only dissenter, Justice Samuel Alito Jr., said, "The First Amendment does not convey the right to *brutalize* private individuals. Our profound national commitment to free and open debate is not a license for the vicious verbal assault that occurred in this case."[1] I could not have said it better myself. Just because you have a right to free speech does not give you the right to verbally abuse someone and defame their character.

If Westboro Baptist Church had any common decency they would keep their vulgar comments to themselves, or at the very least protest elsewhere. Regardless of their First Amendment rights, they should understand that voicing their opinion in this manner is absolutely unacceptable. The last place anyone wants to hear their ridiculous comments is during a time of grieving. Of all the locations they could choose to protest, it should never be at someone's funeral. I can guarantee you that no matter what your feelings are regarding homosexuality, Westboro's message is being lost when they choose to protest in this manner. No one is going to sympathize with a group, or their message, when they cause further suffering to families already in tremendous pain. Considering that neither of these events is even remotely related (protesting gays by assembling at a funeral), just adds credence to the fact that this group is completely out of touch with reality. I understand that they are doing this to get media attention, but at what cost? All the attention they are receiving is completely negative. This tells me they have no sense of decency and do not care who they hurt while spreading their message of hate.

Their First Amendment right gives them the ability to speak freely, no matter how heinous their message, but it does not give them the right to intentionally inflict emotional distress. The Supreme Court got this one wrong in my opinion. While I wholeheartedly agree with an individual's right to speak his mind, I do not believe it should be allowed at a venue that would cause further pain and suffering. As the old saying goes, there is a time and place for everything. Laws need to be passed that keep these individuals from assembling anywhere near a funeral. Of course doing so means they will not get the media coverage they desire. What a shame. The states of Arizona, Arkansas, Nebraska, North Dakota, Oklahoma, West Virginia, and Wyoming agree with me. They have already passed laws prohibiting these types of protests anywhere around military funerals, according to the national conference of state legislatures. [IV] Westboro Baptist Church is defiant in their message and says that they will travel around the country challenging these laws one state at a time.

It is clear to anyone with compassion that the First Amendment does not give us the right to speak with total disregard for human emotion. But legally speaking, are there limits to what we are allowed to say? The short answer is yes; there are some limits. Any words that provoke violence, libel, slander, and certain obscenities have all been challenged in court and are not protected by the First Amendment. In Chaplinsky versus the State of New Hampshire, 315 U.S. 568 (1942) the Supreme Court established the fighting-words doctrine. This case centered around a Jehovah's Witness, Walter Chaplinsky, who was arrested after purportedly telling a New Hampshire town marshal, "You are a God-damned racketeer" and "a damned fascist" when the marshal tried preventing him from preaching on a public street. Chaplinsky appealed the decision citing his First Amendment rights, but the court unanimously upheld the charges against him, explaining in their decision that there are certain well-defined and narrowly limited classes of speech, the prevention and punishment of which have never been thought to raise any constitutional problem. These include the lewd and obscene, the profane, the libelous, and the insulting or *fighting* words—those, which by their very utterance inflict injury or tend to incite an immediate breach of the peace. It has been well observed that such utterances are no essential part of any exposition of ideas, and are of such slight social value as a step to truth that any benefit that may be derived from them is clearly outweighed by the social interest in order and morality. [v]

There have also been instances during times of war in which certain speech was restricted. In Schenck versus the United States, 249 U.S. 47 (1919) the Supreme Court upheld the Espionage Act of 1917. The court concluded that the defendant, Charles Schenck, did not have a First Amendment right to print and distribute leaflets advocating opposition to the draft during World War I. They unanimously decided that when a nation is at war, many things that might be said in time of peace are such a hindrance to its effort that their utterance will not be endured so long as men fight, and that no court could regard them as protected by any constitutional right. It seems to be admitted that, if an actual obstruction of the recruiting service were proved, liability for words that produced that effect might be enforced. [vi] The court basically stated that during a time of war, greater restrictions on free speech would be allowed than during peacetime.

Since our nation's inception there have been many court cases challenging what constitutes free speech. Given that society's definitions for what is considered right and moral are constantly evolving, it appears this will be an ongoing struggle for our nation. The bottom line is we should use common sense when exercising our First Amendment right to free speech. If our intent is to verbally assault someone, then we should take a deep breath and think twice before acting. Chances are the same message can be achieved with calmer heads prevailing. More than likely the message will mean more as a result. Since free speech envelopes so many avenues of our society, there will never be a strict definition of this portion of the First Amendment, nor should there be. We never want government dictating what they feel is moral and decent when it comes to the spoken word, and we definitely do not want them limiting our ability to speak freely and openly about their policies.

Within the First Amendment, the freedom of speech and press are tied closely to each other. For without one you could not have the other. In order to have a free press it was absolutely necessary that one's speech be unfettered and free from the confines of government oversight. Before the Revolutionary War, those who wrote or spoke critical of government were subject to imprisonment under English law. The Crown considered the criticism as evil. They believed it cast doubt on the integrity and reliability of public officers. [VII]

The Founding Fathers understood that in order to have a working democracy, freedom of the press was essential. It was imperative that the press be allowed to scrutinize government so they could inform the colonists if government was acting against their best interests. Thomas Jefferson wrote, "The basis of our government being the opinion of the people, the very first object should be to keep that right; and were it left to me to decide whether we should have a government without newspapers, or newspapers without a government, I should not hesitate a moment to prefer the latter." [VII]

He and others understood that without freedom of the press it would be impossible to create a truly free nation. Government had to be kept in check, which meant having a press that was allowed to speak freely without fear of prosecution. But just because the press is free does not mean they always report things accurately and fairly. They have the ability to manipulate their message and push an agenda onto an unwary public by selectively picking and choosing stories, and wording them in ways that best suits their own interests. This means they have the potential to influence the public's opinion on politics by reporting stories that side with one particular party over another.

This is not even close to what our Founding Fathers envisioned when they wrote this amendment. They believed that by allowing the press to be free from government oversight and retribution this would produce a press that was critical of government policies. The Founders wanted to ensure our politicians remain just and utilized our tax dollars responsibly. If the Founders were alive today they would definitely be upset with the path most of the media has taken. One of deceitfulness and, in some cases, outright corruption regarding their coverage of government policies in an objective manner, to the point that they ignore certain stories altogether just to pursue their political interests. Not true you say? There is no proof the media is actually biased? Believe it or not, it is, and the hypocrisy behind those on the left and their connection to the mainstream media's agenda will astound you.

National Public Radio (NPR) is a nonprofit public broadcasting media outlet that receives partial funding from the government. More specifically, the government appropriated $420 million for the corporation of public broadcasting in 2010. About ninety million dollars of that went to public radio, to which a portion went to NPR and other local public radio stations that used some of that money to buy NPR programming. [VIII] This means you, the taxpayer, are partially funding a news organization, a company that should be reporting the news objectively and free from bias. Forget about the bias for now; we'll get back to that in a moment. Let us first deal with the fact that government is partially funding a media outlet that delivers news to the private sector. The government should in no way be involved with funding any type of media outlet, directly or indirectly. This could generate a huge conflict of interest simply by the government's involvement. With this type of influence it is very possible for government to dictate programming, although this has not occurred. But the mere association allows for the possibility of state-run media, something that should never exist in a free society. On merit alone, funding for NPR should be withdrawn. There is no reason that they cannot compete in the private sector just like everyone else. Public funding is not the only problem I have with NPR. As I mentioned earlier, they are extremely biased as well.

In late 2010, News Analyst Juan Williams was fired from NPR because of a statement he made on the O'Reilly Factor.

> "Look, Bill, I'm not a bigot," Williams said. "You know the kind of books I've written about the civil rights movement in this country. But when I get on a plane, I got to tell you, if I see people who are in Muslim garb and I think, you know, they are identifying themselves first and foremost as Muslims, I get worried. I get nervous." [IX]

Vivian Schiller, NPR's former president and CEO defended the firing by stating,

> "Juan Williams is a news analyst; he is not a commentator and he is not a columnist. We have relied on him over the years to give us perspective on the news, not to talk about his opinions." She also stated, "…we expect anybody that appears on our air, either as a

> journalist or as a news analyst, to conduct themselves according to
> our journalistic rules of ethics—wherever they might be, in any
> form and in any venue. [IX]

While these statements may appear admirable on the surface, if we look a little further into NPR's past we can see clearly they are not adhering to their own standards.

In June 2010, during a discussion on the Gaza flotilla incident, Tom Ashbrook interviewed five guests on NPR, asking for their perspective on the story. The Gaza flotilla incident occurred when six ships with more than 600 *peace activists* left Cyprus bound for Gaza. Before these ships reached Gaza they were intercepted by the Israeli Navy and Special Forces Commandos. The first five ships complied with Israeli forces, but the passengers aboard the sixth vessel, the Mavi Marmara, attacked Israeli commandos with steel poles, knives, and pepper spray, provoking a battle that claimed at least nine lives. [X] Not one of the guests on NPR defended Israel's actions according to the Committee for Accuracy in Middle East Reporting in America (CAMERA). "So there you have it—five perspectives and not one voice to present the mainstream Israeli perspective," CAMERA officials said in a June 17 press release. "That's Ashbrook's and NPR's version of a balanced discussion on Israel." [XI] If a news organization claims to be objective, their panel should consist of viewpoints from both sides of the issue.

In October 2010, during NPR's *Fresh Air,* Program Host Terry Gross spent most of the hour-long program insinuating that the Republican Party was dangerously infested with extremists, according to Newsbusters—a conservative media watchdog group. [XI] Ms. Gross was quoted, asking, "Can you think of another time in American history when there have been as many people running for Congress who seem to be on the extreme?" This is unbiased reporting at its best, let me get my checkbook— I would like to make a donation to support this wonderful organization. They are doing such a terrific job of keeping us ignorant citizens informed of the extremist that are rampant within the Republican Party. Yeah, that or they are completely false in their accusation, unless you are an extreme left-wing liberal in which case you would agree with Ms. Gross' opinion. The Republicans Terry was most likely referring to were the Tea Party candidates. The fact that so many of them got elected was because Americans agreed with their message of fiscal responsibility and limited government. Both of these ideas are considered extreme in the liberal mind, which would explain Ms. Gross' liberal viewpoint and why she posed the question.

In 2005, during NPR's *All Things Considered* segment, Andrei Codrescu said that the "evaporation of four million [people] who believe" in the doctrine of Rapture "would leave the world a better place." [XI] NPR later issued an apology for that remark. Also, in 2005 during NPR's "Day-to-Day" program, Author Mark Levin was falsely accused of advocating violence against judges. NPR later apologized for that remark as well. These are only a few examples of bias. That does not mean their whole organization is liberal.

Or does it?

In 2002, the head of NPR issued an apology six months after a report linking anthrax-laced letters to a Christian conservative organization. [XI] In 1995, Nina Totenberg, NPR's award-winning legal affairs correspondent, was allowed to keep her job after telling the host of PBS's *Inside Washington* that if there was *retributive justice* in the world, former Republican North Carolina Senator Jesse Helms would "get AIDS from a transfusion, or one of his grandchildren will get it." [XI] I wonder if Ms. Schiller remembered any of these stories when she stated that Juan Williams was outside NPR's *journalistic* boundaries. Sounds like blatant hypocrisy to me, and a prime example of intolerance toward anything that does not fit their liberal ideals. It is no wonder that she resigned after yet another story surfaced exposing even more liberal bias.

During an undercover sting operation by Conservative Activist James O'Keefe, a top fundraiser for NPR was secretly recorded making defamatory remarks against Republicans and the Tea Party. Former president of the NPR Foundation Ron Schiller, no relation to Vivian, met with what he thought were potential donors, the Muslim Education Action Center. Unbeknownst to Schiller, this was a fictitious group made up by James O'Keefe specifically to expose NPR's liberal ideology. As Mr. O'Keefe and Mr. Schiller were eating lunch, Mr. Schiller was recorded stating the Tea Party was *xenophobic* and contained *seriously racist people* who are *fanatically involved in people's personal lives*. [XII] After this video was posted online by Mr. O'Keefe, and it reached the eyes and ears of the people, it set off a firestorm regarding the public funding of NPR. Senator Jim DeMint, Republican South Carolina, said,

> Besides calling the members of the Tea Party Movement *uneducated* and *racist*, he [Schiller] also admitted that NPR did not need taxpayer money. Let's take his advice and pass legislation to defund this biased news organization that is clearly out of touch with the American people.[XII]

If they have readily admitted that taxpayer money is not needed, then we should comply with Schiller's statement. There is no reason to provide money to an organization that admits it does not need the money. Now is definitely the time to defund the Corporation for Public Broadcasting. The House of Representatives agreed with this sentiment and voted to cut funding for this group. Unfortunately, a democratically controlled Senate killed the bill almost as quickly as it arrived. So it appears NPR will continue to receive taxpayer dollars for the time being. Since we are still partially funding this organization I say it is time to call our local senators and representatives and ask them to pull this item from the federal budget once and for all.

NPR is just one example of many regarding mainstream media's liberal agenda. In 2010 CNN produced a list of their most memorable political moments.[XIII] I find most of this list lacking any real political substance.

> *Number 6:* Texas Republican Congressman Joe Barton apologizes to BP CEO Tony Hayward.
>
> *Number 5:* Tea Party candidate Christine O'Donnell's campaign ad claiming she's not a witch, she's nothing you've heard, she's you.
>
> *Number 4:* A clip from Sarah Palin's reality show, Sarah Palin's Alaska, showing her shooting a caribou.
>
> *Number 3:* A quote from Sarah Palin during an early moment of the 2010 political campaign at a Tea Party rally where she asks, "How's that hopey changey stuff working out for ya?"
>
> *Number 2:* During a town hall meeting with President Obama, Velma Hart, an Obama supporter, tells the president she's exhausted of defending him and his administration.

> *Number 1*: Former President Bill Clinton taking questions during a White House press briefing, instead of President Obama, defending the need for extending the Bush era tax cuts to everyone.

These are CNN's most memorable political moments of 2010? To be fair, CNN host John King did make a distinction between memorable and important. He stated that these were not the most important, but what CNN's staff perceived as the most memorable. So it appears CNN is putting ratings over substance. Rather than reporting hard news they chose to go with more of a fluff piece, thinking that Americans would rather see their version of entertainment over actual news. The irony however is that showing entertainment pieces is not working for CNN. Their ratings are absolutely horrible. Not one of their shows made it into the top ten most viewed news programs as of February 2012. Apparently Americans are more intelligent than CNN would give them credit, as is illustrated by viewers abandoning their format and going elsewhere for their news. One could also argue that their bottom four items portray Republicans in a negative light. If they were trying to truly be objective they would have picked three moments from each party, negative or positive, or just listed moments not portraying any kind of political slant. A more balanced and substantive list would have looked like this.

> *Number 6*: Tea Party influence help get a large number of Tea Party candidates elected in the 2010 election.
>
> *Number 5*: America's dissatisfaction with the federal government resulted in more Republicans being placed into office during the 2010 mid-term elections than any time since the 1960s.
>
> *Number 4*: Health care reform passed by a Democrat-controlled White House and Congress.
>
> *Number 3*: Lawsuits filed by more than twenty states declaring health care reform unconstitutional, rejecting the overreach of federal government.
>
> *Number 2*: The national debt reaching $14 trillion due in part to out of control government spending.
>
> *Number 1*: The proclamation by some economists and our government that the economy has been recovering since June 2009, even

> though the unemployment rate is at 9.8 percent and has been
> for fourteen months; the housing market continues to slide
> with no sign of recovery; foreclosures are at an all-time high;
> and more banks closed in 2010 than any time since 1992. [XIV]

A more complete list if I do say so myself. This, however, is not the only example of bias I have seen on CNN.

During a report on the union protests in Wisconsin, a reporter for CNN stated, "We have been told that doctors are writing notes for some of those teachers so they won't be penalized, fined by staying away from school. They are helping out the teachers." [XV] This was in reference to some teachers receiving doctor's notes, from actual doctors, stating that they were too sick to work. Yet they were okay to go protest at a rally. Apparently these teachers and doctors are not familiar with the word fraud. This took place during a huge union protest in Wisconsin regarding the changes Governor Scott Walker was making to public unions to rein in government spending and Wisconsin's out of control state debt. He campaigned heavily on this and promised that if elected he would balance the state's budget. To do so, one of the items he tackled was reducing the benefits that public unions received. He also wanted to control their collective bargaining rights so they could not ask for these benefits again in the future. He wanted to be certain the state's money was not spent in this manner now or in the future.

As this bill weaved its way through the legislative process, there were massive protests by the unions at the state capitol. The story made national news; however, when it was covered by FOX News it was reported a little differently. One of their newscasters stated that this was fraud by doctors, incidental to the breach of a teacher contract, which prohibits them from calling in sick to protest. FOX reported the story more accurately, in my opinion, simply because it was fraud, while CNN stated these doctors were trying to help out the unions. CNN spun it with more empathy— that's for sure—because these doctors were not helping anyone. CNN's most memorable moments, NPR's long list of verbal tirades, and the different ways a story is reported, are all examples of media bias and hypocrisy. Unless of course you are liberal, then you probably would not agree. As was the case when self-proclaimed liberal Jon Stewart was asked if bias exists in the media.

He appeared on an episode of Fox News Sunday [XVI] with Chris Wallace, where he was questioned about the media's perceived liberal bias. Jon Stewart is the host of Comedy Central's *The Daily Show*, a political satire program that injects humor into day-to-day political events. This is important to understand because it explains one of the reasons for having him on Fox News Sunday, to get a liberal person's viewpoint regarding the media. I do, generally, like Jon Stewart and think he is an intelligent and funny comedian. However, the fact that he offers a mostly liberal perspective on his show is somewhat off-putting and makes it difficult to watch. During the interview Mr. Wallace asked Jon what his views were regarding *The New York Times* and their agenda and if he believed they had a liberal bias. To which Mr. Stewart replied, "Uh, *The New York Times*? No… Do I think they are relentlessly activist? No. In a purely liberal and partisan way? No I don't." Within that same interview Chris Wallace stated that he would provide some examples that he believed illustrated their bias. One such example was the document dump of 24,000 emails from Sarah Palin's governorship. He asked Jon to explain how *The New York Times* and *The Washington Post* could ask their readers to go through these emails to dig up dirt on the former governor but would not ask them to read through the 2,000-page Obama health care bill. Mr. Stewart replied that he believed their bias was toward sensationalism and laziness and not a liberal agenda. While I do agree with Mr. Stewart regarding the media's tendency toward sensationalism, I believe he is completely wrong when it comes to recognizing their bias. Liberal columnists at *The New York Times* outnumber the conservatives and moderates, ten to one. [XVII] Does this seem balanced and objective to you? Maybe if Mr. Stewart read *The New York Times* with a slightly more open mind he might have a better understanding of the problem. Later in the interview Chris Wallace gave yet another example of liberal bias, this time coming from ABC's World News. On an episode that aired April 23, 2010, Diane Sawyer was explaining the Arizona immigration law. She stated, "If a stranger walking down the street or riding the bus does not seem to be a U.S. citizen, is it all right for the police to stop and question them?" She totally mischaracterized the law, which clearly states an individual could only be asked for legal status if stopped for an infraction. In other words, the person had to be performing some type of illegal activity first. They could not be stopped randomly on the street without probable cause. Prior to showing this example, Mr. Wallace stated that this clip clearly demonstrates liberal bias and he believed it was proof of yet another organization with a partisan agenda. Jon replied, "I'm not suggesting there's no liberal bias in the media..." So which is it, Mr. Stewart? Earlier in the interview you stated that the media was not biased but lazy, then, minutes later, you admit that it does in fact exist.

I fully believe that media bias exists, and I am not the only person who believes so. Others are starting to realize it as well. A September 2010 Gallup poll found that the majority of Americans, 57 percent, say they have little or no trust in the mass media to report the news fully, accurately, and fairly. [xviii] When asked which news outlet they trusted the most, a 2011 Suffolk University poll [xix] found that 28 percent said FOX News, with CNN, NBC, and MSNBC fairing much worse at 18 percent, 10 percent, and 7 percent respectively. The reason behind this distrust is simple—the media's failure to cover things in a balanced manner. In 2008, a study [xx] by the Center for Media and Public Affairs found that the broadcast news' election coverage of Barack Obama was twice as favorable as that of John McCain. In fact, it was more favorable than any other presidential nominee since they began tracking election coverage back in 1988. That same study found that Barack Obama received 68 percent positive evaluations versus John McCain's 33 percent and Sarah Palin's 34 percent. Below is a breakdown of how those in the media covered the 2008 presidential campaign.

	Positive Coverage of Obama	Positive Coverage of McCain/Palin
NBC	73%	31%
CBS	68%	33%
ABC	68%	36%
FOX	37%	42%

2008 Campaign Coverage by Network
Center for Media & Public Affairs study of 2008 campaign coverage.

NBC was the most unbalanced organization, providing 42 percent more positive coverage of Barack Obama than of John McCain. While CBS and ABC faired just slightly better with 35 and 32 point differences. FOX was the only media outlet that came close to covering the candidates in a balanced manner. But even FOX is not always completely balanced. It is also guilty of some media bias, although nowhere near as much as the other networks.

One tactic used by the media to push their agenda is the way they word a headline of a story. One such headline that existed on FOX News' website, *Is Bulletstorm the Worst Video Game Ever in the World?* [XXI] Simply by adding a question mark to the end they can claim objectivity because they are leaving it up to the reader to decide. But the wording itself does, in fact, make a statement against the game, regardless of the question posed. They could have easily titled this story, *Bulletstorm Video Game, for Adults Only!* My headline more accurately represents the contents of the story without conveying any bias for or against the game. It plainly states the facts and briefly describes the story.

Bulletstorm is a video game that is rated Mature, meaning no one under the age of seventeen should have access to it; the same concept as going to an R-rated movie. This game contains many mature themes, including: adult language, sexual situations, and extreme violence. This is definitely not something for minors. When you read the story on FOX News' website it clearly conveys a bias against the game, at least initially. It is not until you get half way through it before you read an alternate view. Understand that news stories are written in a specific format, which places the writer's context, specific facts, and the summary up front, because they know most people do not read through the entire story. So they try and give you the overarching message up front while providing details later. This is common practice with all news organizations. They do the same thing with story placement in a newspaper as well as their website. Headline stories go on the front or home page and the remainders are buried within the paper or website. For the Bulletstorm story, FOX News interviewed psychiatrist Carole Lieberman who stated, "The increase in rapes can be attributed in large part to the playing out of sexual scenes in videogames." Let us put aside for a moment that this video game is intended for use by sane-minded adults that can differentiate between fiction and reality; the statistic Ms. Lieberman cited regarding rapes does not seem to exist. According to the Bureau of Justice, they estimate there were 126,000 rapes and sexual assaults in the U.S. in 2009 (the most recent year available)—less than half the 2006 total of 272,000. In fact, the number of rapes and sexual assaults has been trending downward for decades. The bureau estimates there were 607,000 incidents of rape or sexual assault in 1992. [XXII] So, did the folks at FOX news forget to fact check Ms. Lieberman before posting the story, or were they just trying to push a specific agenda?

The article went on to quote other experts who warned that exposing this game to children could have resounding negative effects on their psyche. My question to these *experts* is, "Where are the parents?" The current rating system provides a more than adequate warning. Mom and Dad need to be held accountable regarding what they purchase for their children, just as if they were going to a movie. It is clearly marked on the packaging and fully explains why it received a Mature rating. If you read through the entire story on FOX's website it does give the other side of the story and does offer suggestions to limiting the game to minors, such as creating more legislation to penalize store clerks for selling the game to minors—which I fully disagree with because it is not the job of government to restrict something based on their perception of what is considered objectionable. That is called censorship and a clear violation of the First Amendment. There is no need for this legislation either because the current rating system is enforced at all video game outlets. If a parent is not present and the kid is not over seventeen, he is not allowed to purchase the game. However, if a parent does purchase this game for their small child, then, in my opinion, they are doing a disservice to all responsible parents and the industry as a whole. If they feel their child is mature enough to understand the game at fifteen or sixteen, then it is their prerogative to purchase it as they see fit. It really boils down to common sense; the video game industry has changed substantially since its inception and caters to people of all ages. You can no longer go into a store and blindly purchase a game for your child without first reading the rating. The bias contained within this story was much more conservative than liberal, but it existed nonetheless. As I stated, it should be the primary goal of any news organization to eliminate bias and provide complete objectivity. FOX News is in the minority when it comes to conservative bias, and they do a much better job at covering the news in a balanced manner, especially their hard news broadcasts. Most all other news organizations lean left, some unabashedly so.

Liberal bias is not just some anomaly that exists in the media. It exists elsewhere as well. Hollywood is rife with liberal folks. Author and Lawyer Ben Shapiro wrote an entire book on the subject called Primetime Propaganda. In it he writes that the industry's elites use television to "shape America in their own leftist image." He also said that he was shocked by how open the Hollywood crowd was to admitting their liberal bias. "They weren't ashamed of it. In fact, some were proud of it," he stated. [XXIII] This does not surprise me, after all, why would someone by ashamed of their beliefs? But the fact they are pursuing their agenda to the point of activism concerns me deeply, and it should concern the viewing public as well. It is not imperative that Hollywood be unbiased, of course—as the media should be—but we need to be aware of their agenda when paying to see a movie or when supporting their television programs through advertising. After all, if your viewpoint differs from theirs, is it not in your best interest to fully understand where your money is going? Ben Shapiro interviewed seventy people in Hollywood for his book and asked if the liberal agenda was something tangible or if it was merely speculation. What he found confirmed his belief, that it absolutely was a mostly liberal town.

Marta Kauffman, co-creator of *Friends*, said she "hired a bunch of liberals" to "put out there what we believe." She went on to say, "When we did the lesbian wedding, we knew there was going to be some flack. I have to say, when we cast Candice Gingrich as the minister of that wedding, there was a bit of a 'f–- k you' in it to the right-wing, directly." [XXIII] Ah, the progressive mind of a liberal. They are so accepting of people with opposing views. The producer of *MacGyver*, Vin DiBona, agreed that there was a liberal bias in Hollywood, stating, "I'm happy about it, actually." *MASH, Happy Days*, and *Sesame Street,* are other shows mentioned in Shapiro's book that also push liberal agendas. Their bias goes beyond projecting their viewpoints onto an unsuspecting public. They push their agenda with their pocketbooks as well. Approximately 1,160 employees, including senior executives, on-air personalities, producers, reporters, editors, and writers of ABC, CBS, and NBC contributed more than 1 million dollars to Democratic candidates and campaign committees in 2008, according to an analysis by *The Examiner* of data compiled by the Center for Responsive Politics. [XXIV] By contrast, only 193 employees gave to Republican candidates, totaling $142,863. The liberal movement is alive and well in our society, even though only 20 percent identify themselves as such. How can such a small minority have such a large voice? They are rooting themselves in areas of high visibility and influence, such as our schools, television, and the news. Liberal teachers and professors espousing their beliefs on our children, Hollywood injecting their viewpoints into television and movies, and the mainstream media reporting the news in a biased manner, all spread the liberal agenda, which permeates society and is forced upon us to the point of indoctrination. It is no wonder more and more people are growing up with a sense of entitlement. At this rate, America will be a fully socialist state within a few generations. If this occurs it will completely destroy the ideals on which this country was founded, and the American dream of achieving greatness through hard work and determination will be no more.

Think rampant liberalism in our social and cultural mediums is not having a resounding effect on how people view their political party? Starting on the next page is a conversation I had with some friends on a popular social networking website. It revolved around a graphic posted on Sarah Palin's website and the supposed hateful rhetoric surrounding it. The posting contained a map with gun sights targeting Democrats that Governor Palin wanted voted out of office. My friends, and those in the media, stated that this graphic somehow played a part in the shooting of Congresswoman Gabrielle Giffords. They suggested that since Republicans use this type of inflammatory posturing on a regular basis, they were partly responsible for the violence—while Democrats were the party of acceptance and never utilized this type of language when deriding their opponents. I exposed the left's hypocrisy and proved that this type of behavior exists in both parties and that none of it had anything to do with the shooting. To provide full disclosure, I am not currently a Sarah Palin supporter. I do believe, however, that when a person tries demeaning someone based solely on ideology while totally disregarding the facts, he should be called out on the matter, regardless of political affiliation.

Brad: Good job, Sarah Palin, what did you think would happen? Hope all my Republican friends start to wake up to the hate, crap, and ignorance their politicians stand for and even more so their media blowholes.

Kirk: Yeah the lunatic that shot those people in AZ did it because of what Sarah Palin puts on a website. Come on, the guy is a freakin' nutcase.

Brad: Didn't say that, just showing the obvious bad judgment Palin has. Good thing she isn't in a VP spot right now. Her type of rhetoric, as well as Becks, Rush's, and everyone else on Fox is bad for everyone.

Let's call a spade a spade here. A hardcore red city in a hardcore red state and a Dem gets shot. Hm…I wonder what Beck and Rush's ratings are in Tucson?

Come on, her saying things like, "Let's not retreat let's reload." That is just stirring the pot. She is a lunatic. Glad to see her show cancelled. But we all knew that was going to happen

Kirk: Well I completely disagree. For one, you are saying this was a political shooting and as far as I've heard, it's not. It's the left that started this whole political thing. It's B.S. if you think Sarah is the first to use comments like that; well, you must not listen to too much political rhetoric, well except for Colbert, Olbermann, and the likes.

Brad: They don't say things like "reload" or "I want you to come armed and dangerous." Their followers don't show up to political events with guns.

Kirk: So who relayed to you that this was political?

Brad: I didn't say he was specifically politically motivated. I am just saying you have a right wing party that uses a lot of violent talk and *never* denounces things like this image or Nazi talk, or bringing guns. And they show zero respect for the current president, shouting liar, etc. It creates a bad environment and it just takes one nutjob to take it too far.

Chris: Loughner had been "described by classmates as a very liberal pothead" whose "favorite video shows a burning American flag."

He sounds like a huge Palin fan. But then again does that lady really have fans? Seriously—this guy is a nutjob and whether he watched Palin or followed *The Daily KOS* doesn't matter. As for rhetoric, how about all of the violent, hate-filled speeches against Bush! Was that justified, because you (and the media) agreed with that view?

There is a price for freedom—we all get a voice and many of the loudest ones say the dumbest things. The minute we start linking dumb comments to insane acts of violence, we'll quickly start restricting what people can and can't say. Talk about dangerous and scary.

Brad: I don't recall people calling for the death of Bush, just the prosecution of him.

Me: You don't recall people calling for the death of Bush? Are you kidding me? Did you forget the movie that was made about the assassination of Bush, *Death of a President?* It was released at all major theaters in 2006 during his presidency. Can you imagine what the media would say if someone released a movie like this about Obama? Political rhetoric of this sort has been used on both sides, not just by Republicans. I direct your attention to this website for further proof: http://bigjournalism.com/dloesch/2011/01/09/the-blame-game/

Even Democrats have used a map with targets on it. This has nothing to do with Republican or Democratic ideologies or blaming one side over another for the ridiculous actions of one person. This has everything to do with a mentally disturbed man shooting innocent people, period. No one is at fault, but the nutcase that pulled the trigger. We need to grieve for the deceased and quit trying to politicize this.

*Brad***:** It's one thing for a filmmaker to do something like that and something else for a VP candidate to do it. And for the record, not blaming the Republicans for the shooting, just saying that if leaders use language like what Palin and some others have, it's only a matter of time before someone does something stupid.

Me: For the record, there's absolutely no difference. The makers of the film were liberal and had an agenda, just like the people pointing fingers at Palin, advocating she's somehow responsible for the actions of a nut. Furthermore, if you're defining Palin's photo as hateful rhetoric, then what about the map Democrats posted with targets? You state that you're not blaming Republicans, yet all your examples were Republican/Conservative. In fact, your first post states that all your Republican friends need to wake up to the hate, crap, etc., their politicians stand for, yet I proved rhetoric exists on both sides of the aisle. Sounds like you're blaming Republicans to me, this leads me to believe you have an agenda and aren't taking this tragedy for what it is, a tragedy and nothing more.

Brad: The shooter is responsible period, but Republicans appear to be more violent, rude, and angry to me.

There is no comparison between what Democrats have said and done vs. what Republicans have. Palin's map is the famous one; we have two recent, disgraceful shouting incidents by Republicans in Congress. Republicans show up with guns at political events not Democrats. Can't remember an event where a Democrat stomped on a Republican's head. What's with all the tea bagger Nazi stuff? Democrats aren't the ones suggesting tax breaks for the rich while trying to take health care and other benefits away from those in need. Democrats didn't get us into what is now the longest war in US History. Democrats didn't ruin the economy. Just seems to me that the Republicans embrace hatred, fear, greed, and anger a lot more often than Democrats. Just making an observation.

Me: Where to begin, where to begin? Let me, one more time, direct you to the website I posted earlier as one example of how many things Democrats have said/done that are just as inflammatory. Did you even read the article?

Not sure what you're referencing regarding Republicans showing up to events with guns. Regardless, I take it you don't believe in the Second Amendment? If more law-abiding citizens carried guns the nut that shot all those innocent people may have thought twice before doing so.

Do you remember liberals calling Bush a Nazi, and posters made to Hitler's likeness? Like I said, it happens on both sides.

Your belief that tax breaks for the rich and taking health care from those in need is also flawed. Who hires people in this country? Our country has one of the highest corporate tax rates in the world. Making those people pay more taxes will only stifle the recovery because they'll be less likely to hire. Furthermore, when did it become the responsibility of the government to redistribute wealth? This country was founded on hard work, determination, self-reliance, etc.—not government handouts.

Name one time someone was turned down from going to an emergency room? Don't get me wrong, our health care system does need some serious refinement, but not by the hands of government.

Democrats absolutely had a hand in the recession; Bill Clinton repealed the legislation that regulated improper lending practices, which was one of the primary causes of the great recession. Both parties were to blame, along with some greedy corporate executives, all outlined in detail in my brother's book.

And I state, yet again, none of this has anything at all to do with the tragedy that took place last weekend. Yet, you're going out of your way to draw a connection.

Brad: Wow, Lou, I can't possible keep up with all this. You out typed me :)

Me: All in good spirits, Brad, nothing like a lively, healthy debate. I hope you and your family is doing well. Take care.

Brad: You as well. LOL.

So which person do you agree with more? Now think about where you receive most of your news. What do they generally report when covering these types of issues? Which side of the argument does your news outlets support—liberal, conservative, or are they truly objective? If you are honest with yourself you are not going to be able to place your media outlet in the objective column. Most media outlets tend to skew one way or the other. And some are just downright corrupt in their approach to covering the news from a biased perspective. I understand that no one is truly unbiased, but it is the responsibility of any good news organization to be as objective as possible. They should not be presenting the news with an agenda. They should strive to present both sides of the story so you can make an informed decision based solely on the facts. When the media tries to force an agenda on you, they are basically stating that you are too stupid to make up your own mind. They believe they know what is best for you and, therefore, present the news in such a manner that depicts their vision of how the country should be. This is yet another example of *intellectual* elites trying to tell us they know best, which sounds eerily similar to big government's agenda. Could it be possible that they both have the same ideological motive? I will leave that up to you to decide.

If after reading this chapter you are still not convinced the media bias exists, I highly recommend reading *Bias* and *A Slobbering Love Affair*, by author and news analyst Bernard Goldberg. There are other books as well, but these two provide plenty of examples and explain the issue in great detail. So it appears people are finally taking notice. Evident by the studies that show most Americans no longer trust most major news outlets, which is why I find it amazing that media bias still exists, even to this day. If the poll numbers are any indication, this should not continue much longer. People are now getting their news from many different sources, not just mainstream media. Blogs, news websites, cable news, social networking sites, and RSS feeds all create an environment that allows us to gather our news quickly and efficiently, which means anytime a major news network decides to spew their rhetoric, we now have options.

My prediction—the liberal mainstream media's advertising revenue will inevitably dry up, simply because most people are tuning out and going elsewhere for their news. MSNBC, CNN, and CNBC are consistently way behind in the ratings. FOX News dominates the cable news market on a daily basis, sometimes quadrupling their competition's total viewers. [xxv] For everyone other than FOX, their diminished viewership will mean less advertising dollars, less advertising means less revenue, and continued revenue decline equates to a failed business model—a pretty simple concept. The organizations that thrive will ultimately be the ones that folks trust.

The Right to Bear Arms

The Second Amendment to the Constitution deals with an individual's right to own a firearm and a state's right to maintain a militia. As written, it states: *A well regulated Militia, being necessary to the security of a free State, the right of the people to keep and bear Arms, shall not be infringed.* The meaning of this amendment has been the subject of debate for quite some time. Does it pertain to an individual's right to own a gun or a state's ability to form and maintain a militia as a means of defense? To answer this question effectively we need to examine the historical context behind the creation of this amendment.

During the late 1700s, around the time the Declaration of Independence was being written, many states were forming their own constitutions to institute new rules from which to govern. Within each state's constitution, the right to bear arms was defined a little differently. Massachusetts and North Carolina guaranteed the right for an individual to bear arms in order to provide defense for the states. [1] Since the government did not supply weapons for defense it was assumed that an individual would retain his own firearms to assist with defending the state in a time of need. Pennsylvania's constitution guaranteed this right for the defense of the individual as well as for defense of the state, *That the people have a right to bear arms for the defence of themselves and the state; and as standing armies in the time of peace are dangerous to liberty, they ought not to be kept up; And that the military should be kept under strict subordination to, and governed by, the civil power.*[II] Regardless of the differences between each state's constitutions, it was either inferred or specifically written that each person had a right to own and use firearms for the purpose of defense. The colonists' attitude toward gun ownership never changed, even after the Revolutionary War was won.

After the defeat of the British, memories of the king's tyrannical rule were fresh in the minds of the Founding Fathers. It was imperative their new government be reflective of the people's wishes and not those of one single ruler. When they met to discuss the creation of this new government during the spring of 1781, one of their primary goals was ensuring no such absolute power could exist. They even went as far as denying the new federal government the ability to maintain a standing army. Instead, giving all the power to the states, making sure their militias remained intact. This meant each state would not have to rely on big government for defense, nor would they have to be concerned with a government that had its own army, one that could be used to enforce supreme rule, something they were all too familiar with under King George III.

As they drafted the first constitution, the Articles of Confederation, the Founders ensured states' rights to defense by creating Article VI, which states: *No vessel of war shall be kept up in time of peace by any State, except such number only, as shall be deemed necessary by the united States in congress assembled, for the defense of such State, or its trade; nor shall any body of forces be kept up by any State in time of peace, except such number only, as in the judgement of the united States, in congress assembled, shall be deemed requisite to garrison the forts necessary for the defense of such State; but every State shall always keep up a well-regulated and disciplined militia, sufficiently armed and accoutered, and shall provide and constantly have ready for use, in public stores, a due number of field pieces and tents, and a proper quantity of arms, ammunition and camp equipage.* This Article is very clear and concise in its message. The states would each maintain their own militia, and in times of peace would only keep the number necessary for proper defense of the state. Nowhere was it mentioned that a national army should exist. In order for states to defend themselves and form militias, it was understood that an individual must procure his own firearms since they were not being provided by the state.

In time, the Founders began to realize the Articles of Confederation were failing at maintaining an effective government. To combat the problem and keep the fledgling nation from collapsing, the Founders decided to meet and discuss possible solutions. At first the intent was just to ratify the original Articles of Confederation. But it was soon discovered simple ratification was not sufficient, given all the changes that were needed to fix the current system, so the decision was made to create an entirely new constitution.

Of the many problems the Founders faced, one in particular caused sufficient struggle within the group; how best to address problems regarding national security. Their solution of forming a national militia to repel foreign invaders was worrisome to anti-federalists, because in order to do this a federal government would have to be created. The anti-federalists feared the creation of a new federal government and national army. They believed it would inevitably lead to the disarmament of the state militias. Another problem that had to be rectified was the lack of an organized security force to repel insurrections, something that was becoming all too prevalent under the new nation. Within the new Constitution these issues were both addressed with Article 1, Section 8. Some representatives were not satisfied and worried about enlarging federal powers and the inherent risks associated with centralizing power. The federalists and anti-federalists did eventually come to an agreement by explicitly spelling out government's duties and by creating a separate bill of rights for the general populace.

There was tremendous opposition to the Constitution in the beginning. The transfer of power to arm the state militias at the federal level rather than the state was a major concern for the Founders. They believed this new arrangement would allow the government to neglect the states militias, causing them to fall into disrepair and leaving them vulnerable in the event of a government confrontation. This transfer of power was in direct conflict to Article VI in the Articles of Confederation. By creating Article 1 Section 8 in the new Constitution, it appeared to some that the state's primary means of defense were being stripped away. You have to remember that during this time period there was well-justified concern of government tyranny and political corruption. Even the federalists recognized the risks of tyranny, and they were the ones who pushed for the new Constitution. Because of this the Framers believed the right to bear arms was a necessary right from which to protect all other rights, as well as to provide for public defense against tyranny. Founding Father Patrick Henry stated, "Guard with jealous attention the public liberty. Suspect everyone who approaches that jewel. Unfortunately, nothing will preserve it but downright force. Whenever you give up that force, you are inevitably ruined." [III] People were concerned about the new government becoming something similar to Europe's model. The father of the modern dictionary Noah Webster said:

> Before a standing army can rule, the people must be disarmed; as they are in almost every kingdom of Europe. The supreme power in America cannot enforce unjust laws by the sword; because the whole body of the people are armed, and constitute a force superior to any band of regular troops that can be, on any pretence, raised in the United States. [IV]

Founding Father James Madison reassured his fellow patriots that our government could never become like Europe, simply because we have the advantage of being armed. In Federalist paper number forty-six he wrote:

> Let a regular army, fully equal to the resources of the country, be formed; and let it be entirely at the devotion of the federal government; still it would not be going too far to say, that the State governments, with the people on their side, would be able to repel the danger. ...To these would be opposed a militia amounting to near half a million of citizens with arms in their hands, officered by men chosen from among themselves, fighting for their common liberties,... [V]

Madison believed our government would never be able to overthrow the will of the people by force, simply because there was no way its army would ever outnumber the armed citizenry. Of course, he never imagined the amount of power and weaponry that would be developed by our modern government. Regardless, just because the threat of government tyranny in the physical sense seems nonexistent today does not mean we should ever lose site of the Founders' concerns.

By the end of the ratification convention, the Framers were so evenly divided between those for and against the Constitution it appeared it would never get approved. To break the stalemate, federalists agreed to the amendments proposed by the anti-federalist and the Constitution was ratified on June 21, 1788, with the Bill of Rights following suit on December 15, 1791. Samuel Adams proposed that the Constitution,

> Be never construed to authorize Congress to infringe the just liberty of the press, or the rights of conscience; or to prevent the people of the United States, who are peaceable citizens, from keeping their own arms; or to raise standing armies, unless when necessary for the defence of the United States, or of some one or more of them; or to prevent the people from petitioning, in a peaceable and orderly manner, the federal legislature, for a redress of their grievances: or to subject the people to unreasonable searches and seizures.[VI]

He specifically stated the Constitution should never be used to prevent peaceful citizens from keeping their own arms. The belief held by our Founding Fathers regarding an individual's right to bear arms is obvious to me and has been demonstrated clearly by the quotes provided herein. Firearms were a part of everyday colonial society and there can be no argument to the contrary regarding the meaning of the Second Amendment, especially when historical context is considered. Plainly put, every citizen has the right to own a firearm, just as Samuel Adams stated. Had the Framers been able to foresee the modern debate surrounding this amendment they probably would have worded it differently, if only to clarify the portion regarding a well-regulated militia.

After the introduction of the Second Amendment, for the better part of a century, it was given little attention. However, near the end of the nineteenth century and up through the twenty-first century, people's interest regarding its true meaning has grown substantially. So much so that the courts' involvement has become somewhat commonplace. There have been many cases at the state and federal levels regarding this amendment. The Supreme Court tried some notable cases dating back as far as 1886. In Presser versus Illinois, 116 U.S. 252 (1886), the Court ruled the State was not violating Herman Presser's Second Amendment right by barring him from organizing and marching in a private militia. They stated such a right "cannot be claimed as a right independent of law." [vii] This meant that just because he had a right to own a firearm did not give him the right to form and march in a private militia when State law specifically forbade it. In Robertson versus Baldwin, 165 U.S. 275 (1897), it was ruled that laws regulating concealed weapons were not a violation of the Second Amendment. Within the text of the case it was stated "…the freedom of speech and of the press (Art. I) does not permit the publication of libels, blasphemous or indecent articles, or other publications injurious to public morals or private reputation; the right of the people to keep and bear arms (Art. II) is not infringed by laws prohibiting the carrying of concealed weapons." [viii] Just because a person cannot carry a concealed weapon does not infringe upon his right to own a gun—although some states now allow a person to conceal and carry. In United States versus Miller, 307 U.S. 174 (1939), the Court ruled that Jack Miller and Frank Layton unlawfully transported a twelve gauge, double-barrel shotgun, with a barrel shorter than eighteen inches, across state lines. This violated a law enacted in 1934, the National Firearms Act, which regulates the manufacture and transfer of certain firearms as well as mandating their registration. The defense claimed this act was unconstitutional and was a violation of their Second Amendment rights. The Court rejected this claim outright and ruled against the defendant, stating:

> In the absence of any evidence tending to show that possession or use of a 'shotgun having a barrel of less than eighteen inches in length' at this time has some reasonable relationship to any preservation or efficiency of a well-regulated militia, we cannot say that the Second Amendment guarantees the right to keep and bear such an instrument. Certainly it is not within judicial notice that this weapon is any part of the ordinary military equipment or that its use could contribute to the common defense. [ix]

Most of these early cases restricted firearms in some capacity, slowly stripping away at the foundation of the Second Amendment.

More recently, however, two landmark decisions by the Supreme Court proved encouraging for gun enthusiasts everywhere. In District of Columbia versus Heller, 554 U.S. 570 (2008), the Court decided that the Second Amendment does protect an individual's right to possess a firearm in federal enclaves, such as a home within the District of Columbia. It did not address whether gun rights extended beyond federal enclaves to the states. This case set an important precedent and was the first in United States history to protect a person's right to bear arms for self-defense. The lawsuit was brought by Robert A. Levy, chairman of the Cato Institute. One of the plaintiffs he represented was Dick Heller, a police officer for the District of Columbia. Mr. Heller was allowed to carry a gun in federal buildings but was not allowed to keep one in his home for self-defense, per the Firearms Control Regulations Act of 1975—which banned handguns, automatic firearms, and high capacity semi-automatic firearms. There were exceptions that allowed police officers to carry a gun, or any citizen that registered their firearm prior to 1975. But here is the kicker—this Act also required that all firearms kept in a home be "unloaded, disassembled, or bound by a trigger lock or similar device."[x]

The fact that the government made a person keep any weapons inside the home, unloaded or trigger locked, is just plain ridiculous. What purpose does an unloaded weapon serve in a time of crisis? I can just envision how this would play out in real time. A thief breaks into an occupied home carrying a loaded weapon, at which point the homeowner reaches for his gun to confront the attacker and politely asks, "Can you please hold on a moment while I load my gun?" What is in the minds of politicians that pass these types of incomprehensible laws? I would also love to know how in the hell they enforced this. I can only assume they performed random surprise inspections of people's homes, asked to see their firearms, and ticketed them accordingly. Give me a break. This overprotective nanny state is exactly what our Founding Fathers warned us about, and the District of Columbia illustrates their concerns perfectly.

The second most recent case decided by the Supreme Court occurred in 2010. In McDonald versus Chicago, 561 U.S. ___ -08-1521 (2010), the Court addressed the uncertainty left over from the District of Columbia v. Heller case regarding gun rights and the states. The case specifically challenged four limits placed on handgun registration by the city of Chicago and a suburb, Oak Park: a ban on the registration of handguns; that all guns must be registered prior to purchase; that all guns must be reregistered annually; and that any lapse in a gun's registration removes it from ever being reregistered.[xi] The Court ruled that the right of an individual to keep and bear arms was protected by the Second

Amendment and does apply at the state level as well, making the Chicago regulations unconstitutional. They based their decision on the fact that they considered this amendment incorporated as per the due process clause of the Fourteenth Amendment, which makes it enforceable at both the state and federal levels.

Thankfully, these recent Supreme Court rulings were more in line with the Framers' intent, albeit by a small margin of 5-4. The view that most gun opponents' hold is one of collective rights. They insist that the Second Amendment was created solely for the purpose of arming a militia, and since militias no longer exist, then neither should an individual's right to own a gun. These folks generally dismiss historical context when arguing their point. They also argue that because of guns we are one of the most violent nations in existence today.

One recent event, which they claim supports their argument, was the shooting of Congresswoman Gabrielle Giffords, a Democrat from Arizona. While holding a meeting with her constituents outside a grocery store in Tucson, Congresswoman Giffords was shot in the head by a deranged lunatic Jerry Lee Loughner. She and twelve others were wounded and six people were killed. Miraculously she survived and is recovering well—a true testament to the human spirit and her strong will to survive. The irony behind this whole incident is Congresswoman Giffords is a gun owner and supported broad Second Amendment rights. In 2008 and 2009, Giffords signed onto briefs to the Supreme Court, urging justices to overturn gun control laws that severely restricted the access of those who sought to purchase and own firearms. In both cases, the Court ruled to roll back the restrictions. At the time, Giffords noted the *long tradition* of gun ownership in the United States, adding, "It is a tradition which every law-abiding citizen should be able to enjoy." [XII]

Of course, you would never know this when debating this issue with someone opposed to gun ownership. Like most people on the extreme left, they tend to debate with their emotions rather than with logic and facts. They would have you believe that guns are the problem rather than the actual people committing the crimes. Representative Carolyn Maloney, Democrat of New York, said, "Guns kill. And those who glamorize gunplay or worship gun ownership do no service to humanity." [XII] Using Congresswoman Maloney's logic we must assume the gun sprouted arms and legs and shot Congresswoman Giffords all by itself.

When are individuals like Ms. Maloney going to realize that guns do not kill people, people do. No matter how much she and others like her try and regulate guns, there will always be individuals that disobey the law in this manner. No amount of gun control is going to curb this. All it will do is make law-abiding citizens less safe. I tried explaining this to some colleagues while chatting online, right after the incident with Giffords occurred in January 2011. Their initial argument was against the size of clip used in the gun. However, as the conversation progressed, their true agenda surfaced.

> *Brad:* Wow, just heard a guy on TV defend the multi-round clips with, "Well when you are at the shooting range it is a difference of a gun enthusiast having to reload fifteen times versus three. You have to use your thumb each time."

> *Really,* that is the defense of them, *wow*!

> *Robert:* Ban the use and sale of clips more than ten rounds. There is no legitimate argument to the contrary.

> *Jim:* We cannot blame guns or gun manufacturers for this tragedy. Cars kill more people than guns. This guy was insane. Gun control is never the issue. One legitimate argument would be police would be out gunned if they had to abide by a 10 round clip when all the gangbangers and criminals are running around with 30 round AK magazines and 15 round pistol magazines.

> *Brad:* Sorry, Jim, that is a weak argument for these clips, and yes AK-47s should be banned also. Both are made for one thing only, to kill lots of people. And this has nothing to do with Tucson, but instead, common sense. And I can blame the manufactures, who you think had all the money to lobby for things like letting the assault rifle ban expire.

> Whoever said the police could not have them? Keep them available for the police or military, just not a crazy to buy them at Wal-Mart.

And do not give me any 2nd amendment stuff either. That was written when we had single shot muskets, pretty hard for someone to mass kill with those. And no I am not worried about needing to protect myself from my government (do not need to match the military with fire power).

Me: Robert and Brad, when are you going to learn that regulation of this type is never good for our country? One primary reason is because criminals do not care about laws or regulations. So all you are doing is limiting the ability of law-abiding citizens to defend themselves against crooks. Jim has a good point regarding the police as well. Once government starts regulating clip size, what is to stop them from taking the next step? It is a very slippery slope. And who's to say what the limit should be—four, three, or even one bullet? Where does it stop? Isn't killing one person just as horrific as murdering six? The end result being that the family members of each victim all feel grief and pain for the loss of their loved ones. And with a ten round clip Loughner still would have had enough bullets to murder six innocent people. I would say those are all pretty legitimate arguments to the contrary.

Jim: Ban guns because they kill people, really? Have you ever bought an assault rifle? It is not against any law to purchase one even with the ban. The ban just allowed people to sell it for more money. I had one when we were in high school and I paid 100 dollars for it. I sold that one for 350 dollars (who was really benefitting). It's not against any law to own an assault rifle or even to sell an assault rifle (person to person). The ban does nothing to stop high capacity magazines or AKs from entering into criminal hands. They have already been produced so there will always be a way to obtain them. So what do you hope to gain by doing this? I can only speak for Missouri, but I cannot buy a high capacity handgun mag, or even a handgun or an assault rifle in Wal-Mart. Finally, I agree we should throw out the Constitution; it is an outdated document (sarcasm) full of things that do not apply in 2011.

Jim: However that was a horrible argument to put on TV. He has to reload less. I agree with you on that point.

Brad: Jim the Constitution is a living document and is changed regularly. And the act in 1994 did prohibit the manufacture of some assault rifles and high capacity magazines.

Lou, let the cops keep the high-powered guns, just make it more difficult for others to get them. And you are right you will not be able to stop criminals from getting it, but why not make it more difficult? You would then agree that we should legalize drugs because people will get them anyway. And I am not worried about precedent (slippery slope), but that is just me. Does one really need an arsenal to *defend themselves?* Is that not what police are for?

And this is not just about Tucson, but all the school shootings, etc. Why is America considered a joke in the eyes of all other first world countries when it comes to this issue? We should look at what our peers are doing. It is why we have the highest rate of gun violence of any developed country in the world.

Me: Brad the only people you hurt when we limit or ban anything is the law-abiding citizen. Banning guns does not make it more difficult for criminals to obtain them because most of them are already being obtained illegally. As far as drugs are concerned, you and I do, in fact, agree. While I have never done them myself, I do believe it is a person's right to do what they want with their body. The drug war we have been waging for years on end hasn't worked anyway. It is costing our country billions of dollars every year; and all-out war at the Mexican border, and for what? In my opinion, if drugs were legal, most of these problems would disappear.

Why are you so concerned with what the rest of the world thinks about us? We are the greatest country on this planet and have helped more nations monetarily than all other nations combined. And for what, most of them still dislike us. I would say if anything they should be more concerned with how we view them, not the other way around.

Jim: Louis is spot on!

Ramak: Jim and Louis—LOL so based on that argument I should be able to own a nuclear bomb, or how about an F16? You live in a civilized society, therefore, certain regulation on certain equipment is necessary for the greater good! And if the argument is that criminals are going to break the law, then let us legalize rape because guess what? Criminals are going to rape anyway! Sorry, but your arguments, at minimum, are fundamentally irresponsible.

Me: Ramak, I love how you try and tie two subjects together that have absolutely nothing to do with one another. This is a typical tactic for someone disagreeing with a subject that he has no legitimate response to. I believe they call this the straw man technique in debate 101 (exaggerate an opponent's position and then claim to fight against a position they do not hold). The argument was not that because criminals break the law we should legalize everything they do, the argument was that by banning or restricting our right to bear arms you embolden the criminal element. For if they are left to run amok, only chaos can ensue. The police cannot be everywhere all the time. No one was advocating that rape should be legalized, but nice try. The bottom line is any person that understands the Constitution knows it is our right to bear arms, and as long as you are a responsible, law-abiding citizen, there should be no infringement upon those rights. And I say if you can afford an F16, more power to you.

Ramak: You say we should not ban them because it will not make it any harder or stop criminals from getting them? Rape laws have not stopped any rapist from raping either! The point of the law is not so much stopping, but the prosecutorial power it provides. As far as Constitution in its original format: it no longer is. We evolve; so does the Constitution. Thus, is called a living document. Otherwise many of the privileges we now enjoy would cease to exist.

Let me get this right: banning the gun ownership creates chaos, but allowing the ownership of nuclear power or F16 by private citizens who can afford them does not? Yeah, I think we see things differently! A private citizen should not have access to certain equipment, period. This would be regardless of financial ability.

I assure you of full pre-funding the moment I am able to legally purchase F16. But money should never be the barrier of ownership for such thing.

Me: So what is your point? What good are prosecutorial powers when they are not acting as a deterrent? Rape still happens does it not? This again, is why I say we need the ability to protect ourselves. If a criminal has a gun and I do not, that gives him a serious advantage over me. I personally believe that a criminal would be less likely to rape a woman if he knew she was carrying a gun. In fact, if more people carried guns I think crime overall would go down, or at the very least criminals might be more reluctant to commit a crime.

Once again, you're arguing a point I did not state. Nowhere did I say that the Constitution still exists in its original format. It has been amended twenty-seven times over the years, as recently as May 7, 1992. So I'm not sure what point you were trying to make. All I stated is the Second Amendment affords us the right to bear arms. Are you, in fact, advocating we repeal that Amendment? I agree with you on one thing, we do in fact see things differently.

Ramak: I used to have a professor in my constitutional law classes who said: you should always know when to rest your case. You don't see my point, that's pretty obvious. But let me try to see if I see yours: more citizens who carry guns would reduce crime! I *rest my case*!

Me: My point was simple; I want the ability to protect myself and my family. The Second Amendment allows me the right to bear arms. I do not want that right infringed upon, nor do 69 percent of the American public, according to a Nov. 22, 2010 Gallup poll.

David: Lou, I agree with you. A ban on guns will make it extremely hard for people like you and me who abide by the law to protect ourselves. They have been making and selling guns for a very long time and there is an ungodly amount out in the public (unlike F16s and nuclear weapons) and the bad guys will not just turn them in and will not care if they are illegal. If they (the bad guys) know that the good guys cannot carry weapons the crime rate will surely go up.

Ramak: David, obviously not! Now if you want to get into predicting criminal behavior, then here you go—the more powerful guns they think citizens have, even more powerful ones they (the criminals) will carry! Also, U.S. has the highest per capita gun, the most number of citizens with guns, and, as a result, the highest per capita crime of any post-industrial nation!

My point: to assume from Second amendment, written some 300 plus years ago, that the Founding Fathers meant anyone should be able to carry any arm without limitation is farfetched. The context of a law is just as important as the law itself. There is no logical argument to be made for a private citizen to own a semi-automatic gun with a 30 plus round magazine. Here is a recipe for chaos: more guns with more firing power, and then more citizens owning them! Plenty of societies out there are living proof that this is a recipe for disaster, while plenty of proof also exists that less guns actually makes it safer.

And here is the icing: gun-carrying citizen with years of training, first, almost shot the wrong guy! Then attacks the wrong guy! At the end, he thoughtfully puts the gun away to proceed and help out others without a gun! http://www.latimes.com/news/nationworld/nation/la-na-zamudio-shooting-20110115,0,7713862.story

David: I used to predict criminal behavior for a living as a Washington county deputy and I have had years of training, along with the other law enforcement officers that I worked with. I never heard of the wrong person getting shot. And as you put it in your last comment, the ones who needed help were the ones without the guns and the guy with the gun was okay. Me, myself, and I would rather be the guy that was okay, wouldn't you?

Also, criminals will not upgrade their weapons based on what citizens are carrying. Most of the criminals are financially challenged and will use whatever they can get, based on my experience.

Ramak: The issue is not the petty theft by financially challenged losers, but those like recent Arizona case that is facilitated but lack of qualification and plenty of time and money to plan and more. As far as Law enforcement officers, past or present, should be allowed to have whatever they like. Hell, there should be a tax on gun sale to fund a program to provide them with what they want. You know what is funny, I see people's rental application get denied for a criminal record everyday but not their license to own or carry a gun. They always call my work and complain—but I have a gun license so your record must be wrong!

Me: Ramak, we can go around and around like this for days, so let's try and end this conversation civilly. After all, didn't you *rest your case?* You see things differently than the majority of Americans, please reference my previous post. And the Second Amendment was ratified Dec. 15, 1791, along with nine other amendments constituting the Bill of Rights. That's just over 219 years ago, not 300 plus as you stated. Either way, it is a long time ago, I get it. But facts are facts and I feel it is very important to get them correct when debating an issue such as this. The bottom line is you think guns should be restricted and by doing so society would be safer. While I contend that by doing so you're actually making it less safe, and there are many studies out there that prove my point.

So which of these individuals do you feel made the better argument? My guess would be whomever you agree with more. I feel it is important to back up any claims made for or against gun control with cold hard facts. To solidify my stance on the subject, that societies with looser gun control laws are actually much safer than those with stricter laws, I researched the issue and compiled what I found.

Former Chicago Mayor Richard Daley, a Democrat, predicted an end to society as we know it when the Washington D.C. gun ban was struck down in 2008. He said that overturning the gun ban was "a very frightening decision" and predicted more deaths along with Wild West-style shootouts, and that people "are going to take a gun and they are going to end their lives in a family dispute." Washington's Mayor Adrian Fenty similarly warned: "More handguns in the District of Columbia will only lead to more handgun violence." [XIII] So was Mayor Daley correct? Of course not, quite the opposite. In 2009, Washington's murder rate fell 25 percent, compared with a national drop of only 7 percent. Their crime rate from January 1 to June 17 of 2010, compared to the same period in 2008, showed a drop in murder of 34 percent. This placed the murder rate back to where it was before the 1977 handgun ban. [xiii]

Mayor Daley also held the distinction of running one of the most violent cities in the nation. The city of Chicago has one of the highest crime rates in the entire country, with one in eighty-nine residents being victims of violent crimes in 2009. In 2010 more Chicago Police Officers were killed by gunfire than any other police agency in the nation. [xiv] Up until the Supreme Court ruling of 2010, Chicago did not allow a private citizen to own a handgun anywhere within the city limits. How, then, did so many police officers lose their life, and why were so many residents victims of violent crimes? How could this occur if guns were banned? Because criminals ignore the law and obtain their weapons by whatever means necessary. This is the fundamental reason that gun opponents' ideology does not work. Outlawing guns does nothing but embolden the criminal element, while law-abiding citizens are left defenseless.

So what about their statement regarding the United States being the most violent nation in the world? Yet another farce perpetrated by those proposing more gun control. When arguing their point, they cite a study that states eighty people a day die from gunshot wounds in our country. What they fail to mention is that 96 percent of those crimes are committed by repeat offenders, according to the Uniform Crime Report by the FBI and United Nations study on violent crime. [xv] These criminals are let out of prison early by judges and prosecutors who know that recidivism is out of control, know that they are likely to commit the crimes again, and yet they still release them through plea bargaining and early release programs. [xv] Plain and simple, most of the people committing these violent crimes are repeat offenders, and instead of being punished accordingly they are being let go. Whatever happened to being held responsible for your actions? Given that some in our justice system no longer understand this concept, by all means, let us remove guns from the hands of the law-abiding citizen.

In Australia, most guns were banned in 1996 and crime shot up across the country. The bans were not just limited to assault weapons or military firearms, but also shotguns and .22 rifles. Lawmakers promised that by banning guns the country would be safer. However, the statistical data tells another story. Homicides rose by 3.2 percent, assaults 8.6 percent, and armed robberies climbed an astonishing 45 percent. [XVI] In the Australian state of Victoria, gun homicides climbed 300 percent. During the twenty-five years prior to the gun ban, crime had been dropping steadily. In Dr. John Lott's book, *More Guns, Less Crime,* he documents account after account of problems that exist due to tighter gun control. In countries with tough gun control laws, more *hot-burglaries* occur than in countries with looser laws. A hot burglary is when a criminal invades a home while the homeowners are present. In Canada and Britain, almost half of all burglaries are *hot-burglaries.* By contrast, the United States, with fewer restrictions on guns than both Canada and Britain, has a *hot-burglary* rate of only 13 percent. [XVII] Dr. Lott's book is an in-depth study using decades of empirical evidence that proves time and again that law-abiding, gun-owning citizens deter violent crime and make society much safer for everyone. Not make it more dangerous, as gun opponents would have you believe. His exhaustive research also showed that states, which passed concealed carry laws, reduced their murder rate by 8.5 percent, rapes by 5 percent, aggravated assaults by 7 percent, and robbery by 3 percent. If those states, not having concealed carry laws had adopted such laws in 1992, then approximately 1,570 murders, 4,177 rapes, 60,000 aggravated assaults, and 12,000 robberies would have been avoided yearly. [XVI] Just like I tried conveying to Ramak, during our online conversation.

Dr. Lott also details studies done with criminals that analyzed their behavior regarding their victims and guns. The study explains how a criminal's apprehension increases dramatically prior to attacking their victims, and in most cases the unknown of carrying a gun is enough of a deterrent to prevent the attack completely. Interviews were also performed on incarcerated violent offenders, when asked their thoughts on an armed citizenry their replies produced the following evidence. In venues where guns are severely limited or completely banned, the criminal in almost every case stated they felt bolder and were more likely to attack. In areas that allow conceal and carry, or where restrictions are much looser, they usually did not attack and instead moved onto areas where the folks were less likely to be armed. In other words, they looked for the weaker target.

The bottom line is that guns in the hands of responsible citizens deter crime and provide for good self-defense. An article on Forbes' website, written by Larry Bell (an endowed professor at the University of Houston), provided even more statistical data supporting this fact. Law-abiding citizens in America used guns in self-defense 2.5 million times during 1993 (about 6,850 times per day), and actually shot and killed two and a half times as many criminals as police did (1,527 to 606). Those civilian self-defense shootings resulted in less than one-fifth as many incidents as police, where an innocent person was mistakenly identified as a criminal (2 percent versus 11 percent). Mr. Bell goes on to state that recognizing clear statistical benefit evidence, 41 states now allow competent, law-abiding adults to carry permitted or permit-exempt concealed handguns. As a result, crime rates in those states have typically fallen at least 10 percent in the year following enactment. [XVIII]

Gun opponents never reference these statistics when arguing their point. Most of them are blinded by the media's portrayal of rampant gun violence in the United States and their belief that a gun-free society is somehow safer. This, of course, makes them completely ignorant to the facts that unequivocally portray the success of legal gun ownership. How many times do you hear a news report about a victim successfully thwarting their attacker with a gun? Those stories almost never make the news. Instead, what you hear is a story about an innocent person who was shot by a gun-toting criminal, followed up by an interview with a person who purports to be an *expert* on the subject, stating that the only solution to this type of criminal activity is legislation for even greater gun control. More often than not the reporter or journalist interviewing this person never even challenges the response. Regardless of the media's portrayal, there are some people that feel strongly about greater gun control for a different reason, other than just clueless ideology. These individuals have experienced a traumatic event in their life that is a direct result of a person wielding a firearm irresponsibly. I can sympathize with these individuals' viewpoint somewhat, given the unfortunate card they have been dealt. At least they have a valid reason, in their minds, as to why they feel society would be safer without guns. Take for example the attempted assassination of Ronald Reagan.

As President Reagan exited the Washington Hilton Hotel and walked toward his limousine, a man in a crowd of Reagan's admirers fired off six shots, attempting to kill the president. The psychopath responsible for this madness, John Hinckley, Jr., failed to assassinate the president but did manage to wound him and three others. Among the wounded was former White House Press Secretary James Brady. He sustained a serious head wound from the attack, which left him permanently disabled. He retained his role as press secretary after his recovery but became a strong advocate for gun control later in his life. Mr. Brady and his wife also became active in the lobbying organization, Handgun Control Incorporated, which was eventually renamed the Brady Campaign to Prevent Gun Violence. They founded the non-profit Brady Center to Prevent Gun Violence and were instrumental in getting The Brady Handgun Violence Prevention Act passed in 1993. [XIX] Again, given his traumatic experience I can empathize with his stance on the issue, even though I completely disagree with it. The notion of any kind of gun control that inhibits law-abiding citizens from protecting themselves and their families is unpleasant to say the least, especially when such laws do nothing to correct the real problem.

The Brady Handgun Violence Protection Act was passed in 1993 and went into effect in 1994. This law required, for the first time, that a federal background check be performed on all people purchasing firearms from a federally licensed dealer. The passing of this law may sound admirable on its face, but when you really think about its intended purpose it becomes useless at preventing another assassination attempt, or any other violent gun crime for that matter. I understand that Hinckley purchased his gun from a pawnshop, which the 1993 law was supposed to address, but even if this law were in place during that time it would not have prevented Hinckley from obtaining a firearm. Either his background check would have come up clean or he would have just gone somewhere else to purchase the gun. He had an agenda and nothing was going to stop him from pursuing it. He had a mentally disturbed obsession with Jodie Foster and was determined to impress her, in his own warped way. Unlike Hinckley, most criminals do not purchase their guns from pawn or gun shops. Most, in fact, are getting them off the black market, which does not require any type of background check other than one's ability to produce cold, hard cash.

Jim Brady found himself in the news again recently when he stopped by Capitol Hill to push for a ban on *large magazines,* which are used in weapons to carry more ammunition. He arrived on March 30, the thirtieth anniversary of the assassination attempt on President Reagan. During his meeting with White House Press Secretary Jay Carney,

President Obama stopped by. According to Sarah Brady, the president brought up the issue of gun control, "to fill us in that it was very much on his agenda," she said.

"I just want you to know that we are working on it," Brady recalled the president telling them. "We have to go through a few processes, but under the radar." [xx]

This statement reinforces an article in the Huffington Post [xxi] describing how his administration is exploring ways to bypass Congress and enact gun control through executive action. The Department of Justice, reportedly, is holding meetings discussing the White House's options for enacting regulations on its own or through adjoining agencies and departments. "Administration officials said talk of executive orders or agency action are among a host of options that President Barack Obama and his advisers are considering." [xxii]

I would love to know why the president and some in Washington feel more gun control laws are necessary when the current laws are doing nothing but making it more difficult for the law-abiding citizen to purchase a firearm. These laws are not acting as a deterrent or making it tougher for criminals to obtain weapons. Surely they understand that limiting our ability to protect ourselves does nothing more than benefit criminals, unless of course they have a different agenda. If that agenda is to eventually disarm the electorate then we must remember what history has taught us regarding other nations' governments that have disarmed their citizens.

- In 1929, the Soviet Union established gun control. From 1929 to 1953, about twenty million dissidents were rounded up and exterminated.

- In 1911, Turkey established gun control. From 1915 to 1917, one and a half million Armenians were rounded up and exterminated.

- Germany established gun control in 1938 and from 1939 to 1945 thirteen million Jews and others were rounded up and exterminated.

- China established gun control in 1935. From 1948 to 1952 twenty million political dissidents were rounded up and exterminated.

- Guatemala established gun control in 1964. From 1964 to 1981, 100,000 Mayan Indians were rounded up and exterminated.

- Uganda established gun control in 1970. From 1971 to 1979, 300,000 Christians were rounded up and exterminated.

- Cambodia established gun control in 1956. From 1975 to 1977, one million *educated* people were rounded up and exterminated.

Defenseless people rounded up and exterminated in the twentieth century because of gun control—fifty-six million. [XVI] This may sound extreme just to prove a point but these examples precisely illustrate our Founding Fathers' concern regarding government and its inevitable decline toward tyrannical rule, which is why the Second Amendment was created. While the logistics behind a total government takeover by force would be difficult today, this should never detract from the notion that it could be achieved by other means. Therefore, it is imperative we retain our inherent right to keep and bear arms. Always remember this one premise as illustrated throughout history—armed men are citizens of an elected government while unarmed men are nothing more than subjects to a king. It is us—the citizens—that control government, not them that control us.

The fact that the two most recent Supreme Court rulings on gun control were not decided 9-0 concerns me deeply. Going forward, these close decisions could sway completely, possibly eliminating our ability and right to defend ourselves. If more judges that oppose gun rights are appointed to the bench, there is a strong possibility that our right to bear arms will eventually be eliminated. There should be no debate when it comes to the meaning of the Second Amendment, period. Given the historical context around which it was created, and the views of the Framers regarding firearms, the Second Amendment should stand on its own. Along with the evidence that clearly shows an armed populace makes for a safer community, no argument can be made against one's right to bear arms. Former Chicago Mayor Richard Daley, Jim Brady,

President Obama, and all gun opponents need to start paying attention to facts and statistics and realize once and for all that an armed society is, in fact, safer. *We the People* have a Constitutional right to own a firearm and no government is going to take that right away from us.

Your *Right* to Health Care

The first ten amendments to the Constitution are known as the Bill of Rights. They were ratified after the Constitution was approved because the anti-federalists believed the rights of citizens were not well defined. Some of the Framers thought these amendments were unnecessary because the Constitution was strictly for detailing government's responsibilities only, thereby deferring all others not listed to the people. They were also concerned that by defining an individual's rights they would, in turn, be creating limitations on his rights. However, the anti-federalists were adamant regarding their inclusion and would not agree to a new constitution otherwise. So to avoid further complications the Founding Fathers agreed and created these amendments *en mass*. They were ratified December 15, 1791.

A basic description of each amendment within the Bill of Rights is shown below.

> *First Amendment:* Grants everyone the freedom of religion, speech, assembly, press, and to petition the government.
>
> *Second Amendment:* The right to bear arms.
>
> *Third Amendment:* The military cannot force homeowners to provide soldiers with room and board.

> *Fourth Amendment:* Protects from improper seizure of property, papers, or people without probable cause and a valid warrant.
>
> *Fifth Amendment:* Protects you from being held for committing a crime unless properly indicted, you cannot be tried twice for the same crime, a.k.a. double jeopardy, you cannot be forced to testify against yourself, prevents property from being seized without just compensation, and contains the guarantee of due process.
>
> *Sixth Amendment:* A guarantee to a speedy trial, impartial jury, accused can confront witnesses against him/her, and right to a lawyer.
>
> *Seventh Amendment:* Guarantees a jury trial in federal civil court cases.
>
> *Eighth Amendment:* Punishments will be fair and not cruel, and that extraordinarily large fines will not be set.
>
> *Ninth Amendment:* States that other rights may exist, aside from those listed and that just because they are not listed does not mean they can be violated.
>
> *Tenth Amendment:* Any power not granted to the federal government belongs to the states or the people.

Nowhere in these amendments, or anywhere else in the Constitution, does it state that we have a right to health care. Nor is it guaranteed in any of our Charters of Freedom. In the Declaration of Independence it states that you have the right to life, liberty, and the pursuit of happiness. Your right to happiness is not even guaranteed; it is left up to you, the individual, to pursue your own happiness. So the next time you hear someone state that he has a right to health care, please refer him to the documents on which this nation was built. Then ask him to point out, specifically, where that right is defined. I guarantee you he will not be able to find it, but he may state that because we have evolved it should be included. While I strongly disagree with that sentiment, I do believe that our current health care system does need some refinement.

We all know too well how much health insurance premiums are rising. Cost is not the only factor; some of the tactics used by this industry are questionable as well, such as not allowing you to enroll with pre-existing conditions. But is the solution to allow government to regulate all or part of this industry wise? I say absolutely not, especially when you consider Washington's track record. For the sake of argument, assume for a moment their track record was impeccable. It is still not the responsibility of the government to take care of our social needs. Not according to our Constitution, and not according to my beliefs or the beliefs on which this country was founded. In this chapter I will discuss the current health care systems run by the government and expose the subsequent misuse of taxpayer money to the tune of billions of dollars. I will also explore the new health care law and its deficiencies and illustrate why government needs to get out of the social engineering business and leave it to the private sector. I will also propose common sense solutions to help bring down costs in our current health care system, solutions that are nowhere to be found in the current law.

There are currently two types of government-run health care programs in this country—Medicare and Medicaid. Medicare was created as part of the Social Security Act Amendment in 1965 and was signed into law by President Lyndon B. Johnson. It is a federally funded health care program that covers health expenses for people over sixty-five. Most of seniors' medical costs are covered by this program, less any deductibles and co-payments. Medicare consists of four parts, A, B, C, and D. Part A covers hospital and nursing care; Part B covers doctors' services; and Part C, known as Medicare Advantage, allows the option of enrolling in a supplemental health care plan while using Parts A and B; and Part D is a prescription drug plan.

Medicare is financed by a portion of payroll taxes paid by workers and their employer, and in part by monthly premiums deducted from Social Security checks.[I] The other government-run health care program is Medicaid. It is designed to help low-income families receive health care. It too is part of the Social Security Act Amendment of 1965. Medicaid offers federal matching funds to states for costs incurred in paying health care providers for serving covered individuals. All fifty states participate in Medicaid even though participation is voluntary.[II] Qualification for Medicaid varies by state and depends on certain levels of income—usually at or around the poverty level, with some exceptions.

Some politicians laud these institutions as terrific examples of how government assistance is necessary for the greater good. I contend, however, they illustrate perfectly how poorly and ineffectively government *assists* the private sector. Once you understand the magnitude of fraud and waste you can decide for yourself if more government-run health care is, in fact, the answer.

It is estimated that abuses of Medicaid alone consume about 10 percent of the program's total cost—about thirty billion dollars a year. [III] Abuses—like pharmacists filling prescriptions for dead people, doctors billing for procedures over twenty-four hours per day, nonexistent companies invoicing for phantom services, home health care companies billing for treating clients that are actually in the hospital—are rampant within the industry. In 2009, Medicare fraud was estimated to total about sixty billion dollars a year.

An excellent piece on Medicare fraud was done by *60 Minutes* [IV] and they found some very troubling facts. A tiny medical supply company billed Medicare two million dollars in July of 2009 and half a million dollars in August of that same year. On the surface this appears legitimate, until you trace the address and find that the building it pertains to is empty. Phone calls were placed to the business as well and were never returned. A pharmacy billed Medicare 300,000 dollars in charges and the actual location of the business does not even exist. The address was traced to the middle of a public warehouse storage facility. The FBI arrested fifty-three people in Detroit, including doctors, for billing Medicare over fifty million dollars in unnecessary procedures. In Los Angeles, the City of Angeles Medical Center took in homeless people to fill their empty beds and offered them cash and drugs while billing Medicare tens of millions of dollars.

It has become one of the most profitable crimes in America and has overtaken cocaine as the major criminal enterprise in South Florida. The piece goes on to illustrate that the fraud is so easy and simple; it is literally like taking candy from a baby. There is a whole industry built around providing names to these fraudulent companies that allow them to fill out the necessary paperwork to submit to Medicare for repayment. You do not even need a legitimate business or have to have any actual equipment or provide any real treatment. Just fill out the forms with a *patient's* information and submit it to Medicare. From there the agency is required by law to process the payment in fifteen to thirty days. The government does not have enough auditors on staff to validate every single claim, which is why fraud is so rampant. In fiscal year 2010, federal officials recovered four billion dollars in taxpayer funds from fraud and prevention efforts. [V]

While the creation of Medicare may have been well intentioned, the extensive fraud exposes its vulnerability while calling into question the effectiveness of its construction. It also reveals government's inability to administer anything efficiently and effectively. For them to create a program that allows fraud of this magnitude just reinforces my belief in government incompetence. No matter what they do or how well intentioned, their programs inevitably become bogged down with red tape and/or rife with corruption, leading to the subsequent misuse of our money.

Both Medicare and Medicaid together made up 21 percent, or 753 billion dollars, of the 2010 U.S. budget. Include Social Security at 20 percent—or 708 billion dollars—and the interest we currently owe on our debt, and that percentage jumps to forty-seven. [VI] Almost half of the U.S. budget is spent on social programs. We also have more people entering retirement now than in the past, which means even more money will have to be spent than is budgeted. Combine that with a 1.27 trillion dollar deficit for fiscal year 2011 and you start to see why government spending has become such a huge issue. Unsustainable programs, budget deficiencies, and massive fraud, are valid reasons to privatize these entities. Or at the very least move Medicare to the states and eliminate it completely from the federal government's budget. Doing so would create fifty laboratories from which best practices would evolve, allowing the market to determine the most efficient and cost effective senior-driven health care system.

All this leads me into the current health care law. Why on earth would we want our government overseeing yet another boondoggle when it is obvious they are incapable of running the current programs? If after reading the first portion of this chapter you still believe that government is the answer, maybe, just maybe, you will change your mind after reading about the massive ineptitude behind the construction of the new health care law.

It is important to note that most Americans are unhappy with the law in its current form. According to a Rasmussen poll, 60 percent [VII] of the electorate want the new health care law repealed. Another poll from Gallop [VIII] stated only one in ten people is happy with the way the law is written. These statistics cut across party lines, as both Democrats and Republicans are dissatisfied with this legislation. It is understandable really, given that most of the people in Congress passed this monstrous piece of legislation without even reading it. When asked specifically what was in the new bill, former Speaker of the House Nancy Pelosi said, "We need to pass the bill to find out what's in it." Do you think this is what our Founding Fathers envisioned when they wrote Article 1 of the Constitution? I highly doubt it. I guess one could be somewhat sympathetic as to why so many in Congress did not read the bill, given that at one point it was over 2,300 pages in length. Twenty-three hundred pages, are you kidding me? This new law has IRS written all over it, and we all know how streamlined and efficient that department operates. Not to mention the fact that you need a law degree from Harvard just to understand the current tax code. Speaking of taxes, when the new health care law is fully implemented it will impose over nineteen new taxes on Americans.[IX] Twelve of which will directly affect the middle class, a direct violation of President Obama's 2008 campaign promise.

Given its complexity and shear breadth, there is no way for me to cover every aspect of this law, unless of course I wanted to devote 2,300 pages to the topic. Who wants to read through 2,300 pages anyway, not Congress, right? Instead I will just focus on the *highlights*.

Kevin Brady, the top House Republican on the joint economic committee, created a flowchart (shown on the next page) that perfectly illustrates the bureaucratic nightmare that will exist under the new health care system. As cited by Bloomberg Columnist Kevin Hassett, this new law will create sixty-eight grant programs, forty-seven bureaucratic entities, twenty-nine pilot programs, six regulatory systems, six compliance standards, and two entitlements. Because this legislation will be next to impossible to get up and running, the Democrats granted Health and Human Services Secretary Kathleen Sebelius the authority to make judgments that cannot be challenged either administratively or through the courts. This protection from challenges is also extended to the person in charge of development for new patient care models, Donald Berwick. He will run the Centers for Medicare and Medicaid services where he can experiment with ways to make the system more like Europe's model, which he himself has embraced.[X]

The Internal Revenue Service (IRS) stated that they will need 1,054 new auditors and staffers, and new facilities, which will cost us—the

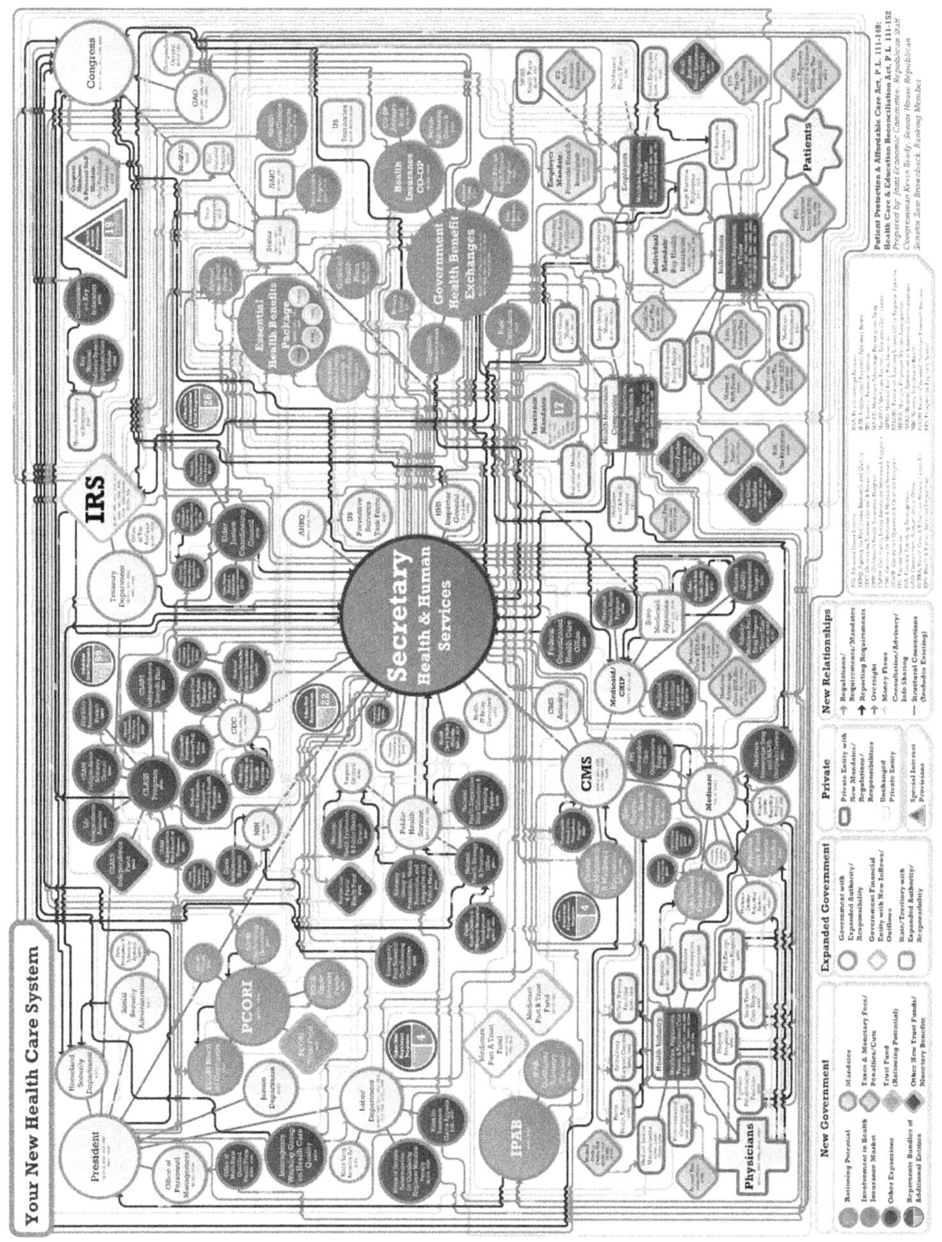

To view this chart in full clarity please visit: http://www.house.gov/brady/
pdf/Press_Packet.pdf

taxpayer—more than 359 million dollars in fiscal 2012. This will all be needed to help with the implementation of the president's health care reforms. Among the new employees will be eighty-one workers whose sole responsibility will be to monitor the new 10 percent excise tax assigned to tanning salons at a cost of 11.5 million dollars. [XI] The huge bureaucracy, massive entitlement spending, and enormous government expansion created by this new law all vividly illustrate how our Constitutional freedoms are slowly and steadily being stripped away by big government. There is no way our Founding Fathers would approve of this type of legislation were they alive today. Regardless, let us take a look at some of the reasons why Washington justified the need for health care reform.

A major problem within the current health care system is the exceedingly high costs that go up exponentially each year, making it more and more difficult for the average American to afford quality coverage. In the United States, expenditures on health care surpassed 2.3 trillion dollars in 2008. [XII] This is more than three times the 714 billion dollars spent in 2009, and over eight times higher than the 253 billion dollars spent in 1980. [XII] Premiums have increased on employer sponsored health coverage by 131 percent since 1999. [XII] Each year insurance rates rise and each year the health insurance companies give us the same excuse. Health care treatment costs are rising; therefore, so too must the insurance that covers these services. Some of the reasons given for the rising costs, according to kaiserEDU.org, are as follows: [XII]

Technology and Prescription drugs—For several years, spending on new medical technology and prescription drugs has been cited as a leading contributor to the increase in overall health spending; however, in recent years, the rate of spending on prescription drugs has decelerated. Some analysts state that the availability of more expensive, state-of-the-art, technological services and new drugs fuel health care spending not only because the development costs of these products must be recouped by industry but also because they generate consumer demand for more intense, costly services even if they are not necessarily cost-effective.

Chronic Disease—The nature of health care in the U.S. has changed dramatically over the past century with longer life spans and greater prevalence of chronic illnesses. This has placed tremendous demands on the health care system, particularly an increased need for treatment of ongoing illnesses and long-term care services such as nursing homes; it is estimated that health care costs for chronic disease treatment account for over 75 percent of national health expenditures.

Aging of the Population—Health expenses rise with age and as the baby boomers are now in their middle years, and some say that caring for this growing population has raised costs. This trend will continue as the baby boomers will begin qualifying for Medicare in 2011 and many of the costs are shifted to the public sector. However, experts agree that aging of the population contributes minimally to the high growth rate of health care spending.

Administrative Costs—It is estimated that at least 7 percent of health care expenditures are for administrative costs (e.g., marketing, billing) and this portion is much lower in the Medicare program (<2 percent), which is operated by the federal government. Some argue that the mixed public-private system creates overhead costs and large profits that are fueling health care spending.

To help control rising costs, Congress and the president told us that new health care legislation was needed, and if passed they promised it would make health care more affordable for everyone. Hence, Washington named the new law the Affordable Care Act. I can say beyond a reasonable doubt that so far the new law has not performed as promised. Some portions that went into effect in 2011 have actually made health care costs rise. One can only imagine what effect it will have on the industry when it is fully implemented in 2014. I know many people whose health insurance has gone up significantly this year. When they questioned representatives from their health insurance companies regarding the increase, they were all told the same thing: a contributing factor to the higher costs was due to portions of the new health care law that went into effect this year, which mandates covering your children until they are 26. So let me get this straight, the new legislation is costing the insurance companies more money and they are passing that cost on to us? Who would have foreseen that outcome? Apparently, not those in Washington. They must have been preoccupied with reading the new law. Or maybe that was their intention all along, rising costs which would slowly drive insurance companies out of business, forcing us all onto a government-run plan.

The American Association of Retired Persons (AARP) is telling its employees their insurance costs will rise, partly because of the very law they supported. AARP endorsed and backed President Obama's signature legislation and was a key supporter while the law was being rushed through Congress. AARP went on to state that it is changing copayments and deductibles to avoid a 40-percent tax on high-cost health plans that take effect in 2018[xiii] under the new law. Boeing also cited the new tax when explaining why their health care costs went up. Blue Shield Health Insurance Company of California increased their rates by as much as 59 percent[xiv] on some of their members. They explained that the increases were the result of rising health care costs and other expenses resulting from the new health care law. The Congressional Budget Office (CBO) predicted that premiums for a small number of families who buy their insurance privately could increase as much as 2,100 dollars.[xv] This means these folks will be forced into health care they may not necessarily want, since they will no longer be able to afford their current plan. I thought the president stated we were going to be able to keep our insurance if we liked it. I guess what he meant was only if we could afford it. Even the CBO has stated that repealing the law would reduce net spending by 540 billion dollars in ten years, 2012 to 2021, along with eliminating 770 billion dollars in new taxes.[xvi] So once again our politicians' incompetency is highlighted by passing a piece of legislation that negates one of the very things it was meant to curtail.

When the president stated that we would not have to change our current health care I really wonder if he was sincere. Because according to Washington's own numbers 117 million people may have to change their health plans by 2013.[x] Some companies, however, will not have to change their employees' coverage, at least not initially. They are receiving waivers from the government, exempting them from a portion of the new law that affects businesses with limited health benefit plans, also referred to as *mini-med* policies. These plans have limits on how much can be paid out, limits that would be phased out under the new law. According to the department of health and human services, over 221 businesses[xvii] have been given waivers exempting them from this portion of the new law. If this legislation is so necessary and designed so perfectly, then why are waivers being granted? Special interests appear to be behind these decisions. Another 204 waivers were approved in April of 2011, 20 percent of which went to luxurious restaurants, nightclubs, and hotels in House Minority Leader Nancy Pelosi's district.[xviii] Some were also given to labor union chapters with vested interest in furthering the Democrat agenda. The remaining waiver recipients included large corporations, financial firms, and local governments. More cases of collusion between business and government, I would even go as far as stating this is outright corruption at the highest level. The government is fraudulently representing this plan as necessary for the greater good by forcing the average American into it while granting a select few exemption, further proof that this bill was never intended to bring down costs. It was only put in place to allow government to take over yet another portion of the private sector. Some politicians have said the new law was just a plan put into place to initiate the process of reform, rather than a final bill meant to change health care as a whole. If one uses that logic then this legislation will be under a constant state of evolution, leaving the doors open for ongoing change, creating more and more government bureaucracy. In other words, I believe it was purposely designed this way so that the government can change the law whenever and however it sees fit. Now that it is law, they will be able to do so at their discretion with or without our approval. This is one more reason why this unorganized mess needs to be fully repealed and is yet another promise broken by our trusting politicians.

What may be the worst piece of the new legislation is the provision that enforces mandatory health care coverage. Everyone living in this country, legally, will be forced to purchase health insurance. If you choose to opt out you will be penalized via the IRS. You read that correctly; for the first time in history you will be forced to buy something simply for being a citizen of this great nation. If you choose to opt out you will be taxed by the government. Congress and the president justify this as being constitutional by stating that it falls under the interstate commerce clause—Article One, Section Eight of the Constitution. I sincerely and emphatically beg to differ. This portion of the Constitution was not created for this purpose. It has been abused by our government almost since its inception. And particularly after the New Deal when the powers of government were vastly expanded during the Great Depression.

Before the Constitution was adopted, under the Articles of Confederation, barriers existed that interfered with the free flow of trade between states. The Framers recognized this problem and created the commerce clause when defining the powers of Congress under Article

One of the Constitution. It was intended to make the United States a free-trade zone, allowing goods to flow between the states under one set of guidelines at the federal level, rather than the chaotic mess that existed between each state. In the beginning, this clause was closely interpreted as such. In 1824, Chief Justice John Marshall's Court, in the first big case involving the commerce clause, Gibbons versus Ogden, struck down a New York law that would have created a steamship monopoly for traffic between New York and New Jersey. Marshall laid down the principle that for the national government to have jurisdiction, the issue must involve interstate commerce; it must involve the trafficking of goods between two or more states. [XIX] Unfortunately it did not take long for this clause to be misconstrued and misinterpreted as something else entirely. In 1870 the Court upheld the inspection of steam ships that remained within a state but carried goods shipped from or destined to other states. In 1887 the Interstate Commerce Commission was created to cartelize the railroads and regulate their rates. The Sherman antitrust law could not be used in 1895 to stop the merger of sugar refiners. A federal prohibition on the interstate trafficking of lottery tickets was upheld in 1903. The prohibition on interstate shipment of goods produced in plants using child labor was struck down in 1918, all glaring examples of the misinterpretation of this clause. Case after case slowly chipped away at the interstate commerce clause. Its definition became more vague and inclusive regarding any and all goods and services transported and/or sold across state lines. As the years progressed, its original intent (that state governments could not create trade barriers) had ultimately been lost. If one looks at the interstate commerce clause as it was written, using its original intent, then it is safe to state that it cannot and should not be used to force you to purchase insurance. Nor should our government be allowed to use this clause as leverage for stating that the new law is constitutional. Therefore, the only conclusion that can be drawn is full repeal of the current law.

Thankfully there are some in our government who agree that the law is unconstitutional and should be repealed. This idea was one of the primary platforms they campaigned on in 2010. They believed that in its current state the law is inefficient, too broad and vague in scope, enlarges an already bloated government, and, most importantly, tries enforcing a mandate upon every citizen in this country. I also believe another reason these politicians want health care reform repealed is because they finally understand how unhappy the electorate is with this law, illustrated by people's discontent at the polls in 2010.

On Tuesday August 3, 2010, Missouri's Proposition C passed overwhelmingly with more than 70 percent of the vote. Proposition C amends Missouri Statutes to deny government the authority to penalize citizens for refusing to buy health care. Missouri State Senator Jim Lembke was quoted as saying, "I expected a victory, but not of this magnitude. This is going to propel the issue and several other issues about the proper role of the federal government."[XX] I could not agree more. The government has overstepped its boundaries and should not be involved in social engineering, and poll after poll shows that most Americans agree. Arizona, Florida, and Oklahoma also proposed similar measures on their ballots in November. It passed in Arizona and Oklahoma but was removed from Florida's ballot by court order because Leon County Circuit Judge James Shelfer said the measure was misleading and could confuse voters. [XXI] I guess he felt the voters in Florida were not intelligent enough to understand a simple measure regarding the government's ability to force one to purchase insurance. In Colorado the people voted down a similar measure in their state by 53 percent. But at least they were able to vote on it without a judge telling them otherwise.

Along with states voting symbolically to eliminate government-mandated insurance there are also twenty states suing the federal government because they too believe the government does not have the power to force someone to purchase insurance. This lawsuit was filed by Florida Republican Attorney General Bill McCollum just minutes after the president signed the 938 billion-dollar health care bill into law. [XXII] The Obama administration will argue that the portion mandating health insurance does not take effect until 2014 and should not be challenged until that time. They have also stated that they have the right to create the insurance mandate under the interstate commerce clause. So, which is it, wait to challenge it because it is unconstitutional, or the government has the right to create it? One statement contradicts the other, does it not? Given the original intent of the commerce clause, I wholeheartedly believe the lawsuit is justified. Waiting until 2014 to challenge, it is out of the question because changes are taking place now that are already having a negative impact on people's coverage. So again, I say the lawsuit must proceed. The other states involved in this lawsuit are Alabama, Alaska, Arizona, Colorado, Georgia, Indiana, Idaho, Louisiana, Michigan, Mississippi, Nebraska, Nevada, North Dakota, Pennsylvania, South Carolina, South Dakota, Texas, Utah, and Washington. As of January 19, 2011, six other states requested to join the suit—Wisconsin, Wyoming, Iowa, Maine, Kansas, and Ohio—bringing the total to twenty-six or just over half of the states in the Union. I would say this is a very strong indication of people's displeasure with the current law.

Views seem to be split among federal judges regarding the new law. In Florida, U.S. District Judge Roger Vinson allowed two major counts against the law to proceed—the states' challenge requiring all Americans to purchase insurance and the expansion of Medicaid, setting the stage for each state involved to decide whether or not this law is constitutional. In Lynchburg, Virginia, U.S. District Judge Norman K. Moon declared that the provision requiring most individuals to obtain insurance is constitutional. This was the second such decision upholding the law— the first coming from Michigan. Another federal judge in Virginia, Henry E. Hudson, ruled with the states' claim that forcing people to purchase health care exceeds the power of Congress. He wrote, "Importantly, it is not the effect on individuals that is presently at issue—it is the authority of Congress to compel *anyone* to purchase health insurance." [XXIII] On January 31, 2011, Roger Vinson, the same judge that allowed the case against health care reform to move forward, ruled that as a result of the individual mandate requiring everyone to purchase insurance, the entire law must be declared void. He wrote:

> I must reluctantly conclude that Congress exceeded the bounds of its authority in passing the act with the individual mandate. That is not to say, of course, that Congress is without power to address the problems and inequities in our health care system. The health care market is more than one-sixth of the national economy, and without doubt Congress has the power to reform and regulate this market. That has not been disputed in this case. The principal dispute has been about how Congress chose to exercise that power here. While the individual mandate was clearly 'necessary and essential' to the act as drafted, it is not 'necessary and essential' to health care reform in general." He continued, "Because the

> individual mandate is unconstitutional and not severable, the
> entire act must be declared void. [XXIV]

President Obama's administration has, of course, vowed to appeal every case that declares the law unconstitutional. It appears most decisions are falling on each judge's interpretation of the Constitution's commerce clause. It is obvious that some judges reviewing the case agree more closely with its original intent while others do not. That is why this was ultimately decided by the Supreme Court. Unfortunately the court's decision was not as I had hoped or expected. The 5-4 ruling was in favor of the law not against it. The only real positive is the high court did agree with my assessment of the commerce clause, that it could not be used to force people to buy a good or service. Chief Justice John G. Roberts Jr. ruled the law was constitutional based on Congress' taxing authority. He stated that Congress had no authority to utilize the commerce clause in such a dictatorial fashion but they did have the authority to levy a tax, and the new law could be enforced as such. As you might expect I disagree completely with Justice Roberts' decision on taxation. I do not believe the law should have been upheld on any grounds.

Polls showing people's discontent, states holding elections to repeal the new law, and all who are involved in the federal law suit—all paint a vivid picture of this country's view regarding government subsidized health care. It was with no surprise that on Wednesday January 19, 2011, a Republican-lead House of Representatives voted to repeal the new health care law, 245-189. They were joined by three Democrats, but otherwise the votes fell pretty much along party lines. The bill then moved on to the Senate where it failed as expected, 51-47, right along party lines. I guess the Democrats forgot about the shellacking they received in November 2010. Regardless, the intent was clear—for the first time in a long time a portion of our government seems to be listening to its electorate. For those who choose not to listen, their time will come soon enough, when they too are voted out of office. If the 2010 election showed us anything, it was that more of the American people are finally becoming engaged and taking their dissatisfaction to the polls.

Some people point to socialized health care in other countries as examples of how those industrialized nations are more civilized and more compassionate than the United States. I say if you want to really look at how effective and *compassionate* these systems are, then let us take a closer look. In a New York Times article [xxv] the dire state of England's socialized health care system, the National Health Service, is explained. Due to the global recession and the poor state of England's economy, their new coalition government was looking for ways to drastically reduce their deficit. They originally stated that they would only make cuts to the public sector and would not cut any services to their massive health care system. However, after reviewing their total spending it was soon realized that they had no choice but to make significant cuts to health care, and that it had to be completely reorganized. So they proposed shifting control of England's 160 billion-dollar annual health budget from a centralized bureaucracy to doctors at the local level. About 100 billion dollars to 125 billion dollars would be doled out to the doctors so they could use the money to buy services from hospitals. They also proposed significantly shrinking their current health care's administrative costs by 45 percent. This would, of course, translate to workforce reductions by the tens of thousands since layers of bureaucracy are effectively being eliminated to achieve these proposed cost saving measures.

The government admitted that the architecture of the current system involves duplication and is unwieldy. It went on to state, "Liberating the NHS and putting the power in the hands of patients and clinicians means we will be able to affect a radical simplification and remove layers of management." Even England's own socialist government admits that their system is a bureaucratic mess and placing the power back in the hands of the people is more beneficial.

We need to learn from England's restructuring, and their statements regarding their government's inability to effectively manage their own system, and understand that this could happen to our country if it continues down the same path. If you want to see what kind of a bureaucratic nightmare our system will evolve into, take another look at the diagram displayed earlier in this chapter. Government is inherently incompetent by its very nature, as is evidenced by England's restructuring and our own government's attempt at socializing health care and their subsequent miscalculations regarding cost and its impact on businesses. Need more proof on how well socialized medicine works? A man in Sweden sewed up a cut on his own leg because he was tired of waiting for emergency room staff to treat him after being admitted. In Canada, a pregnant woman of nine weeks was rushed to the hospital when she started bleeding. She sat in the waiting room of the hospital for three hours, bleeding through her jeans with a room full of people watching, when she and her husband finally became so frustrated they got up and left and drove to another hospital forty-five minutes away. She ultimately lost the baby because of a miscarriage, not because of waiting in the hospital. But she described the incident as completely mortifying, having to sit in a waiting room while going through the whole ordeal.

In Massachusetts, former governor Mitt Romney passed a bill reforming health care in his state in April 2006. It also promised to increase health care coverage while lowering costs. Over five years later, quite the opposite has transpired. Costs in that state are skyrocketing, the number of Medicaid recipients has risen by 25 percent, and insurance premiums have risen significantly since it was implemented. [XXVI] According to a report on *The O'Reilly Factor,* health care costs have grown 600 percent from 2007 to 2010 and the state has added $1.3 billion in debt since 2006. Massachusetts' debt now stands at more than $20 billion and growing. Individual premiums for health care are $480 higher than the national average and family premiums are $893 higher. [XXVII] Congressional Democrats and President Obama have both cited this state's reform as an example of how their new health care law will work. Even with the poor results received from this program—in plain sight mind you—our intellectually superior governing body still decided to implement health care reform at the federal level.

Has anyone besides me lost complete faith in our government's ability to utilize common sense? They see an example of health care that is doing poorly, decide to mold their plan in its image, and proceed to implement it nationwide. The Massachusetts law and the Affordable Care Act both contain very similar promises. Money that was being spent by hospitals on the uninsured could be redirected to insurance premiums via government efficiencies (an oxymoron if I ever heard one). Primary care would now replace emergency room use for those who used to not be covered, and all of this new bureaucracy could be implemented without raising taxes. Each one of these "promises" has proven untrue for Massachusetts. It still spends $414 million on uncompensated care, emergency room use has not dropped, it rose 9 percent from 2006 to 2008, and private insurer costs have continued to rise. A 2010 study published in the Forum for

Health Economics & Policy found that health insurance premiums in Massachusetts, prior to the overhaul, increased at a rate 3.7 percent slower than the national average. After the overhaul, they are increasing 5.8 percent faster. [XXVIII] The individual mandate in the Affordable Care Act requires that a family making $55,000 in 2014 will have to pay $4,428 a year for health insurance or face a $550 fine. Since insurance will be available on demand, there is really no need to buy into the plan until a serious illness arrives. When you have the option of paying a fine of $550 or paying $4,428 for full coverage, it seems pretty straightforward to me what will transpire. So much for the individual mandate forcing every citizen to be covered.

It is obvious to me that the current US health care law will not perform as promised. Therefore, when the current law is repealed, we must employ measures to help bring down costs that will ultimately lead to a better, more cost-efficient health care system. A few solutions that will help bring costs under control, which are not listed in the current law, are tort reform, interstate competition, and small business employee pooling. Tort reform is a broad subject and is not one single idea or law. Instead it is a group of ideas and laws designed to change the way our legal system works. The classic legal textbook about tort is called *Prosser and Keaton on Torts.* [XXIX] Within that book one definition explains that tort is a civil crime; an act that is illegal but not criminal, such as an auto accident or a medical malpractice lawsuit. Tort reform looks to set limits on damages accrued on things like pain and suffering and mental anguish, also sometimes referred to as punitive damages. The reason this is important is because lawsuits on medical malpractice cause physicians' malpractice insurance to be much more expensive in states where tort reform is absent. This expense gets passed on to the patient in the form of higher premiums. Tort reform removes exorbitant rewards and makes it more difficult to get a malpractice lawsuit in front of a judge. It helps weed out "ambulance chasers" and some of the more frivolous lawsuits so that more legitimate ones can be pursued in court.

Physicians who work in states that have tort reform usually pay tens of thousands of dollars less in malpractice insurance, which in turn helps draw quality doctors to that state. People that argue against tort reform usually state that it is not fair because it does not hold doctors accountable for their mistakes. It is in a doctor's best interest to treat you well and effectively without making mistakes. It is how he establishes his client base; his business depends on it. It is also the very foundation of a doctor's Hippocratic Oath. A doctor who makes numerous mistakes will not be in business for long simply because people will stop going to him. This is not to say that if a doctor makes a major mistake he should not be held responsible. But limits need to exist in some cases to ensure doctors can practice without fear of retribution from frivolous lawsuits. It only makes sense that if a doctor can practice medicine cheaper that the savings will be passed on to his patients.

Interstate competition for single payers is an option that would allow insurance companies to compete across state lines. We currently do not have a national market for individual health insurance coverage. Health insurance companies are protected by the federal McCarran Ferguson Act of 1945, which allows states the right to regulate health care within their borders. Large employers are exempt from these state regulations. If this portion of health care were treated like automobile insurance, a whole new industry would be born. Insurance companies would compete for your business nationwide, which would ultimately drive down costs. Since the options would be greater for the individual, it is possible new insurance companies would develop. With all the completion, new services could even be offered, such as covering people with preexisting conditions. One thing is certain: it would definitely drive down rates because competition spurs that type of environment by creating efficiencies between competitors.

On the National Center for Policy Analysis website it states that legislators can require insurers to cover services that drive up premiums simply because each state market is protected. They explain that about one-fourth of states mandate benefit packages that cover acupuncture and marriage counseling. More than half require coverage for social workers and 60 percent for contraceptives. Seven states require coverage for hairpieces and nine for hearing aids. When states force insurers to cover providers or benefits that consumers do not want, both the insurer and the consumer lose. Consumers lose because they are required to pay for amenities they do not want. Insurers lose because mandated benefits and overzealous insurance regulations drive up the cost and reduce the sales of insurance products. Proponents often claim a given mandate costs very little, but they do add up. They go on to state that there are approximately 1,843 state mandates, according to the Council for Affordable Health Insurance, an industry trade group. Some estimates suggest these mandates have priced as many as one-quarter of the uninsured out of the market. [xxx] It is obvious that competition drives down cost. It happens in just about every facet of society, so it stands to reason that this concept would also help reduce costs in health insurance as well.

Allowing small businesses to pool their employees into larger groups is also missing from the current law. The idea behind this topic is to allow small businesses to group their employees with those of other small businesses to form large groups from which to purchase health insurance. The larger the group of employees, the better rates each business can negotiate for themselves and their staff. This would give these businesses access to similar rates and benefits that larger corporations and labor unions currently receive.

The Republicans laid out a ten-point plan that they feel will help positively reform health care without the negative effects the current law is having on businesses and individuals alike. Below is an outline of their ten-point plan as listed on both gop.gov and speaker.gov websites. [xxviii] Each of these goals is explained in detail within the actual 219-page bill they created.

- Lowering health care premiums. The GOP plan will lower health care premiums for American families and small businesses, addressing Americans' number-one priority for health care reform.

- Establishing Universal Access Programs to guarantee access to affordable health care for those with pre-existing conditions. The GOP plan creates universal access programs that expand and reform high-risk pools and reinsurance programs to guarantee that all Americans, regardless of pre-existing conditions or past illnesses, have access to affordable care—while lowering costs for all Americans.

- Ending junk lawsuits. The GOP plan would help end costly junk lawsuits and curb defensive medicine by enacting medical

> liability reforms modeled after the successful state laws of California and Texas.

- Prevents insurers from unjustly cancelling a policy. The GOP plan prohibits an insurer from cancelling a policy unless a person commits fraud or conceals material facts about a health condition.

- Encouraging small business health plans. The GOP plan gives small businesses the power to pool together and offer health care at lower prices, just as corporations and labor unions do.

- Encouraging innovative state programs. The GOP plan rewards innovation by providing incentive payments to states that reduce premiums and the number of uninsured.

- Allowing Americans to buy insurance across state lines. The GOP plan allows Americans to shop for coverage from coast to coast by allowing Americans living in one state to purchase insurance in another.

- Promoting healthier lifestyles. The GOP plan promotes prevention and wellness by giving employers greater flexibility to financially reward employees who adopt healthier lifestyles.

- Enhancing Health Savings Accounts (HSAs). The GOP plan creates new incentives to save for current and future health care needs by allowing qualified participants to use HSA funds to pay premiums for high deductible health insurance.

- Allowing dependents to remain on their parents' policies. The GOP plan encourages coverage of young adults on their parents' insurance through age twenty-five.

While I do not agree with all their points, they do a decent job of dispelling the myth perpetrated by liberals that states all Republicans want to do is repeal the current law without offering an alternate plan. They obviously have a plan, a very concise and practical plan that has some very good ideas.

Health care is not something that our government should be

involved with, no matter how you feel about health care reform. The role of government should not be one of a social nature, nor should it be concerned with redistributing wealth. This country was not founded on those principles, equal opportunity for all—yes, but not equal status or pay regardless of one's willingness to participate. It is up to the individual to achieve fulfillment and happiness, whether you are talking about financial independence or something as basic as a person's health. The bottom line is that our Constitution was designed to minimize the role of government and keep it in check. Our country was founded on self-reliance, hard work, determination, ingenuity, and perseverance, not through government social engineering. Let us hope that this latest travesty regarding the new health care law has taught us all a valuable lesson. Whether or not it taught our government anything is still up for debate. It does appear that one portion of Washington is starting to understand. The House of Representatives listened to its constituents and voted to repeal health care in 2011. As for the Senate and the president, they chose not to listen, so it will be up to us to remind them of our wishes in 2012 when we exercise our right to vote.

Taxes and Government Waste

Article One of the US Constitution defines the legislative branch of our government where Congress' responsibilities and structure are detailed. Section Eight establishes the powers of Congress, one of which includes the right to lay and collect taxes. Section Nine specifies the limits on Congress, a portion of which states the following: *No Capitation, or other direct, Tax shall be laid, unless in Proportion to the Census or enumeration herein before directed to be taken.* This clause basically states the need for apportionment taxes, something that is difficult to comprehend today. The following is an explanation of the Direct Tax Apportionment Clause, written by Supreme Court Justice Paterson in 1796.

> The constitution declares, that a capitation tax is a direct tax; and both in theory and practice, a tax on land is deemed to be a direct tax... The provision was made in favor of the southern states; they possessed a large number of slaves; they had extensive tracts of territory, thinly settled, and not very productive. A majority of the states had but few slaves, and several of them a limited territory, well settled, and in a high state of cultivation. The southern states, if no provision had been introduced in the constitution, would have been wholly at the mercy of the other states. Congress in such case, might tax slaves, at discretion or arbitrarily, and land in every

> part of the Union, after the same rate or measure: so much a head,
> in the first instance, and so much an acre, in the second. To guard
> them against imposition, in these particulars, was the reason of
> introducing the clause in the constitution. [1]

Constitutionally, the term *direct tax* means a tax on land by means of its ownership, such as a property tax. According to Article One, Section Nine, all direct taxes imposed by the national government must be apportioned among the states based on population. This keeps the less populated states from being placed under an unfair burden when being taxed.

During our nation's early history, a series of court cases kept trying to reinterpret the meaning of the Constitution's direct tax clause in an effort to raise revenue for the government. Some of the verdicts from these cases defined this tax as a type of pseudo income tax. However, there was no real income tax in America prior to 1861. That year, the Revenue Act was passed to raise money for the Civil War. It levied a flat tax of 3 percent on all people with an annual income above 800 dollars. Since it was not a tax on property it was considered an indirect tax and, therefore, immune to the confines of the Constitution. The following year this act was replaced by the Revenue Act of 1862, which levied a graduated tax of 3 percent on incomes from 600 to 10,000 dollars and 5 percent on anything higher. It was later repealed in 1872 at the end of the Civil War when the need for government revenue lessened. [2]

Our past government understood what it meant to be fiscally responsible, choosing to eliminate a tax when it was no longer needed, rather than keeping it to spend on unnecessary bureaucracy. How great would it be if our current government understood this concept and repealed the Sixteenth Amendment? In 1894, Congress tried reinstituting the income tax by passing the Wilson-Gorman Tariff Act. A year later, however, this was declared unconstitutional by the Supreme Court in Pollock versus Farmers' Loan and Trust Company, 157 U.S. 429. The Court ruled income taxes on interest, dividends, and rents were a direct tax and unconstitutional because they violated the provision that direct taxes be apportioned. After this ruling, the thought of taxing income was abandoned until 1909, when President William Howard Taft proposed that Congress pass a constitutional amendment that would allow for the creation of a tax without the need for apportionment. Four years later, on February 3, 1913, the Sixteenth Amendment was ratified by thirty-six of the forty-eight existing states. It was on this day that the hopes our Founding Fathers had for a minimally intrusive federal government were all but dashed.

Let me state for the record that in order for a lawful, civil society to exist, I do believe so too must government. Which means by matter of association, so must taxes. I do not believe in an anarchist society nor do I believe that government should be abolished. But the role and size of government should be severely limited and well-defined. In the final chapter I will do just that, by drafting a new amendment to the Constitution that clearly lays out government's role and explains how much of our tax dollars can be used. The need for a new amendment will become apparent after reading how government has wasted our money to the point of bankrupting the country. Their incessant waste has contributed to government's immense size and unbelievable inefficiencies, causing debt to the tune of trillions of dollars. You will learn why I am of the opinion they not receive another dime of our hard earned money until it is proven they can use it responsibly, instead of extorting it from us to use at their discretion.

Back in the early part of the twentieth-century, the Mafia was an expert at shaking down local businesses and demanding *protection* money or a tribute to the Don. If the individual refused to pay, the Mafia would usually do something harmful to him or his shop until he had no choice but to pay. This is a clear example of extortion—per the definition. [III]

> Ex·tor·tion—noun \ik-ˈstor-shən\
> 1: the act or practice of extorting especially money or other property; especially: the offense committed by an official engaging in such practice
> 2: something extorted; especially: a gross overcharge

The similarity between what our own government demands from us each and every pay period, and what the Mafia did to local businesses when they demanded protection money is frightening. The only real difference is one uses the law to enforce its policy while the other used sheer intimidation. For years the government has tried shutting down the Mafia for this and other heinous practices. Yet extortion exists within our government without question, as we are forced to hand over a portion of our pay check or face penalties and/or possible jail time for nonpayment. In a civil society, extorting money from individuals should never be allowed. I believe we can all agree it is unacceptable to allow the Mafia to bully businesses into relinquishing a portion of their assets. And the same should be said of our government as well; extorting money by any means legal or otherwise is unacceptable. Therefore we must do what we can to repeal or severely limit the powers of the Sixteenth Amendment by ensuring politicians are voted in that carry the same beliefs. When you see just how badly the government is misusing our money I am certain you will agree. There is no point in having an income tax if limits on government spending do not exist, allowing them to waste money ad nauseam.

On average, about 30 percent [IV] of our paychecks are *donated* to the government under the guise of a necessary tax. Of course, it all depends on how you define the word necessary. Because if the government downsized and controlled spending there is no reason they could not operate with 20, 10, or, dare I say, zero percent of our income? I would definitely classify taking 30 percent of my paycheck as a form of extortion. When you include the taxes we pay on other items we purchase, this percentage jumps to almost 40 percent. [IV] We are also taxed on our assets when we pass away, via the estate tax. We are literally being taxed to death. I find those percentages absolutely nauseating. Especially when you factor in how much is actually being wasted by our government, items that have absolutely nothing to do with running our country or protecting our freedoms.

To put their taxation in some perspective, we went to war with England for far less when we declared our independence. One of the primary causes of the Revolutionary War was excessive taxes imposed on the colonists by Britain. As an example, the Stamp Act and other parliamentary taxes were created to help offset the cost of placing British troops in America, and because of the huge debt that was incurred as a result of the French and Indian war. The colonists deeply resented these taxes and the way they were instituted without their consent. Protests from the colonists did eventually get the Stamp tax repealed, but it was too late to stop the inevitable. They were at the breaking point and already distrusted Britain, and so these and other factors are what led them to war.

As the Founding Fathers drafted the Declaration of Independence, their sole intent was to make us a sovereign nation with individual liberties, free from tyrannical rule and excessive taxation imposed by the king of England. Now, I am not advocating that we rise up and start another revolutionary war, not at this point and time. But I do believe we need to use the powers granted us by our Founding Fathers—Article Four, Section Four of the Constitution—and vote out any incumbent that does not heed our message regarding less taxation and smaller government.

As of February 2010 there were over 138,000,000 people employed[v] in the United States, and that was with a 9.8 percent unemployment rate. Obviously there is no easy way to calculate the exact amount the government would take home each pay period with my suggested lower tax rates, since they would most likely still be adjusted based on income, dependents, deductions, and a host of other factors, unless of course a flat tax is introduced, or the income tax is eliminated altogether, but I digress. My suggested tax rates should be ample money for government to perform its basic functions, given the number of people working in this country. So why then does our government need so much? For that matter, why is an income tax needed at all? Should not the other items on which we are taxed be enough to sustain government? Is it because the government has grown too large? Are they spending our money on unnecessary expenditures? The answers to all these questions and more are addressed forthcoming.

Our government has accumulated a 16 trillion-dollar debt.[vi] It will most likely climb well above 16 trillion by the time this book is released, unless serious cuts are made. Remember this debt was created by government's mismanagement of our money.

Let me repeat, this is our money they are spending. It is not their money to do with as they please. I cannot stress this enough. So whenever you hear the government state that they are giving us a tax break, remember, it is not theirs to give. Make no mistake, this enormous debt is now our burden to carry; it is ultimately our responsibility since it is our money the government is spending. With a population of over 310,000,000 [vii] people living in the United States, that breaks down to about 51,000 dollars owed per person. To make matters worse, the government has spent and wasted so much of our money that we may never be able to pay back what is owed. Can the average American even comprehend what it would be like to have 16 trillion dollars? When that number is actually put to paper it appears surreal—16,000,000,000,000. That is the number sixteen with twelve zeros behind it! So, what exactly is debt and what does this number really mean? We all understand very well what debt is, but for the sake of our government I am going to explain it so even they can understand. I really doubt they have a firm grasp on its definition given how unmanageable it has become. To put it simply, debt is the total amount of money owed. If the government spends more money in a given fiscal year than it makes in revenue (our tax dollars), it has a deficit. The total of all the deficits is the debt. The deficit is the total amount the government spends minus the total amount the government raises in revenue in a single year. So, for example, say your monthly income is 1,000 dollars. Yet your monthly spending totals 1,100 dollars. Each month you put 100 dollars on a credit card to cover the difference. The 100 dollars owed each month is your deficit. By the end of the year your monthly deficits total 1,200 dollars or your new debt. If you continued this behavior every year for ten years then your total debt would be 12,000 dollars.

Currently, government spending takes up about 20 percent of the Gross Domestic Product (GDP). It is projected that if their spending is not brought under control very soon, by 2082 it will be over 80 percent of the GDP, according to the Congressional Budget Office (CBO) as illustrated in the following chart.

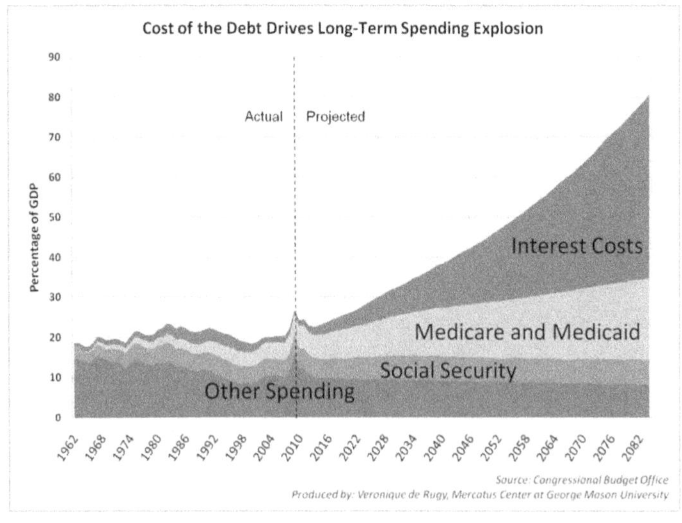

Since this is money we owe, it is essentially a loan, and as with any loan there is interest on the amount owed, shown in the Interest Costs portion of the chart on page 110. When you take out a loan with a bank, you enter into a contract that states the amount owed plus the interest charged over the life of the loan. The interest is the money the bank makes for giving you the loan. It is your responsibility to pay back the total amount of the loan, including interest. Everyone understands this of course because it is basic financing—everyone, that is, except for our government. Below is another graph that shows the projected interest on our debt and the amount of the national budget it will consume by the year 2081, at various different interest rates.

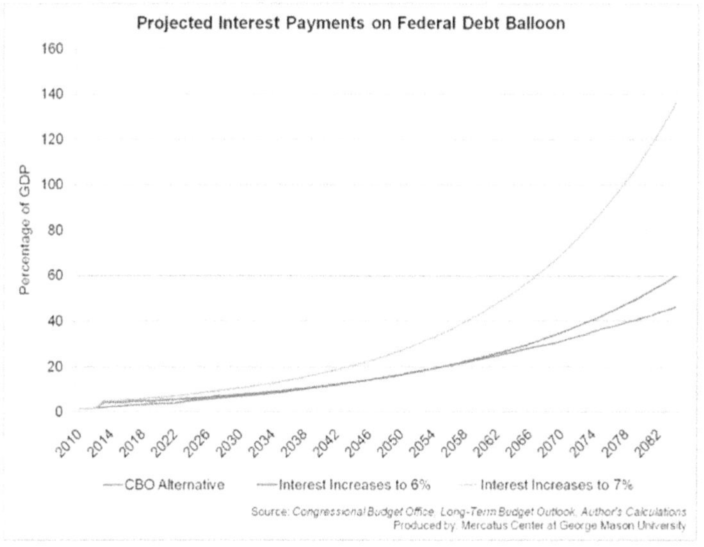

At seven percent, the interest on the debt will consume well over 100 percent[VIII] of the government's budget. At six and five percent the interest payments are a little more modest, but will still explode well beyond anything that is sustainable. Understand that these calculated interest rates are very modest by comparison; back in the 80s interest rates were around 20 percent. At that rate we would be bankrupt in just a few years. If we assume the worst-case scenario, as defined by the CBO, with interest rates at seven percent, the country goes bankrupt in 2081. If spending is allowed to reach that level, the government will no longer have the funds to cover the interest, let alone the remainder of their budget. There will not be enough people employed in the U.S. to tax their way out of this travesty either, no matter how much taxes are raised.

Now let us take a look at a list [ix] of some of the different types of taxes that exist in America. Afterwards I will compile another list that illustrates how some of our tax dollars are being spent, *uh hum*…wasted. Then you can decide for yourself if it is finally time to put the brakes on the government's runaway money train, and finally hold them responsible for their spending. Full definitions for each of these taxes are available in the glossary.

> Accounts Receivable Tax
> Building Permit Tax
> Capital Gains Tax
> Commercial Drivers License Tax
> Cigarette Tax
> Corporate Income Tax
> Court Fines
> Dog License Tax
> Estate Tax
> Excise Taxes
> Federal Income Tax
> Federal Unemployment Tax
> Fishing License Tax
> Food License Tax
> Fuel Permit Tax
> Gasoline Tax
> Hunting License Tax
> Inheritance Tax
> Inventory Tax IRS Interest Charges
> IRS Penalties
> Liquor Tax
> Local Income Tax
> Luxury Taxes
> Marriage License Tax
> Medicare Tax
> Personal Property Tax
> Property Tax
> Real Property Tax

Road, Tunnel, and Bridge Toll Tax
Road Use Tax
Sales Taxes
School Tax
Septic Permit Tax
Service Charge Taxes
Social Security Tax
State Income Tax
State Unemployment Tax (SUTA)
Telephone Federal Excise Tax
Telephone Federal Universal Service Fee Tax
Telephone Minimum Usage Surcharge Tax
Traffic Fines
Trailer Registration Tax
Utility Taxes
Vehicle License Registration Tax
Vehicle Sales Tax
Watercraft Registration Tax
Well Permit Tax
Workers Compensation Tax

This list is by no means complete, rather it is just a sample of some of the taxes that currently exist, and not every one of these taxes applies to all individuals. But you get the idea; we are being taxed beyond all reason. With all the taxes available to our government there should be absolutely no reason they cannot afford to operate within their budget, unless of course they are being irresponsible with our money. The list below details how some of our tax dollars are being spent. See if you agree with my assessment regarding the rampant misuse of tax dollars—some of which you will not believe. Trust me, these are real cases of abuse, they were researched thoroughly to ensure their accuracy.

> *African Male Genital Washing:* The National Institute of Mental Health (NIMH), a division of the National Institutes of Health (NIH), spent 823,200 dollars of economic stimulus funds in 2009 on a study by a UCLA research team to teach uncircumcised African men how to wash their genitals after having sex. [x]

Something that is common sense to most of us had to be taught to some men in Africa at a cost of almost a million dollars. I would have been more than happy to fly to Africa and teach these men for much less, say a hundred thousand. Seriously though, with all the problems here in the United States how can our government justify spending any money on this type of activity without first considering how that money could have been better spent here?

Alaska Airlines: Congress recently gave Alaska Airlines 500,000 dollars to paint a Chinook salmon on a Boeing 737. [XI]

A sum of 500,000 dollars to paint a fish on a plane, was the paint made of gold?

Bailout/Stimulus Spending: This is too broad a topic to mention here; therefore, I devoted an entire chapter to it—Government Bailouts and Stimulus. My brother Robert Srote also wrote a book detailing how this subject pertains to the recent recession, *Wildfire—The Legislation that Ignited the Great Recession.* Available everywhere books are sold. Visit www.wildfirebook.com for more information.

Chinese Prostitutes: Washington will spend 2.6 million dollars training Chinese prostitutes to drink more responsibly on the job. [XI]

Getting paid to drink, it appears our entire government is drunk with corruption.

Clean Cooking Stoves Given to Developing Countries: Secretary of State Hillary Clinton announced a U.S. contribution of more than 50 million dollars toward providing clean cooking stoves in developing countries to reduce deaths from smoke inhalation and fight climate change. [XII]

When the government can justify spending 50 million dollars on stoves for people in other countries, it is time to hold their feet to the fire. Everyone that approved this expenditure needs to be voted out of office.

Congress' Offices: Members of Congress have spent hundreds of thousands of taxpayer dollars supplying their offices with popcorn machines, plasma televisions, DVD equipment, ionic air fresheners, camcorders, and signature machines—plus 24,730 dollars leasing a Lexus, 1,434 dollars on a digital camera, and 84,000 dollars on personalized calendars. [XI]

Congress' Food Tab: During the nine-month period between late 2009 and early 2010 various members of Congress spent a total 2.6 million dollars on food and beverages for themselves and their staffers. Some of the items purchased were 604,000 dollars worth of bottled water, 397,000 dollars on catering, 135,000 dollars on meals, 9,374 dollars spent by the GOP with coffee companies, 4,543 dollars spent by the Democrats with Coca-Cola Enterprises, just to name a few. [XIII]

I bet everyone wishes they had an endless food budget from which to consume anything they desire. Apparently congress is not familiar with brown bagging it.

Democratic Fundraising Spree: It has been estimated that Obama's five-state, three-day tour across the country to help raise money for his party to retain power in the 2010 election cost taxpayers two million dollars. [XIV]

Department of Energy: The Department of Energy spent nine years and 153 million dollars on an obsolete cyber-security project that was supposed to safeguard America's nuclear weapons information. [XI]

Let me get this straight, 153 million dollars on obsolete technology, yet another brilliant example of government incompetency at work.

Federal Employee Taxes: Federal employees owe more than three billion dollars in income taxes they failed to pay in 2008. [XI]

We get penalized, and possibly jailed, for not paying our taxes. I guess since they are federal employees the same rules must not apply.

Flying First Class: The refusal of many federal employees to fly coach costs taxpayers 146 million dollars, annually, in flight upgrades. [XI]

Grateful Dead: Washington will spend 615,175 dollars on an archive honoring the Grateful Dead. [XI]

Impact on Government Programs: Government auditors spent the past five years examining all federal programs and found that 22 percent of them, costing taxpayers a total of 123 billion dollars, annually, fail to show any positive impact on the populations they serve. [XI]

Misplaced Equipment: The U.S. Centers for Disease Control and Prevention lost or misplaced more than 8 million dollars in property in 2007, losing track of items including computer and video equipment, government auditors say. [XV]

How many people actually have 8 million dollars, let alone trying to comprehend what it would be like to lose that amount of money?

Nancy Pelosi's In-flight Services: House Speaker Nancy Pelosi and her staff have charged taxpayers 101,000 dollars for *in-flight services*, including food and liquor, during trips on Air Force jets over the last two years. Charges reportedly include: "Maker's Mark whiskey, Courvoisier cognac, Johnny Walker Red scotch, Grey Goose vodka, E&J brandy, Bailey's Irish Crème, Bacardi Light rum, Jim Beam whiskey, Beefeater gin, Dewar's scotch, Bombay Sapphire gin, Jack Daniels whiskey, and Corona beer." [XI]

No wonder Washington thinks they are an elite class. They treat themselves to the best of everything on the taxpayer's dime. I too would feel entitled if I could spend money without consequence.

NASA Conference: During a recent three-day conference, NASA spent 62,611 dollars on *light refreshments* for its 317 attendees, sixty-six dollars per person, per day. NASA officials said such expensive snacks were needed to keep its officials from wandering away from the conference. [XI]

National Broadband: The stimulus set aside 350 million dollars for a national broadband coverage map, even though one private firm stated it could create one for 3.5 million dollars. [XI]

We can spend 3.5 million dollars and let the private sector prosper, or spend ten times that amount with the government's involvement. I propose we do the latter; after all, we are working with an endless supply of money given to us generously by the taxpayer.

Overstaffing: Because of overstaffing, the U.S. Postal Service selects 1,125 employees per day to sit in empty rooms. They are not allowed to work, read, play cards, watch television, or do anything. This costs fifty million dollars annually. [XI]

Getting paid to do nothing, yep this pretty much sums up my impression of our government.

Photo Op: Washington spends 60,000 dollars per hour shooting Air Force One photo-ops in front of national landmarks. [XI]

Our intellectually superior, governing body must be oblivious to the popular photo editing software Photoshop. It retails for around 700 dollars, just a little cheaper than 60,000 dollars. You can also find similar software online for free. But we cannot expect them to do something for free; otherwise they might be viewed as acting in a fiscally responsible manner. What a novel idea.

Raises for White House Staff: Seventy-four percent of White House staffers got a raise in 2010, according to a Gawker analysis of the White House's annual salary reports to Congress. *USA Today* published an analysis of the federal workforce, showing that the number of federal workers making more than 150,000 dollars a year has increased tenfold since 2005 and the number earning above 180,000 dollars has increased twentyfold. [XVI]

It is good to see that most of the White House staff received raises in 2010. They definitely deserve it considering how well they have handled the economy. While most of America has not received a raise in years, or lost their jobs entirely, government workers are making more money and receiving raises. Does anyone see anything wrong with this scenario?

Rearranging Furniture: The Securities and Exchange Commission spent 3.9 million dollars rearranging desks and offices at its Washington, D.C., headquarters. [XI]

Rebuilding Iraq: The U.S. has wasted billions *rebuilding* Iraq. A forty million-dollar prison sits in the desert north of Baghdad empty; a 165 million-dollar children's hospital goes unused in the south; a 100 million-dollar water treatment system in Fallujah has cost three times more than expected, yet sewage still runs through the streets; and the U.S. is leaving behind hundreds of abandoned or incomplete projects as it draws down in Iraq, with an estimated cost of more than five billion dollars. [XVII]

If you are an opponent of this war then this definitely should add fuel to the fire. Why is it that the government feels we should trust them with more when they have such a horrible track record with what they already manage?

Sandy Beaches: Washington has spent three billion dollars re-sanding beaches, even as this new sand washes back into the ocean. [XI]

Our money is literally being washed out to sea.

Scientists to Study Cow Burps: University of New Hampshire has been awarded a 700,000-dollar U.S. Department of Agriculture grant to create a computer model that measures the amount of greenhouse gases an organic dairy farm produces, such as methane created by cow burps, and thus provide ways to cut those emissions. [XVIII]

I am utterly disgusted (no pun intended) with the mismanagement of our money.

Self Portraits: Taxpayers are funding paintings of high-ranking government officials at a cost of up to 50,000 dollars apiece. [XI]

Who are they hiring, Leonardo De Vinci?

State Department: The State Department will spend 450,000 dollars on art shows in Venice, Italy. [XI]

Stimulus Payments Made to Dead People: The Social Security Administration's inspector general said in a report Thursday that 18 million dollars went to 72,000 dead people. The report estimates that a little more than half of the payments were returned. The report said 4.3 million dollars went to a little more than 17,000 prison inmates. [XIX]

Free money for everyone—even for those who are in no position to spend it. When is this nightmare going to end? Apparently never, not even after we are dead.

Studying Dinosaur Eggs in China: The National Science Foundation gave a 141,002-dollar federal stimulus grant to Montana State University to fund a six-week, student trip to Hangzhou, China, to study dinosaur eggs and other fossils. [XX]

Subsidizing Sanctuary Cities: The State Criminal Alien Assistance Program, a report from the Center for Immigration Studies, found that the federal grant program commonly known as SCAAP allocated 62.2 million dollars—more than 15 percent of its 400 million-dollar total—to twenty-seven jurisdictions that are widely considered to be *sanctuary communities.* [XXI]

Sanctuary cities adhere to policies that allow illegal aliens to setup camp without fear of deportation. A safe haven if you will, where immigration laws are not enforced. Yet these cities are requesting money from the government to combat the influx of illegal immigrants. Does anyone in our federal government have any common decency? What is happening to this money if it is not being spent on the problem? For that matter, why are they receiving any money at all? I smell the stench of corruption.

Super Bowl Ads: The Census Bureau spent 2.5 million dollars on Super Bowl ads. [XI]

We are in the greatest recession since the depression, yet our government has no problem spending our money on a useless ad to run during the Super Bowl. It is required by law for every adult living in the United State to fill out a census report. Therefore there is no need for the government to advertise these services.

Unaccounted for Defense Spending: According to a study published by the Special Inspector General for Iraq reconstruction the Defense Department is unable to account for 8.7 billion dollars of the nine million dollars. One billion in Development Fund for Iraq monies. [XXII]

That's 8.7 billion dollars lost; oh well, we will just raise taxes to cover the loss. The stupid electorate will never know the difference. They never keep track of what we spend. I have news for you, Washington—we are on to you. The rise of the Tea Party is just the beginning.

Unused Flight Tickets: The Defense Department wasted one hundred million dollars on unused flight tickets and never bothered to collect refunds even though the tickets were refundable. [XI]

Why bother to get a refund when we have an endless supply of money coming in from the gullible taxpayer? Not after reading this book. You are being exposed for the frauds you are.

Unused Properties: Washington spends twenty-five billion dollars, annually, on unused properties. [XI]

U.S. Aid Going to Taliban: As much as one billion dollars in U.S. aid has been diverted from programs meant to stabilize Afghanistan and has wound up in the hands of the Taliban and other insurgency groups, war analysts and government auditors say. [XXIII]

By all means let us keep funding this war—nothing like indirectly supplying money to our enemy and assisting them in their endeavors to defeat us.

Wasteful Stimulus Spending: Senators John McCain, R-Arizona, and Tom Coburn, R-Oklahoma, generated a report that highlighted one hundred stimulus projects that they say have *questionable goals* are *being mismanaged or were poorly planned* and are even *costing jobs and hurting small businesses.* One hundred and seventy-five million to Hydrogen Energy California (a BP subsidiary) to build a power plant that is not breaking ground for over two years; one million dollars to the California Academy of Sciences to send researchers to the Southwest Indian Ocean Islands and East Africa to photograph exotic ants, $500,000 to the U.S. Forest Service in Washington state to replace windows at a visitor center that is currently closed with no set reopen date, $300,000 to Wake Forest University to study whether yoga can reduce hot flashes in breast cancer survivors, $71, 623 to Wake Forest University to see how cocaine affects monkeys. [XXIV]

Approximately, $175 million to build a power plant that is not being used, $1 million to photograph ants, $500,000 to replace windows, $300,000 to study whether or not yoga reduces hot flashes… Are you getting the picture yet? Have you read enough to demand that our government cease and desist with this out of control spending? It is time we take matters into our own hands and vote these incompetent *leaders* out of office and replace them with people willing to get this country back on the right path.

Welfare Stimulus: New York distributed $140 million in stimulus money into the individual accounts of families on welfare, yet neglected to mention it was intended for school supplies. Local a.m. were depleted, and a lot of the money was reportedly spent on "flat screen TV's, iPods, and video gaming systems" as well as "cigarettes and beer." [XI]

Again, this was just a small sample of how our tax dollars are being squandered. As is typical fashion in Washington, some of these items were snuck into other bills that had absolutely nothing to do with the original legislation. Placing provisions such as these into larger bills, regardless of association, is known as adding an earmark to a bill. Earmarks are a provision in Congressional legislation that allocates a specified amount of money for a specific project, program, or organization. [XXV] Earmarks are also sometimes referred to as pork barrel legislation, although the two are not synonymous. One congressperson's earmark is another's pork. The term pork barrel spending usually refers to spending that is intended to benefit constituents of a politician in return for their political support, either in the form of campaign contributions or votes. [XXVI] The term *pork barrel* dates back to the 1870s and was believed to have derived from different sources. It was not given a negative connotation until after the Civil War when it was tied to giving slaves a barrel of salt pork as a reward requiring them to compete amongst themselves to get their share of the handout. [XXVI] No matter how you define it, our government is wasting our money on some pretty outrageous things. If the items in my list, and the subsequent misuse of our taxpayer money, are not enough to outrage every citizen then I fear all hope is lost. It is imperative we ensure every politician is aware of our views regarding wasteful pork spending. The wasteful mentality that exists in Washington cannot be tolerated anymore. Our nation's survival depends on it. The really sad fact in all of this is most of what I listed as waste is actually located in the discretionary portion of the government's budget. The big items that are bankrupting the country were not included. Social Security, Medicare, Medicaid, and defense spending consume most of the budget. Those items, along with the debt and the interest on the debt, when combined, make for an economic disaster.

So why has the debt reached such catastrophic levels? Wasteful spending, entitlements, and defense spending all have contributed. Social programs alone made up 47 percent of the 2010 budget, including interest. Defense spending took up another 20 percent, and some discretionary spending totaled between 10 and 18 percent. [XXVII] It is imperative that we get wasteful spending and entitlements under control. Social Security, Medicare, Medicaid, and the new health care law must all be reformed and/or repealed. Social Security can be fixed by privatizing it through attrition. Allow people that are currently enrolled the option to stay in the plan if they desire or move their vested money into some type of private portfolio. Then set a date for anyone entering the work force, say this year, and make Social Security no longer available from that point going forward. Leave it up to the individual to plan for their retirement. Do not force them into a plan by taxing their paycheck.

To prove just how bleak the Social Security situation has become, congressional budget experts have projected that it will become insolvent by 2037. [XXVIII] It went into deficit for the first time in 2010 and will continue to do so until its funds are depleted. This year alone it will be paying out $45 billion more than it collects in payroll taxes according to the Congressional Budget Office. The government has promised to pay back any lost revenue but that's hardly reassuring when you consider the $1.5 trillion deficit already budgeted for fiscal 2011. As you can clearly see, it is essential that we get a handle on this now or face a very bleak future as a nation. I suggest not only privatizing Social Security but all entitlements. The government cannot and should not be in the business of social engineering. I also stated that defense spending was a major contributor to the debt. The difference here is that this is one of the primary functions of government—to protect us, as defined in the Constitution. So while I do believe there are areas that could be improved upon, as illustrated in my wasteful spending list, I do feel strongly that if the government is going to spend our money this is where it should be spent. This does not mean, however, they have a blank check to do with as they wish. Our money still needs to be used in a responsible manner; waste of any kind is uncalled for and unacceptable.

Our government has grown to an unsustainable size, and way beyond anything our Founding Fathers envisioned. Because of this, it is important we put a stop to their irresponsible behavior immediately. As stated earlier, the best way for us as citizens to deal with this is to vote every incumbent out of office that promotes entitlement or wasteful spending. If someone is voted in and promises one thing but delivers another, vote them out during their next election cycle. Our politicians need to get the message that we are not going to sit idly by and watch them destroy our country. It is time they start working for us again, pushing our interests and agendas rather than their own. They need to concentrate on cutting government spending by shrinking government and eradicating waste, and it is not going to be easy. But it has to be done at all levels, and trustworthy people must be elected into office who share our ideals of fiscal conservatism. I believe we have proven we are way more responsible with our money than the government. Or has this chapter taught us nothing?

Government Bailouts and Stimulus

Article One, Section Seven of the United States Constitution states that *all bills for raising revenue need to originate in the House of Representatives*. Section Eight gives Congress *the power to lay and collect taxes, duties, imposts, and excises to pay the debts and provide for the common defense and general welfare of the United States*. It goes on to state that *they can borrow money on the credit of the United States, and regulate commerce with foreign nations as well as among the states*. It gives Congress the capacity to *establish laws regarding bankruptcies*, and the ability *to coin money and regulate its value*. Article One, Section Nine states that *no money shall be drawn from the Treasury, but in consequence of appropriations made by law*, and definitely does not state that this money can be used for the purpose of bailing out businesses and stimulating the economy. The Sixteenth Amendment gives Congress the power to collect income taxes, and we all know too well how effectively this horrible piece of legislation has been managed by our government, as explained previously.

Nowhere in any of the aforementioned articles or amendments, or anywhere else within the Constitution, does it state that the government has the right to take taxpayer money and use it to bailout or stimulate the private sector. Sure, Article One, Section Nine states that money can be withdrawn when laws are passed stating an appropriate need for the money, but to what end? Based again on historical context I do not believe our Founders would approve of any laws that allow the treasury to be used in this manner. Therefore, I can only conclude that by matter of exclusion our government decided it was allowed simply because it was not specifically stated. They have forgotten this principle only applies to us, the citizen, and government should only be using the Constitution as our Founders intended, as a strict guideline for limiting government's powers.

Take some time to familiarize yourself with this amazing document, located in the appendix of this book. After you have finished reading it, ask yourself one question: is it the responsibility of our government to provide bailouts or stimulus in times of economic strife? My answer is absolutely not. We already have laws in place that allow companies in financial trouble to reorganize and restructure their debt. The government has no business cherry picking companies they deem too big to fail, simply because of the impact they may have on the economy. Politicians should never have influence over which companies are allowed to exist and which are allowed to become insolvent. The government also has no business stimulating the economy by dolling out our tax dollars where they see fit. If they want to provide a stimulus, drastically shrink the size of government, reduce spending, balance the budget, and cut our taxes.

The cause of the latest financial meltdown, known as the Great Recession, started quite some time ago and would require an entire book to explain. That is why I recommend reading *Wildfire—The Legislation that Ignited the Great Recession*, written by my brother Robert Srote. He explains in detail the cause of the recession, where and when it started, what was done to rectify it, and gives common sense solutions that, if followed, will ensure the future success of our nation. Rather than focusing on a detailed analysis of what caused the recession I am going to concentrate my efforts on the specific act of providing stimulus and bailing out the private sector, and why I believe doing so defies the very foundation of the Constitution. I will also provide examples that illustrate how ineffective the stimulus was at creating jobs, one of its supposed primary functions. I will examine government's propensity for wasting our money on these types of programs, and how this was not the first time in our nation's history this has occurred. By the end of this chapter you will have a complete and concise understanding of just how unsuccessful the government is at managing your money and the economy.

The Troubled Asset Relief Program (TARP), or bailout as it is more commonly referred to, was enacted under President George W. Bush, October 3, 2008, with the signing of the Emergency Economic Stabilization Act. The acronym TARP was derived from the United States Department of Treasury's purchase of $700 billion of "troubled assets." These were defined as commercial or residential mortgages and "any securities, obligations, or other instruments that are based on or related to such mortgages," issued on or before March 14, 2008.[I] Some of the companies that received TARP funds were AIG, Citigroup, Wells Fargo, Goldman Sachs, Bank of America, JPMorgan Chase, Morgan Stanley, GMAC, Chrysler, and General Motors. To put it simply, most of these companies were in extreme financial trouble because they allowed consumers access to credit they ultimately could not afford, then repackaged those loans to be sold globally as mortgage backed securities with deceivingly high AAA ratings.[II] Given the severe impact these actions had on the economy, the Bush administration enacted TARP because they felt the potential for an economic collapse and another Great Depression were highly probable. Understand that there is no way for us to really know whether or not this is true, but according to their experts it was absolutely necessary. Other economists, however, have come forward, after looking back on the *success* of this program, and stated our economy would have been better off had we just let these corporations file for bankruptcy and let capitalism run its course. I agree, especially if success is gauged on the amount of treasure that was spent minus the amount that will never be repaid. TARP was highly controversial because taxpayer money was being used to bailout companies in the private sector, companies that did not manage their assets properly. In other words, they were being rewarded for bad behavior, simply because of the impact their company had on the economy. The fact that many executives continued to collect large salaries and bonuses, even after their companies were rescued, also added to people's discontent. I guess if there's any consolation to any of this it would be that $169 billion of the $245 billion invested in banks has been paid back, as of midyear 2010.[I] Only time will tell as to what will happen with the remaining $531 billion.

In 2008, the Economic Stimulus Act was also set into motion and consisted of tax rebates for every taxpayer, projected at $152 billion.

Whether or not this amount should be considered as contributing to the national debt is debatable. Remember, it is the government's out of control spending that is adding to the debt with their yearly budget deficits. Giving you more of your own money only adds to the debt when the government does not reduce their spending. When the government's revenue is affected by a recession and they do not adjust accordingly and control spending, providing tax breaks exacerbates an already bloated budget. This is why most government officials are against cutting taxes during an economic downturn. It is that thinking that causes our nation to continually slide deeper into debt.

But it is, unfortunately, the way most people in government react to a fiscal crisis. They are of the belief that raising taxes is the answer to a financial downturn, taking their increased revenue and redistributing it where they see fit. Rather than focusing on the problem, the incessant squandering. Reducing spending and providing tax breaks would inevitably help the economy take care of itself by placing more money in the hands of the people, rather than taking more away by means of taxation. We as Americans are expected to reduce our expenditures when times get tough and we should expect no less of our government. I truly believe that cutting taxes and controlling spending at the federal and state levels are always good ways to spur an economic recovery. The alternative only increases our debt, which has continued to grow every year exponentially to the point it is no longer manageable or sustainable.

Shortly after Barrack Obama was elected president in 2009, the American Recovery and Reinvestment Act was signed into law to provide stimulus to the economy to the tune of $787 billion. It was comprised of many different programs ranging from tax incentives to transportation. A portion of the money was dispersed among the states to spend on *shovel ready* projects. "Shovel ready" refers to projects that will have the most immediate impact on employment and the economy, projects that are in the advanced stages of development and past the planning stage. It was later discovered that some of these infrastructure projects, totaling $105.3 billion in stimulus, ended up being somewhat formidable as states struggled to find resources to get projects off the ground. Some of the money was also spent on transportation at $48.1 billion; water, sewage, and the environment at $18 billion; low income aid including extending unemployment totaling $82.2 billion; education at $100 billion; health care at $155.1 billion; investments in infrastructure at $105 billion; and tax incentives for individuals and corporations totaling $288 billion. In addition to the $787 billion spent on the aforementioned programs, Congress appropriated $3 billion on the "Cash for Clunkers" program, yet another colossal waste of taxpayer money. Edmunds.com conducted a detailed analysis [III] using doctors and statisticians to study the actual impact the cash for clunkers program had on the recession. Nearly 690,000 cars were sold during this program. While this seems like a large number, understand that only 125,000 cars were considered incremental, which means the remaining 565,000 would have been sold regardless of the program's existence. So while sales did spike during the program, it had only a temporary effect on the economy, because immediately afterward sales plummeted, which means people just purchased cars earlier than they would have had this program not existed. The net result being that each car cost the taxpayer $24,000 with no real gain in sales.

Thus far there has been about $3 trillion spent on stimulus and bailouts with around $11 trillion guaranteed [IV] for future commitments. That sum almost equals the amount of our 2011 national debt, which stood at $14.5 trillion. Add the guaranteed stimulus dollars to the 2011 debt and our future debt jumps to $25 trillion, assuming nothing is repaid by the time the guarantees are spent and balanced budgets are actually proposed and adhered to. Of course, if deficits are allowed to continue each year to the tune of trillions of dollars, that total will be much higher, especially when inflation is calculated into the equation.

To put this in some perspective, the New Deal, under President Franklin D. Roosevelt, cost about $50 billion [V] or about $500 billion in today's money, roughly one-third of the 2011 deficit. The New Deal was a series of economic programs implemented from 1933 to 1938, during the Great Depression, which were meant to provide economic recovery and relief to a seriously ailing economy. The term *New Deal* originated from Roosevelt's 1932 Democratic presidential nomination acceptance speech where he pledged himself to "a new deal for the American people."

When President Roosevelt took office unemployment had reached 25 percent, up sharply from 4 percent in 1929, and peaking around 28 percent in 1933. [VI] As prices fell by 20 percent, deflation skyrocketed, while manufacturing output plummeted by one-third. The nation was devastated and anxious for a solution to the economic crisis. President Roosevelt's first order of business would be to close all the banks so money could not be withdrawn. He was afraid that given the economic climate people would rush the banks and withdraw their remaining funds, causing the banks to crumble. He then convened with Congress to develop a plan to put the country back on the path to prosperity. For the first one hundred days of his administration he and Congress hammered out new laws they felt were needed to get the country back on track. This one hundred-day benchmark is now used to judge current presidents on how much they accomplish during their first one hundred days in office. The banks remained closed until President Roosevelt was able to implement new laws guaranteeing their stability and reassure the public. On March 9, the Emergency Banking Relief Act was signed into law and within three days three quarters of the banks within the Federal Reserve System were open for business. This legislation would allow the banks that were strong enough to survive to reopen and reorganize while other insolvent banks were closed.

Throughout the Great Depression, government regulations and oversight were expanded like never before. Programs for business and agricultural regulation, inflation, price stabilization, and public works were all being drafted at a feverous pace. Congress established many organizations, including but not limited to: the National Recovery Administration (NRA)—not the NRA we are familiar with today; the Federal Deposit Insurance Corporation (FDIC); the Agricultural Adjustment Administration (AAA); the Civilian Conservation Corps; and the Public Works Administration. The Tennessee Valley Authority, Securities and Exchange Commission, Federal Communications Commission, Trade Agreements Act, National Housing Act, the Social Security system, National Youth Administration, Work Project Administration, Fair Labor Standards Act, Wealth Tax Act (to redistribute wealth), and Revenue Acts were also developed. Some of these programs were eventually repealed while others were changed with new laws because they were deemed unconstitutional and the remainders were left in place, some of which are still in existence today. Regardless, the damage had been done; the New Deal increased the government's share of the economy from 4 to 10 percent. In comparison, the 2009 American Recovery and Reinvestment Act spent much more money over a much shorter period of time, increasing the government's share of the economy from 20 to 25 percent.[I] Are you beginning to see the bigger picture here? The government's share of the economy has grown from 4 percent to 25 percent in less than eighty years. When the new health care law is fully implemented it will jump even higher.

Historians and economists have argued whether or not the New Deal was successful. Some have stated that it exacerbated an already terrible situation because it prolonged the depression. Others said that it was absolutely necessary to keep the economy from falling off the cliff. Whatever side you believe, if success is gauged on FDR's intent for complete economic recovery, then it can easily be determined that the New Deal did not perform as expected. Because one fact is certain; his goal for a complete recovery was never realized. While unemployment did decrease, it never fell below 14 percent and remained high during the entire Great Depression. The average unemployment rate throughout the 1930s hovered at 17 percent.[VI] Almost double the current unemployment rate. It never returned to its pre-depression level of 4 percent until after the United States entered World War II in December 1941. A couple of years into the war it shrank to an unbelievably low 2 percent. That is why I believe it was the war, not the vast expansion of government that helped dig the nation out of its slump. Even FDR's own Treasury Secretary Henry Morgenthau, Jr., admitted the New Deal was a failure. In 1939, when unemployment was still around 20 percent, he said, "We have tried spending money. We are spending more than we have ever spent before and it does not work."[VII] Just as the New Deal took government oversight to a whole new level, so did the stimulus and bailouts of 2008 and 2009.

The list [VIII] below contains some examples of other major purchases made throughout our history and adjusts each cost for inflation so you can see for yourself how much was spent compared to the latest government atrocities, which are currently estimated at $3 trillion.

- Marshall Plan—Cost: $12.7 billion, Inflation Adjusted Cost: $115.3 billion

- Louisiana Purchase—Cost: $15 million, Inflation Adjusted Cost: $217 billion

- The New Deal—Cost: $50 billion, Inflation Adjusted Cost: $500 billion

- Race to the Moon—Cost: $36.4 billion, Inflation Adjusted Cost: $237 billion

- Savings & Loan Crisis—Cost: $153 billion, Inflation Adjusted Cost: $256 billion

- Korean War—Cost: $54 billion, Inflation Adjusted Cost: $454 billion

- Vietnam War—Cost: $111 billion, Inflation Adjusted Cost: $698 billion

- Invasion of Iraq—Cost: $551 billion, Inflation Adjusted Cost: $597 billion

- NASA—Cost: $416.7 billion, Inflation Adjusted Cost: $851.2 billion

Total Inflation Adjusted Cost: $3.93 trillion.

The total adjusted cost of all these massive projects combined is just over the amount spent by our government on the bailouts and stimulus. Amazingly, those in Washington were able to spend $3 trillion in about two years' time, whereas previously it had taken them around two hundred years.

In his book, *Wildfire*, Robert stated it best when he defined the acronym TARP as Taxpayers Accosted, Raped, and Pillaged. What a terrific description of government's treatment of the taxpayer through the subsequent misuse of funds. That is the only thing that can be gleaned from the inept practice of rewarding a company that should have declared bankruptcy. Our government explained that the stimulus was not only needed to help prop up a faltering economy, but to also quell the surge of unemployment. Companies were laying off employees by the thousands; unemployment numbers were growing with no sign of subsiding, as hundreds of thousands became unemployed each month. Our government also stated that if the stimulus was enacted, unemployment would never rise above 8 percent. Not only did it not remain below 8 percent, it climbed to 9.8 percent and remained above 9 percent for over nineteen months[IX], the longest period above that level since World War II. Some conservatives will argue that this statistic is the primary reason for stating the stimulus was a failure. I believe that reasoning is flawed and should never be used to explain why the stimulus was unsuccessful. The very idea of taking tax payer dollars and utilizing them to pump money into a failing economy is socialistic in nature, that in and of itself is reason enough to declare the stimulus a failure. Forget about the broken promise made by our government.

As if taking taxpayer money and using it to *stimulate* the economy was not bad enough, reports have surfaced that show it being used for somewhat questionable projects. Projects that, in my opinion, have absolutely nothing to do with helping the economy recover and were a complete waste of our money. Senators John McCain, R-AZ, and Tom Coburn, R-OK, created a report[X] that illustrated massive waste found in the stimulus. Approximately $71,623 spent on studying how cocaine affects monkeys, $1 million to send researches to the Southwest Indian Ocean Islands to photograph and study thousands of exotic ants, $300,000 to study how yoga affects hot flashes, and $175 million given to Hydrogen Energy California to build a power plant that will not break ground for another two years. According to Jordan Feilders of Hydrogen Energy California, forty-seven jobs were created or preserved through this program, and $14 million of the allocated stimulus funds have been spent thus far. That breaks down to over $297 thousand dollars spent per employee. A pretty impressive salary for each job created or saved, would you not agree? Obviously this is a partisan report, given that it was written by two Republicans, regardless the validity of their concerns ring true. Whether or not the jobs listed were actually created or saved is worth calling into question. As well as understanding the type of jobs our illustrious government help save, and this report is just the tip of the iceberg. A simple search on the Internet revealed many other news articles sighting taxpayer dollars wasted on the bailout and erroneous stimulus projects.

In 2008 and 2009, the Federal Reserve rushed trillions of dollars in emergency aid to not only Wall Street, but motorcycle makers, telecom firms, and foreign banks.[XI] Some of the banks that received our stimulus dollars were the Korean Development Bank, the French BNP Paribas, the Swiss UBS, and the German Deutsche Bank. I understand that we are part of a global economy now, and when one country suffers a major economic downturn, it can have a resounding effect across the globe, but do we really want our tax dollars being used to bailout private banks in foreign countries when our government cannot even manage its finances at home? Senator Bernard Sanders, I-VT, does not believe so. He said,

> The American people are finally learning the incredible and jaw-dropping details of the Fed's multitrillion-dollar bailout of Wall Street and corporate America. Perhaps most surprising is the huge sum that went to bail out foreign private banks and corporations. As a result of this disclosure, other members of Congress and I will be taking a very extensive look at all aspects of how the Federal Reserve functions. [XI]

In Cook County, Illinois, near President Obama's hometown of Chicago, the Department of Energy found serious problems in stimulus funded weatherization work. [XII] The Weatherization Assistance Program was implemented with $242 million in stimulus money. It was expected to make 27,000 homes more energy efficient. Surprisingly, it did just the opposite and actually made some houses less efficient and uninhabitable. Energy Department inspectors looked closely at a specific portion of the project where $91 million dollars of the money was allocated to the Community and Economic Development Association (CEDA) in Cook County, which was the largest recipient of weatherization money in Illinois and responsible for weatherizing 12,500 homes. They visited fifteen homes and found that fourteen had failed final inspection because of bad workmanship and/or inadequate initial assessments. Some of the brilliant plans executed under this project were placing insulation in the attic of a house with a leaky roof, billing for labor that had not been incurred and materials that were not installed, heat barriers around chimneys that were not installed, a furnace that was not vented properly, a gas shutoff valve that was not installed on a stove, and carbon monoxide detectors, fire extinguishers, and smoke detectors not installed as planned. The inspectors also discovered fraud and found examples where CEDA was billed for a 200,000 BTU boiler even though only a 125,000 BTU boiler was actually installed; another contractor billed for four times the amount of drywall used; and another billed CEDA for twenty light bulbs but only twelve were installed. They also found CEDA paid almost three times the retail price for each light bulb.

Another report by *USA Today*[XIII] found that $162 million of stimulus funds have not been disclosed. I believe it was President Obama who promised us transparency in government, the likes of which we have never seen. If this is his idea of transparency, one can only imagine what else he is keeping under wraps. We all have a right to know how our money is being spent. According to the Office of Management and Budget (OMB) there are currently 352 recipients of federal stimulus dollars that have not reported how they spent the money, the status of their projects, or how many jobs were funded. OMB stated that those recipients who have not reported are less than 1 percent of the 88,000 stimulus projects, which is an improvement over last year's results when 8 percent did not file. However, it appears little is being done to hold those recipients responsible. The *USA Today* review found that only one of the non-reporting recipients was suspended, International Trading CCT LLC of Livonia, Michigan. The irony here is that this company was not suspended by the U.S. Department of Agriculture, it was suspended by the Defense Logistics Agency for delivering substandard construction materials and then forging documents to cover it up; and they still owe the Defense Department $305,256. The very department in charge of overseeing the stimulus dollars was not competent enough to take action, instead it fell to another department entirely, one that had no affiliation with the stimulus process. How can we expect competency from our government when they do not have the ability to perform accurate and concise audits against jobs they initiate? I believe most, if not all, publicly traded companies have to comply with strict audit standards that are tested each and every year to provide full transparency to their shareholders. We should demand no less from our government. *USA Today's* analysis shows that the Department of Agriculture has the biggest problem with missing reports—one hundred recipients receiving $103 million. On the next page is a breakdown[XIII] of the agencies that have stimulus recipients who have not yet filed reports detailing how and where the money was spent.

**Department or agency Awards not reporting Total
(in millions)**
Agriculture 100 $103.3
Health & Human Services 73 $22.4
General Services Administration 6 $8.5
Education 48 $6.2
Justice 38 $3.7
National Science Foundation 8 $3.4
Bureau of Land Management 21 $3.1
Bureau of Indian Affairs 19 $2.5
State 3 $2.1
Housing & Urban Development 2$1.7
Homeland Security 3 $1.2
National Oceanic &
Atmospheric Administration 3 $1.0
Others 28 $3.7
Total 352 $162.8

This includes Economic Development Administration, U.S. Army Corps of Engineers, Transportation, Energy, National Park Service, Fish and Wildlife Service, U.S. Geological Survey, Federal Communications Commission and Labor.

So once again we are enlightened with more examples of how irresponsibly our government handles our money. The amount of waste being generated by our politicians should have all Americans incensed to the point that they demand a complete restructuring of the current government.

Someone else who believes our system is wrought with fraud, Bernie Madoff. He recently told New York magazine that the government is a big Ponzi scheme. [xiv] While no one should ever trust Mr. Madoff regarding investment advice, there is no one alive that understands a Ponzi scheme better than him. A Ponzi, or pyramid, scheme is a scam in which people are persuaded to invest their money through promises of high returns, with early investors being paid from money put in by later investors. The major reason Ponzi schemes collapse is because they require a constant stream of money to work. When it becomes difficult to recruit new investors, or when a large number of them cash out, that stream is broken, resulting in limited to no funds left for the remaining investors.

So is Mr. Madoff's assessment correct? Is our government really a big Ponzi scheme? If you look at the recent bouts of stimulus and bailouts, one could state that simply enacting legislation of this nature without the funds to cover each is in fact similar in nature to a Ponzi scheme. Money our government does not have ($3 trillion spent while $14 trillion in debt) was taken from us, the taxpayer, to help bailout companies and stimulate the economy, all while hoping the bailouts would reap a full return on investment. That obviously has not occurred, and it is now being projected we will never recoup all of our money. When you factor in the amount we're spending on Social Security, Medicare, Medicaid, and the interest owed on our debt compared to how much revenue the government is accruing, it is starting to resemble a Ponzi scheme more and more with each passing day.

We heard time and time again that the bailouts and stimulus were absolutely necessary. Any other solution was not practical and would lead to economic devastation. So did the bailouts work as promised and were they really necessary, or were they just a stopgap that prolonged an already bad situation, as some historians have claimed was the case with the New Deal? There is no doubt that the stimulus and bailouts both had some effect on the economy. However, it could definitely be argued that the positive effect was minimal at best and did little to nothing to reverse unemployment or help some of the companies that were rescued. I would even go as far as stating these programs were a colossal waste of money. As of the first quarter of fiscal year 2011, just over 229.4 billion [xv] stimulus dollars have been sent to all 435 Congressional Districts within all fifty states. With a total of 580,417 jobs created or saved. That many jobs may sound impressive, until you take a closer look at the numbers. The total cost spent per job was 395,386 dollars. Of the total stimulus allocated around $123.2 billion went to the public sector, with just over $105.6 billion going to the private sector. Here is where it gets real interesting, of the total stimulus spent over $166 billion went to Democratic entities, while only $59.7 billion went to Republicans. Almost three times more went to Democrats than Republicans. Does anyone see a conflict of interest here? Is President Obama trying to prop up his Democratic machine or was this all just a huge coincidence based on the number of Democratic districts versus Republican districts? When you look at how many Republicans won in 2010 I find it hard to believe that this much money went to Democrats on merit alone, by that large of a margin, with absolutely no ulterior motive. Another very good example of why our tax dollars should never be used in this manner.

If we look even closer at some of the cities that received stimulus dollars, things only look worse upon further review. In Los Angeles California the city controller Wendy Greuel released a report[xvi] detailing how the city spent its share of the stimulus. It found that only fifty-five jobs were saved or created after receiving $111 million. That breaks down just over $2 million per job. How many of you make $2 million a year, or for that matter in your lifetime? The report details that the Los Angeles Department of Public Works spent $70 million and only generated 45.46 jobs (the fractional value correlates to the number of actual hours worked), total cost to the tax payer per job $1.5 million. The city's department of transportation did not fare much better. They received $40.8 million and created only nine jobs, their goal was twenty-six. Whichever way you break it down the total cost to the taxpayer was exorbitant, nine jobs costing $4.5 million apiece or had they reached their goal of twenty-six, $1.5 million per job. The dismal numbers were blamed on a number of factors. Bureaucratic red tape caused four highway projects to be delayed seven months after they were authorized. Projects that were supposed to be bid in the private sector ended up going to city workers instead. Stimulus money was not tracked properly within departments. Departments had difficulty reporting jobs created or saved in a timely manner (more ineptitude at work everyone; the government is not fiscally responsible, period). The sooner we all realize this, the better off we will be.

Billions of dollars were sent to states to help prop up their budgets, keep government workers employed and state programs running. Two years later those same states are still drowning in debt and now contemplating or implementing the very cuts that were saved. The end result being the same as if the state bailouts had never occurred, and I would be willing to bet that had these cuts been made two years ago we would be in a much better place now, possibly on a path to recovery.

It appears the government made yet another slight miscalculation when they *invested* our money. Billions wasted to help boost employment, and unemployment is still just slightly better than it was when this all began.

Or is it? If you look closely at the statistics regarding unemployment, it appears things may not actually be improving. A report from the Bureau of Labor Statistics[XVII] shows the "Labor Force Participation Rate" equal to that of last month. The government does not include *discouraged* workers, retirees, or students when defining the labor force. It only includes people at or above sixteen years of age that are employed or seeking employment. The participation rate is the comparison of the labor force and everyone else. In February 2011 that ratio was at 64.2 percent, the same level as the month before. That percentage is holding at a twenty-seven year low, which means the percentage of Americans not working, or trying to find work, is at a near thirty-year high. The ten-year average is usually above 66 percent, last seen in August of 2008. So while the unemployment numbers appear to be improving, the overall outlook is dim at best. I do not believe unemployment has improved. When factoring the Bureau of Labor Statistics report with the way the unemployment rate is actually calculated it actually appears to be getting worse. If more people quit looking for work, and this is not being factored into the equation when reporting unemployment, then it stands to reason that unemployment is not actually improving. Just more people have quit looking. The real way to factor unemployment would be to total how many people are eligible to work, how many want to work, and how many are actually working.

Stimulus waste has permeated all levels of government. I have explained how the government has wasted our money at the federal and state levels; now let us take a look at how it is being wasted at the local level as well. The stimulus was divided among several cities in and around my place of residency in St. Louis County, Missouri.[XVIII]

Missouri Department of Transportation—$21 million to expand Highway 141, estimated to create 1,304 jobs. However, some of those jobs include restaurant and retail jobs that are expected to be generated when the project is finished. They are counting jobs that may or may not be created based on the possibility that retail and restaurant spaces will be built and occupied afterward. This seems a little loose with the facts as far as I am concerned, especially when you factor in the current poor economic climate.

Ballwin—$121,000 for retrofitting public buildings to make them more energy efficient. Jobs created—zero; most work was done by existing companies.

Chesterfield—$219,500 awarded by the department of energy to be used for trail construction and resurfacing. Job growth calculations were not necessary for this project, which is just another way of stating zero jobs created, in my opinion.

Creve Coeur—This city and fourteen other local municipalities received $247,000 to retrofit lighting in forty-five municipal buildings. Jobs created 1.74 collectively, including needed materials and installation labor.

Ellisville—$9,700 for police equipment and $4,800 to refurbish lighting in Ellisville's municipal buildings. Ellisville Mayor Matt Pirrello was quoted by *West Newsmagazine* as saying, "The work performed on either account kept someone employed somewhere I am sure." Using Mayor Pirrello's logic, I can just as easily state that the total number of jobs created was zero—I am sure.

Manchester—Submitted projects for stimulus funds that were "shovel-ready" but were turned down by the federal government.

Wildwood—$1 million went to the Manchester Road Corridor Great Streets Initiative planning, which also included the cities of Manchester, Winchester, Ballwin, and Ellisville. The money received went toward consultant services. No jobs were created from this portion of the stimulus.

It is easy to see from the examples cited above that the stimulus did little to retain or create jobs locally either.

It is not just our nation that is facing problems with this type of government spending. Other countries are experiencing very similar issues with their budgets as well. In Great Britain their whole socialist model is in peril of collapsing due to a £115 billion deficit ($184.5 billion as American currency). They are being forced to reform their welfare system and cut 490,000 jobs. [xix] Items from all types of government programs are being slashed. On Britain's Government Spending Review website [xx] they clearly state that if government spending is not brought under control by reducing their deficit they will not be able to secure sustainable economic growth. It goes on to state, the consequences of not acting could be serious: higher interest rates, business failures, and rising unemployment. In Greece they are faced with a €300 billion debt ($416.8 billion as American currency), now their government is under extreme pressure to raise taxes and make drastic cuts to their entitlement programs, which caused rioting in the streets. Spain, Italy, and Portugal are also dealing with extremely high debts. They too are taking the necessary steps to make their nations solvent again.

All of these European nations are being faced with a similar reality, which is forcing them to realize their spending on entitlement socialist models are not sustainable, so much so they now have no choice but to make drastic cuts to their budgets by restructuring their government. Yet our own government is pushing us closer and closer to a socialist state with each piece of legislation that comes through Congress, all while completely ignoring the fact that we are already $16 trillion in debt. Our debt plus more entitlements only points us in one direction, and I fear if we do not change direction soon we are headed down a very dark road in our nation's history. Even though our government believes in programs of this nature, such as bailing out companies and/or stimulating the economy with our tax dollars, it is evident to me that in the long run these programs do more harm than good. Just ask Great Britain, Greece, Italy, Spain, and Portugal. This is why I am so dumbfounded by government's inability to see what is coming down the pike regarding the effect our debt will have on the nation's economy. They proceeded with the bailouts and stimulus spending knowing full well our dire economic condition, and seeing firsthand what massive debt spending has done to countries across the Atlantic.

Most liberals that favor and believe in the bailout and stimulus will argue that it is way too soon to state whether or not these programs have worked as expected. Furthermore, they will state that unemployment is slowly declining which is a sure sign that both are starting to heed results. I contend, however, that unemployment will eventually improve regardless of the stimulus and has not yet done so because of government's overreaching policies. I would also be willing to bet that if Washington would have made the environment more suitable for small businesses this whole disaster could have ended much sooner instead of being prolonged, as is currently the case.

Small businesses have a huge impact on our economy. They provide just over half of all private sector employees and have generated over 64 percent of new jobs over the last fifteen years. [xxi] As I stated earlier, unemployment was above 9 percent longer than any time since World

War II, and that was just the people the government counted. The real unemployment rate was said to be around 18 percent, [XXII] when you factor in the folks who became completely frustrated and quit looking for work and those who were underemployed. The solution to this downturn would have been to cut taxes heavily across the board for both the individual and businesses, provide a balanced budget by cutting government excess, and immediately introduce plans that reduce spending to help eliminate our national debt. That is the way you stimulate an economy. Giving the folks more of their own money so they can pump it back into the economy, and making government responsible are two very basic ideas that our forefathers understood. Of course liberals will argue that taxes need to be raised on the rich to fix the economy, and forget about having a civil conversation regarding a responsible smaller government. My counter on raising taxes is simple; anything that negatively impacts a business' revenue stream will only stunt growth. Since businesses need to be confident in their profits to hire new employees—something that is difficult to do when you are spending more on taxes and giving more to the government because of increasing regulation. Getting Washington and liberals to understand this philosophy, however, is a lost cause because all they believe in is big government and more taxation. If liberals like paying taxes so much then I suggest they start writing extra checks each tax season and leave the rest of us out of it. I doubt the government would oppose their kind gesture. Liberals do not seem to understand that Washington is employed by us and like any good business does when times get tough, you cut back on your expenditures to balance your budget.

The very idea of taxing people to fix a problem the government caused is ridiculous. Our government is responsible for mismanaging their funds, not us. This is like punishing the older brother for something the younger brother did simply because he is the oldest and should know better. We are all adults now and our government should treat us as such. We do not need to be taken care of like children and I resent the fact that our government views us in that manner. This is one of the inherent problems within the structure and philosophy of government and it needs to be changed. The rest of American businesses do not operate this way, and neither should Washington. The government has grown so large it can no longer operate within its proposed budgets. Each year more and more deficits are realized and the government continues operating as if nothing is wrong. The 111th Congress accumulated more debt than the first one hundred Congresses combined. It even outstripped its closest competitor the 110th Congress by an astonishing $1.262 trillion. [XXIII] We as a nation need to start holding the government accountable and demand they operate within their means. But first we need to define those means by shrinking the size of government and then limiting its ability to grow.

I have given you example after example, which clearly illustrates government's ineptitude and wasteful tendencies. It is imperative that we change their behavior now or face a very bleak future. Our Founding Fathers said we should always be skeptical of government because the institution breeds corruption. Think of it this way: a business exists to provide a service to its clients. They remain in business by providing a service or product that the consumer wants or needs. We purchase these products and provide revenue to the business as long as the demand exists. It is in a business' best interest to ensure quality service is provided at a competitive rate so that they remain prosperous and grow. They are relying on us to exist because we are providing them with revenue. The government is not modeled in this fashion. They are taking our money to operate and do not have to concern themselves with providing a valid service. Since we are required by law to provide them with income via taxes, there is absolutely no incentive for them to operate efficiently. If they spend too much or waste our money, no big deal, they just raise taxes and continue taking more of our money to cover the shortfall. Each time they spend in excess or grow in size they take more. This pattern has existed for quite some time. Those in Washington are never held accountable for their actions, except when we vote them out of office. But since this process takes time and is not as immediate as the business model, corruption and waste ensue. Well I say enough is enough, the time has come for us as a nation to stand up and demand better from our government, or we can choose to continue down the same path of destruction and watch our great nation fade into obscurity.

A New Amendment

The United States Constitution has not been amended since May 7, 1992. Given the unprecedented growth in government during this century and last I believe a new amendment is long overdue. It must be designed to restrain government and control its propensity for growth. There are many reasons to rein in our behemoth of a government, not the least of which is the irresponsible use of our money. But the most important reason, the one that supersedes all others, is the eventual decline of the American dream. It will cease to exist the day this nation fully adopts the socialist policies being slowly introduced into our culture by the entitlement class. If their vision of a socialist utopia comes to fruition, our country will devolve into a state that is one step above tyrannical rule. This assessment is not just pure conjecture on my part; it has been fully realized in other nations around the globe. The more people depend on government the more government grows and the less folks depend on themselves and each other. Eventually government encompasses so much of society that the majority become completely subservient, such as those within a monarchy; something Alexander Hamilton, James Madison, and John Jay knew all too well. They were directly opposed to an intrusive federal government and made this abundantly clear when authoring the Federalist Papers. Between 1787 and 1788 they collectively wrote eighty-five essays detailing the need for a new model government. The idea was to convince the states that a new system was needed because the current government, under the Articles of Confederation, was failing. Each essay thoroughly explained how the new bureaucracy would operate and why a new constitution was needed in order for the union to survive. Mr. Hamilton focused on taxes and the judiciary while Mr. Madison covered general issues of government and representation. John Jay was the eldest of the three and an expert in foreign policy; his primary focus was covering international affairs. Each essay was published in newspapers in plain English so every citizen could easily understand the authors' explanations for the proposed government. It was about transparency, something that is severely lacking in today's government, given that you need a lawyer to interpret any bill sent through congress. Madison, Hamilton, and Jay made it clear that their suggested government was to be very limited in scope and serve a specific purpose, nothing like what has transpired in modern times.

Federalist Papers 17, 28, 33, 45, 46, 47, and 69 all explain the limit on government's power by way of strict enforcement of the Constitution and the balance of power that should exist between the federal and state governments. In Federalist 17 it explains how state government works better at understanding the needs of its people based on proximity to its population. The idea is that law should be enforced at the local level, thereby creating a tighter bond between the people and their state government. It goes on to explain that the states should always retain more power than that of the federal government. Even questioning why the federal government would ever want to take power away from the states when it was clear the balance of power was necessary for the good of the union. The very fact that our Founders did not comprehend the idea of federal encroachment on states' rights is unequivocal proof they would never accept the expansive role government has taken today. An excerpt from the end of this essay explaining this very concept is as follows:

> The separate governments in a confederacy may aptly be compared with the feudal baronies; with this advantage in their favor, that from the reasons already explained, they will generally possess the confidence and good-will of the people, and with so important a support, will be able effectually to oppose all encroachments of

the national government. It will be well if they are not able to counteract its legitimate and necessary authority. The points of similitude consist in the rivalship of power, applicable to both, and in the *concentration* of large portions of the strength of the community into particular *deposits*, in one case at the disposal of individuals, in the other case at the disposal of political bodies.

Federalist Paper 46 reaffirms the Founders' belief in limited government by emphasizing a state's power and the relative insignificance the federal government should have in our daily lives. A portion of it reads:

> It has been already proved that the members of the federal will be more dependent on the members of the State governments, than the latter will be on the former. It has appeared also, that the prepossessions of the people, on whom both will depend, will be more on the side of the State governments, than of the federal government. So far as the disposition of each towards the other may be influenced by these causes, the State governments must clearly have the advantage.

A segment from the beginning of the next paragraph reads:

> Were it admitted, however, that the Federal government may feel an equal disposition with the State governments to extend its power beyond the due limits, the latter would still have the advantage in the means of defeating such encroachments.

It is evident from these two excerpts alone that James Madison believed in limited federal power and greater state power. I recommend reading all of the Federalist Papers to fully comprehend the true meaning behind the Constitution and the authors' intent for government's role in society. If these essays were required reading in school people's views regarding federal government's purpose would change substantially.

Thomas Jefferson warned of government expansion many times in his writings and stressed that limits on Federal government's power are essential for the protection of people's liberties.[1] Limited government was something the Founders believed in strongly. Its significance was defined by describing its purpose as it related to liberty. The larger government grows the more it takes of our liberty, our freedom. This belief is well noted within the Declaration of Independence as well:

> We hold these truths to be self-evident, that all men are created equal, that they are endowed by their Creator with certain unalienable Rights, that among these are Life, Liberty and the pursuit of Happiness. —That to secure these rights, Governments are instituted among Men, *deriving their just powers from the consent of the governed,—That whenever any Form of Government becomes destructive of these ends, it is the Right of the People to alter or to abolish it, and to institute new Government,* laying its foundation on such principles and organizing its powers in such form, as to them shall seem most likely to effect their Safety and Happiness.

The Tenth Amendment to the Constitution asserts the rights of the people and state over the government by limiting federal power to the laws of the Constitution and no further. It reads: *The powers not delegated to the United States by the Constitution, nor prohibited by it to the States, are reserved to the States respectively, or to the people.* Not only did the Founders believe that government expansion was a direct infringement on our freedoms, but that it was the duty of citizens to control its expanse for fear of losing such liberties. In 1785 James Madison wrote *Memorial and Remonstrance* in opposition to a bill introduced into the general assembly of Virginia. In it he wrote:

> Because it is proper to take alarm at the first experiment on our liberties. We hold this prudent jealousy to be the first duty of citizens, and one of [the] noblest characteristics of the late Revolution. The freemen of America did not wait till usurped power had strengthened itself by exercise and entangled the question in precedents. They saw all the consequences in the principle, and they avoided the consequences by denying the principle. We revere this lesson too much, soon to forget it. [11]

The time has come for us to comply with Madison's message and get government back in line with the limitations proposed by our Founding Fathers. To do this I recommend adding a new amendment to the Constitution. It must be drafted in a clear and concise manner, redefining government's role in society. On the following pages I have scribed what should be included in this amendment to limit federal power, with the specific text shown in bold and an explanation on why each addendum is necessary.

The president cannot commit troops or treasure to any battle foreign or domestic, or declare war on any nation, without first seeking and getting congressional approval, unless our nation is directly attacked.

The War Powers Act was created in 1973 to clarify Article 1 Section 8 of the Constitution. It was passed because Congress believed the president was taking too many liberties with our armed forces by committing them to long, drawn-out engagements without ever declaring an act of war, specifically during Korea and Vietnam. While the president is defined as the commander in chief in the Constitution I believe this title gives him the power to command our troops during a time of war. I do not believe being the Commander grants him the authority to place our troops in harm's way, especially without a declaration of war. That responsibly is reserved solely for Congress, as stated in the Constitution. If the president sought Congress' approval every time he engaged in a conflict, there is a very good chance our involvement in some wars would have been avoided. I believe if a country is threatening our sovereignty or housing terrorists that attack our country, as was the case with Al-Qaida in Afghanistan, then we should strike without hesitation. But the mission should be precise and the strategy should only include eradicating the enemy. Once complete we should leave and return home, only going back if the terrorists resurface. We should not attempt to stay and nation build after thwarting the enemy. It has cost our country too many lives and too much money. Furthermore, we should not be stationing our troops all over the world to protect our countries interests. Doing so is costing us money we do not have, billions of dollars every year. We still have 50,000 troops stationed in Germany. I thought World War II ended in 1945. If our presence in these countries is to ensure our safety then I believe we should be able to protect our nation covertly, with special-ops soldiers, CIA operatives, and the like. Of course I do not have access to classified intelligence regarding our national security, so I could be completely wrong in my assessment. In this instance, and this instance only, I am willing to give our government the benefit of the doubt. This is, after all, the primary function of government as instructed by our Founders. But that still does not excuse wasting billions of dollars on nation building in Afghanistan and Iraq and involving our troops in wars such as Libya.

The federal government may not propose any deficit spending in their budget, unless approved by two-thirds of Congress for emergency purposes only.

That emergency must be defined as a drastic incident, such as an act of war committed on our soil by a rogue nation. The government must comply with a balanced budget each year, similar to all fifty states. The reason for this is obvious—government's propensity for deficit spending, which has dug us into a $16 trillion hole. The best way to fix this is to cut spending and eliminate unnecessary government programs and departments. In 1995 Canada's debt consumed 68 percent of their GDP. [III] This frightened investors, so Canada's government did what was necessary to get their debt under control—they cut spending. To put this in perspective, America's debt has now grown to 100 percent [IV] of the economy, equal to the sum of all the goods and services sold in the U.S. in a year. Apparently our fearless leaders must know more than Canada's investors, which can be the only explanation for continuing down this reckless path to bankruptcy. Washington needs to take the appropriate steps to dramatically curb spending immediately and follow Canada's lead. Their government eliminated 22 percent of its agriculture department, reduced its fisheries by 27 percent, natural resources by 49 percent, transportation by 51 percent, and human resources by 35 percent over a period of three years. Doing so shrank their debt from 68 percent of the economy to just 29 percent by 2007.

The Canadian government instituted a small tax increase as well, but the cuts in government spending were six to one when compared with the increase. Unlike our liberal friends in America, Canada understood that you cannot just raise taxes to fix a nation's debt problem. A study by the nonpartisan tax foundation proved this as well and discovered that taxing every individual making more than $10 million at 100 percent would only reduce the nation's deficit by 12 percent and its debt by 2 percent. [V] Liberal Billionaire Warren Buffet believes the government should raise taxes on everyone making $1 million or more.

The problem with Mr. Buffet's suggestion, however, is doing so would do practically nothing to reduce our debt and deficit. According to that same study taxing those individuals at 50 percent, along with eliminating all loopholes and deductions, would only reduce the deficit by 8 percent and our nation's debt by 1 percent. Increasing taxes is clearly not the solution to Washington's growing debt. Canada understood this, apparently better than our politicians, which is why they cut spending. Doing so allowed their economy to improve dramatically, and their unemployment levels dropped as a direct result. Their dollar went from being worth 71 cents of our dollar to one cent more. In 2000, Canada eliminated their small tax increase, something that is almost unheard of in government because it was no longer needed due to the improvements in their economy.

Canada is now ranked the freest economy in the Western hemisphere, sixth in the world according to Heritage's Economic Freedom Index. [III] The United States has dropped to number nine while Hong Kong is number one. The bottom five freest economies are countries that are all very repressed—Venezuela, Eritrea, Cuba, Zimbabwe, and North Korea—finishing last at 179. This tells us that the freer the economy the more prosperous the nation and its people. There is a direct correlation between the growth of government, its subsequent spending and our nation ranking ninth on the list. We are not a high tax nation by comparison, yet our ranking has dropped over the last two years. Simply because our government has grown larger, regulated more, and spent too much. Our government could learn a very good lesson from our neighbors up north.

The size of government can never exceed 10 percent of the economy, bringing it back in line with levels that existed under FDR.

To achieve this, our federal government will need to shrink considerably. They will need to perform massive cuts in spending and eliminate many unnecessary bureaucracies. The news program Stossel [VI] dealt with this topic as it pertained to eliminating our deficit. The host of the show John Stossel is an investigative journalist, author, columnist, and consumer reporter who has been an advocate for protecting liberty for decades. His show on the Fox Business channel exposes big government from a Libertarian's perspective. To start we would privatize air traffic control, just like Canada did when they restructured. We would then privatize Amtrak and remove all subsidies for rail, which would save us $12 billion annually. We would then end subsidies for public broadcasting and eliminate the small business administration. Businesses should be borrowing money from banks not the Fed. Repeal the Davis-Bacon Act, which forces government to pay more for union workers. Cut foreign aid in half; really, it should be cut even more, but cutting it in half is a start. These items combined will save us another $20 billion. Next we would eliminate the federal education department, saving us another $94 billion. This department is failing miserably anyway, wasting billions of dollars. We have increased spending every year, yet our test results, graduation rate, and SAT scores have not improved since 1970. Not to mention we already pay taxes for school at the local level. There is no need to be taxed for education twice, nor should this be managed by the federal government. To save another $30 billion we should cut agriculture subsidies. These just increase the cost of food anyway because farmers are given tax dollars to reduce their crops, thus causing the price of food to be artificially controlled. Next we would eliminate HUD, the Department of Energy, and the war on drugs, which combined would save us another $120 billion. The war on drugs has produced zero results. Drug use continues at a rampant pace and shows little signs of subsiding. The war on drugs is clearly failing and must be handled in a different manner. Dare I say legalization? Even with all these cuts government would still be too large and continue to run up deficit spending.

In order for us to really get a handle on government we need to tackle entitlements and social programs as well. When social security was first implemented it was not designed to provide payouts to such a large aging population. The average age was much lower than today and most people did not live long enough to collect it. It was originally setup as an insurance program. Now people are living much longer and the retirement age for collecting benefits within the program has not increased incrementally. Which means many more people will be drawing from it than can be sustained. So the only answer is to increase the retirement age to a reasonable level. Doing so would save another $93 billion. Privatizing it would really be the way to go and save even more money, but we have to start somewhere.

Medicare and Medicaid will also have to be addressed. The health and human services department should also be eliminated. They alone manage over 400 subsidy programs. Then there is our runaway defense spending. Billions of dollars are spent each year to support our troops abroad. Like the 50,000 still stationed in Germany, the 30,000 in Japan, and the 9,000 in Britain. Those countries should be paying for their own defense or reimbursing us for our service. If we implement the CATO Institute's proposed military cuts [VII] it would save us another $1.2 trillion over the next ten years. The Founding Fathers never envisioned a military that would be used for policing the world. They wanted to ensure we had the ability to properly defend our country when attacked and to maintain freedom by the existence of a strong military power. They certainly did not want it to be used to spread our ideals of freedom and democracy throughout the world by interfering with other nation's sovereignty. Even if those nations are in direct contrast with our beliefs.

Cutting spending and eliminating excessive bureaucracy will allow us to reach our goal of reducing the size of government to 10 percent of the economy. It will also give us a surplus in revenue and finally rid government of deficit spending. Reducing the size of government is absolutely necessary to put us on a path to prosperity. Raising taxes will not generate the revenue needed for government to close the deficit gap.

Government may never use tax dollars to bailout any business or stimulate the economy.

Some economists have claimed that TARP was a success because it gave companies deemed "too big to fail" a second chance. You already know where I stand on this issue; if these banks would have stuck with safe lending practices they would have been fine. Instead they chose to lend money in a scrupulous manner, which in my eyes means they deserve to be punished for their misdeeds, not rewarded. We already have laws in place that handle companies that mismanage their funds or fall upon hard times, it is called bankruptcy. Some companies are able to restructure and liquidate some of their assets and survive. Lending them taxpayer money only justifies their bad behavior. Even if regulatory laws are implemented afterward to stop them from doing it again, and those laws need to hold every offender accountable. In 2010, Washington implemented the Dodd-Frank Act, which created new regulations for banks that were meant to curtail bad lending habits. However, two of the biggest culprits involved in the mortgage crisis, Fannie Mae and Freddie Mac, are both exempt from this regulation. [VIII] This is yet another example of government protecting its own. It is no wonder the general populous has lost all faith in the political process.

Providing tax dollars to *stimulate* the economy was another brilliant solution implemented by our government that failed miserably. As of June of 2011 about fourteen million Americans were still out of work. The unemployment rate rose from 9.1 to 9.2 percent while the underemployment rate remained steady at 19 percent, according to Gallop. The economic recovery has been so slow and stagnant that many economists are predicting a double-dip recession. Furthermore this president's own administration admitted that the stimulus bill cost taxpayers approximately $278,000 per job saved. Does this seem like a cost effective way to spend your tax dollars? How many of you make $278,000 a year? President Obama admitted that the shovel ready projects he so proudly touted as a solution to the downturn were not as shovel ready as expected. All these indicators are a clear sign of failure, not success as the liberal talking heads would have you believe. The reason for this is simple; government cannot stimulate a capitalist economic system. Businesses in the private sector are the only entities that can. They must be free to invest in their company and hire more employees. The only way they will ever feel comfortable hiring is when they are not drowning in endless regulation. Regulation created by our government that is costing businesses more of their bottom line, such as the new health care law. The more money they have to spend on taxes and regulations the less they have to invest, which means hiring fewer or no employees. Pretty simple concept when you get right down to it. Unfortunately, Washington has no idea what simple means.

Collusion between the government and any business is illegal.

We hear of collusion often, but what does it really mean? It is a secret agreement or cooperation, especially for an illegal or deceitful purpose. Collusion is rampant throughout the political process with regard to big business and politicians. Jobs are offered in return for preferential treatment regarding certain laws or for appropriating funds for specific projects. Believe it or not this is all 100 percent legal. Under my proposed amendment it will no longer be allowed. Below is just one example of why it should be outlawed.

Jeffrey Immelt is the chief executive officer of General Electric (GE). He was recently assigned to President Obama's Council on Jobs and Competiveness, a board specifically created by the White House to generate job growth and competiveness in the downed economy. In 2010, GE made $14.2 billion in profits and paid zero dollars in taxes. GE has laid off 21,000 American workers under Immelt's command and closed twenty factories. [IX] So GE paid zero taxes last year, laid off 21,000 workers, and closed down a bunch of factories, and he is on Obama's jobs board? I thought President Obama was the one pushing for corporate tax reform, declaring that the system is too complicated and that companies pay too much. In February of 2010 Mr. Obama stated, "Simplify, eliminate loopholes, treat everybody fairly." Apparently he meant treat everyone fairly except those in his administration, they must deserve special treatment. Either that or the president has an entirely different agenda regarding jobs, like pushing for clean energy. To understand the connection with Immelt, clean energy, and President Obama, one must first understand the proposed cap-and-trade legislation. Cap-and-trade places government-generated limits on carbon emissions produced by companies. Each company would have to get an emissions permit from the government for every ton of carbon dioxide they produce. These limits, or carbon credits, can be sold by companies that fall below their allowance to companies that produce too many emissions. As long as these companies purchase enough credits to place them below the expected level they will avoid paying a huge fine. It is a huge scam that will make the government and certain companies billions of dollars while never truly addressing the problem of pollution. Think about it, if larger companies are allowed to purchase credits and still pollute, who is this really benefitting? Mr. Immelt is a big fan of the cap-and-trade legislation that has been floating around Washington. He said, "Some people argue for a simple tax on carbon. But I just think cap and trade is the more practical approach." Cap-and-trade would let Washington impose a national ceiling on carbon emissions, and companies could buy or sell emission rights. GE, by gaining rights in a windfall as a result of the legislation, would have many rights to sell. [x] This would make their company a ton of money in the process, a perfect example of collusion. Every leading economist states that if this proposed legislation ever becomes law it will cause energy costs to rise substantially. All we need is more bureaucratic red tape that negatively impacts business and their consumers. Is it any wonder our economy is stagnant? With agendas and policies such as these hovering around Washington I too would be afraid to hire or invest if I were a company. Thankfully, this disastrous piece of legislation has not yet become law. But do not think for a second that it has fallen off the president's radar. It is still front and center on his agenda. I am all for clean air but not when our government and a select few stand to benefit monetarily from the process.

The current income tax structure will be revamped. In its place a new flat tax of 10 percent will be temporarily imposed on everyone, eliminating all tax loopholes and deductions, leading the way for the eventual repeal of the Sixteenth Amendment.

The department of the IRS will shrink drastically and the tax code will be completely restructured to allow for the implementation of a flat tax. Once the government achieves a surplus the income tax shall be abolished and never reinstated, effectively repealing the Sixteenth Amendment. There is no reason the government cannot live within its means, especially when you consider the huge amount of taxes that are collected each year. The Sixteenth Amendment was an abomination and should have never been ratified by the states. It was in direct opposition to the wishes of the Framers. They had already accounted for government's ability to collect revenue via a direct tax, or by apportionment among the states. The fact that this amendment actually passed the two-thirds state requirement when it was ratified in 1913 absolutely astonishes me. There is no way something like this would pass were it introduced today. Yes, congress has the ability to lay and collect taxes, but taxing our income is wrong and unnecessary. There are plenty of other avenues from which the government can raise revenue.

Since eliminating the income tax is highly improbable, implementing a flat tax will most likely be the only acceptable solution. This would go a long way in eliminating the class warfare that exists today between rich and poor Americans. Everyone would be required to pay their fair share of taxes as a small percent of their income. This also means eliminating all tax loopholes and deductions. Removing the current tax code and rebuilding a much simpler structure, one that does not allow large corporations to circumvent the law and avoid paying taxes, as the example cited earlier regarding GE's profit. If middle and upper class Americans are required to pay a portion of their income to the government, then so should all Americans, wealthy or poor. If it is based on a smaller percentage than is currently being paid, most everyone wins, including the government because they will be tapping into markets that are currently not contributing.

The federal government cannot publicly fund any business, or provide them with any subsidies or tax breaks.

The playing field must be leveled for all companies so the free market can work. Government and business should always be at arm's length, not intertwined as is currently the case. Subsidies are wrong for the economy because they give unfair incentive to businesses that the government handpicks to promote their agenda. As one example, some farmers are given tax dollars not to plant crops. [XI] Yes, you read that correctly—to plant less crops or in some cases not to plant any at all. This may sound ludicrous but by controlling prices, or keeping them up, this attracts more people to farming because they receive more money, more income, and for doing less work. How many companies do you know that pay their employees based on their lack of performance? None; in fact it is quite the opposite. Providing subsidies of this nature also ties these farmers directly to the politicians that voted for these tax breaks. This has an impact on elections because these politicians are essentially buying votes from these farmers. Elections should be completely void of this type of monetary influence, which is why it is essential all subsidies must be eliminated. Not to mention the fact that they are providing an incentive to produce less of a product to control prices.

Government spending can never exceed 10 percent of the GDP, unless in a time of war in which case it will be capped at 18 percent.

Government spending needs to be capped because people in Washington do not know how to live within their means. On average they take in about 18 percent in revenue, yet they continue to spend way beyond that, currently around 25 percent. The interesting factor in all this is no matter how much the top tax rate is raised, the government's revenue remains consistently flat and has done so since 1950. [XII] In the 50s and 60s the top tax rate was around 90 percent. During the 70s it dropped just below 80 percent. Then it fell to just below 60 percent in the 80s and eventually bottomed out around 40 percent where it stands today. During this entire period the government never took in more than 20 percent. This tells us that no matter how much someone is taxed, government never really makes any more revenue, as some of our politicians would have you believe. Businesses and people find ways to avoid paying taxes, or just quit spending altogether.

In 2011, Illinois raised state income tax from 3 to 5 percent and its corporate tax from 4.8 to 7 percent. It also passed a new law that forced online retailers to collect taxes. All these increases caused online retailer, FatWallet.com, to move north to Wisconsin. [XIII] The new taxes were costing them one-third of their revenue so they packed up all their equipment and moved fifty employees out of the state. These tax increases also had a negative impact on Illinois unemployment rate. Before they went into effect the rate was actually declining. As of July 2011 it has risen to 9.5 percent, [XIV] worse than the national average. Rising unemployment can be directly attributed to raising taxes because companies need to account for their loss in revenue. In San Francisco, Twitter threatened to move its $4 billion company because of the city's high taxes. [XIII] So politicians quickly passed new legislation that exempted companies within a certain part of the city from its payroll tax. These are just two examples of the lengths companies will go to avoid paying higher taxes. So whenever the politicians in Washington tell you the only way out of a fiscal crisis is to raise taxes, you now know better. It is amazing that after sixty years our government still has no clue that higher taxes does not equal more revenue, even with all the evidence in plain sight.

Another reason government spending needs to be capped is because the government is inherently inefficient. Washington is overrun with redundant programs. They have fifty-six financial literacy programs alone. When they were questioned about the total cost of these programs, the United States Government Accountability Office (GAO) could not come up with an estimate. [XV] The government has programs that supposedly serve a specific purpose and the GAO cannot account for their cost? It is no wonder duplicates exist; they have no idea how to estimate their cost. With record keeping like this I now understand why we are $16 trillion in debt. I guess the next time my mortgage payment is due I will just inform the bank that I cannot account for the money because I have too many bills. I am sure they will understand, after all, they are in business to accommodate my needs and not the needs of their shareholders. If we are expected to be responsible with our finances then we should expect the same from our government. If we cannot, then it is time we foreclose on them by voting them out of office. The government also has forty-seven job programs at a cost of $18 billion and eighty economic development programs that are costing us $6.5 billion. Given the current state of the economy it is pretty safe to say we have been bilked out of $24.5 billion.

The federal government can never infringe upon our right to bear arms. Guns are to be allowed for sport and for protection without restriction.

All of the empirical evidence surrounding gun control, and how less of it actually makes for a safer society, should give pause to anyone arguing against the Second Amendment. Firearms are just as much a necessity today as they were during the dawn of our nation. The Founding Fathers understood that we not only needed firearms for protection but also for defending ourselves against the possible advance of a tyrannical government. Even if the day comes when gun violence ceases to exist, we still need to maintain our right to bear arms. The reason is simple; a government can never overthrow the will of an armed populous. To remain a free republic it is essential the Second Amendment never be abolished and its intent never is misconstrued.

Government cannot create legislation that makes it mandatory for an American to purchase a good or service.

The commerce clause is not to be used by those in Washington as a means of forcing Americans to purchase a service, as they are currently doing with the Affordable Care Act. The commerce clause can only be interpreted as the Founders intended and as it was interpreted by Chief Justice John Marshall in 1824. Which is, the states cannot create trade barriers and the federal government has the right to create guidelines that all states must follow. However, those guidelines should only pertain to goods transported across state lines, not services interwoven into legislature designed by Congress to *improve* society. The very idea that government believes it knows best and deems it a necessity to purchase something for the betterment of the collective is completely antithetical to the beliefs on which this country was founded.

Final Thoughts:

In order to get our enormous debt under control, serious action must be taken by the citizens of this great country. Our government must understand that we expect them to control spending. Every year their budget grows larger and larger and our mounting debt never gets factored into the equation. The fiscal 2011 budget is already $1.3 trillion in the hole. That is above and beyond the money we already owe. With this type of attitude in Washington we will never get out of debt. If the average person is in debt, does he continue to run up deficits each year? Of course not, he buckles down and cuts unnecessary expenditures.

With my suggested amendment it will be against the law for

government to do so otherwise. It bears repeating, but to get the deficit under control we will have to make serious cuts. We must privatize all social programs, including Social Security, Medicare, and Medicaid. Doing so, according to the 2010 budget, would immediately save us $1.46 trillion. [XVI] We must also cut other bureaucracies as well, departments that should have never been created in the first place. Of course this will have to take place over time and through attrition. I am not advocating that all these be dismantled immediately, leaving innocent people stranded without assistance. But they do need to be eliminated at some point, if we wish to remain a productive nation and fall in line with our Founding Fathers' message regarding limited government.

This may sound extreme and somewhat harsh, but if their message is taken at face value then not one of these departments should have ever been established. It is not the job of government to take care of its citizens' social needs. This is the responsibility of the private sector, primarily because it does a much better job and is way more efficient and cost effective. The private market also allows for competition which helps drive down costs, something that cannot exist when these entities are controlled by government. As soon as we start eliminating certain portions of the government you will of course hear all sorts of misconceptions from groups that claim to benefit from these services. Similar to what has occurred in the past.

Back when Bill Clinton was president, we were told if we reformed welfare, "We'll see trauma we haven't known since the cholera epidemic," said Democratic Senator Patrick Moynihan; "One million children could be forced into poverty," said Democratic Representative Dick Gephardt. [XVII] So did all those children get forced into poverty as Mr. Gephardt stated? Of course not; in fact, quite the opposite. Over 2 million children rose up from poverty and their parents became productive members of society. You see, when people are forced to become self-reliant then their lives are usually better for it. The idea that people need permanent government assistance is false and has been disproven time and time again throughout history. In April 2011 Nancy Pelosi stated that if the current proposed Republican budget cuts passed, over six million seniors would be deprived of their meals. [XVIII] When a phone call was placed to Pelosi's office asking where she received those figures no one on her staff could provide an answer. *The Washington Post* fact-checked her statement and found only 2.6 million seniors were actually on the program she referenced. I guess some politicians will say anything to keep their special interests in the budget, even if it means lying to our face.

With each new program that is instituted, our nation moves further away from being truly free, because more and more people become dependent on the government. Something the current president and the liberal mindset believe in strongly. They have a very different view of government's responsibility to its people. On Wednesday April 14, 2011, President Obama gave a speech outlining his goals for addressing the countries mounting debt. Within his speech there were many telling signs of Obama's ideals on social fairness. But one paragraph in particular stood out more than the rest, in which he said,

> Part of this American belief that we are all connected also expresses itself in a conviction that each one of us deserves some basic measure of security. We recognize that no matter how responsibly we live our lives, hard times or bad luck, a crippling illness or a layoff, may strike any one of us. "There but for the grace of God go I," we say to ourselves, and so we contribute to programs like Medicare and Social Security, which guarantee us health care and a measure of basic income after a lifetime of hard work; unemployment insurance, which protects us against unexpected job loss; and Medicaid, which provides care for millions of seniors in nursing homes, poor children, and those with disabilities. We are a better country because of these commitments. I'll go further—we would not be a great country without those commitments.

If he is not a president with a socialist agenda, I'm not American. The fact that he believes that we are a better country because we *contribute* (as if we have a choice) a portion of our payroll to a government-run money pit of a social program is absolutely ridiculous. When I help others who have fallen on hard times it is of my own volition, using private charities, churches, or one-on-one assistance. Not through a forced obligation created by government, money that is taken from me via a tax and used by our government in a manner they deem fair. This redistribution of wealth, or Robin Hood syndrome of taking from the rich and giving to the poor, is not the cornerstone on which this country was founded. You become wealthy in this country by working hard and applying yourself, not by scratching a lottery ticket and having your fortunes handed to you by the lottery commission known as big government.

There is no reward for relying on government. Doing so creates a type of stagnation that never breeds ingenuity or the willingness to prosper. Being self-reliant, however, is its own reward. Because when you strive to be the best at something you love it is very self-gratifying—something no amount of government engineering could provide. Compare it to a sporting event if you will. When one team plays better than the other, what is the typical outcome? The team that really applies itself comes out victorious. The same concept holds true in life as well, and it is imperative that this concept not be lost. Just as those who are rewarded with a win in a football game, you are rewarded in life for having a strong work ethic and by persevering through the hard times. The very principles of our society were founded on hard work, determination, perseverance, and self-reliance, not government handouts. When President Obama stated, "We are a better country because of these commitments," proves he believes government assistance is something everyone is entitled to and because of it our country is somehow better. He actually thinks it is the responsibility of the government to take care of its citizens' social needs. I hate to break the news to you Mr. President, but according to the Constitution the only responsibility the government has to its citizens is to protect them from threats foreign and domestic. This in no way translates to protecting us by means of engineering our private lives, it means protecting us from violent people and nations threatening our very existence. The only things we are entitled to is life, liberty, and the pursuit of happiness.

I am all for helping people who are less fortunate than me, but not by way of the government. It is not their responsibility and they are not entitled to my money. People need to be able to rely on themselves and each other, not big government. Until we as a country fully welcome this notion we will continue down the road to ruin and ultimately end up like Greece, Spain, Italy, and all other financially strapped socialist countries. For the sake of our republic, I hope it is not too late to rein in government. The folks in Washington need to wise up and utilize my findings as a guide to get America back on the right track. If they choose to ignore all the evidence presented herein, continuing instead with the status quo, then we must assume their arrogance has rendered them incapable of refinement. Their behavior must be the catalyst that drives us to instill change in the way government fundamentally operates. Continuing to ignore the problems we face should only be perceived as blatant disregard for the well-being of our country and these politicians must be removed from office immediately, before their arrogance destroys our economy. For everyone that believes none of this really matters, let my words be a warning on what to expect going forward if we remain complacent:

No nation can succeed when its politicians are blinded by greed and succumb to corruption. This type of behavior only leads in one direction and will cause destruction the likes of which we have never seen. The complete and total collapse of the greatest nation the world has ever known.

Appendix

The Declaration of Independence [1]

Officially Adopted July 4, 1776

The unanimous declaration of the thirteen united States of America, When in the course of human events it becomes necessary for one people to dissolve the political bands which have connected them with another and to assume among the powers of the earth, the separate and equal station to which the Laws of Nature and of Nature's God entitle them—a decent respect to the opinions of mankind requires that they should declare the causes which impel them to the separation.

We hold these truths to be self-evident, that all men are created equal, that they are endowed by their Creator with certain unalienable Rights, that among these are Life, Liberty and the pursuit of Happiness. —That to secure these rights, Governments are instituted among Men, deriving their just powers from the consent of the governed,—That whenever any Form of Government becomes destructive of these ends, it is the Right of the People to alter or to abolish it, and to institute new Government, laying its foundation on such principles and organizing its powers in such form, as to them shall seem most likely to effect their Safety and Happiness. Prudence, indeed, will dictate that Governments long established should not be changed for light and transient causes; and accordingly all experience hath shewn, that mankind are more disposed to suffer, while evils are sufferable, than to right themselves by abolishing the forms to which they are accustomed. But when a long train of abuses and usurpations, pursuing invariably the same Object evinces a design to reduce them under absolute Despotism, it is their right, it is their duty, to throw off such Government, and to provide new Guards for their future security. —Such has been the patient sufferance of these Colonies; and such is now the necessity which constrains them to alter their former Systems of Government. The history of the present King of Great Britain is a history of repeated injuries and usurpations, all having in direct object the establishment of an absolute Tyranny over these States. To prove this, let Facts be submitted to a candid world.

He has refused his assent to laws, the most wholesome and necessary for the public good.

He has forbidden his governors to pass laws of immediate and pressing importance, unless suspended in their operation till his assent should be obtained; and when so suspended, he has utterly neglected to attend to them.

He has refused to pass other laws for the accommodation of large districts of people, unless those people would relinquish the right of representation in the legislature, a right inestimable to them and formidable to tyrants only.

He has called together legislative bodies at places unusual, uncomfortable, and distant from the depository of their public records, for the sole purpose of fatiguing them into compliance with his measures.

He has dissolved representative houses repeatedly, for opposing with manly firmness his invasions on the rights of the people.

He has refused for a long time, after such dissolutions, to cause others to be elected; whereby the legislative powers, incapable of annihilation, have returned to the people at large for their exercise; the state remaining in the meantime exposed to all the dangers of invasion from without, and convulsions within.

He has endeavored to prevent the population of these states; for that purpose obstructing the laws for naturalization of foreigners; refusing to pass others to encourage their migrations hither, and raising the conditions of new appropriations of lands.

He has obstructed the administration of justice by refusing his assent to laws for establishing judiciary powers.

He has made judges dependent on his will alone, for the tenure of their offices, and the amount and payment of their salaries.

He has erected a multitude of new offices and sent hither swarms of officers to harass our people and eat out their substance.

He has kept among us, in times of peace, standing armies without the consent of our legislatures.

He has affected to render the military independent of and superior to the civil power.

He has combined with others to subject us to a jurisdiction foreign to our constitution and unacknowledged by our laws; giving his assent to their acts of pretended legislation:

> For quartering large bodies of armed troops among us;

> For protecting them, by a mock trial, from punishment for any murders which they should commit on the inhabitants of these states;

> For cutting off our trade with all parts of the world;

> For imposing taxes on us without our consent;

> For depriving us in many cases of the benefits of trial by jury;

> For transporting us beyond seas to be tried for pretended offences

> For abolishing the free system of English laws in a neighboring province, establishing therein an arbitrary government and enlarging its boundaries so as to render it at once an example and fit instrument for introducing the same absolute rule into these colonies;

> For taking away our charters, abolishing our most valuable laws, and altering fundamentally the forms of our governments;

> For suspending our own legislatures and declaring themselves invested with power to legislate for us in all cases whatsoever.

He has abdicated government here by declaring us out of his protection and waging war against us.

He has plundered our seas, ravaged our coasts, burnt our towns, and destroyed the lives of our people.

He is at this time transporting large armies of foreign mercenaries to complete the works of death, desolation, and tyranny, already begun with circumstances of cruelty and perfidy scarcely paralleled in the most barbarous ages and totally unworthy the head of a civilized nation.

He has constrained our fellow citizens taken captive on the high seas to bear arms against their country, to become the executioners of their friends and brethren, or to fall themselves by their hands.

He has excited domestic insurrections amongst us, and has endeavored to bring on the inhabitants of our frontiers, the merciless Indian savages, whose known rule of warfare is an undistinguished destruction of all ages, sexes, and conditions.

In every stage of these oppressions we have petitioned for redress in the most humble terms: Our repeated petitions have been answered only by repeated injury. A prince whose character is thus marked by every act which may define a tyrant is unfit to be the ruler of a free people.

Nor have we been wanting in attentions to our British brethren. We have warned them from time to time of attempts by their legislature to extend an unwarrantable jurisdiction over us. We have reminded them of the circumstances of our emigration and settlement here. We have appealed to their native justice and magnanimity, and we have conjured them by the ties of our common kindred to disavow these usurpations, which would inevitably interrupt our connections and correspondence. They too have been deaf to the voice of justice and of consanguinity. We must, therefore, acquiesce in the necessity, which denounces our separation, and hold them, as we hold the rest of mankind, enemies in war, in peace friends.

We, therefore, the representatives of the United States of America, in General Congress, assembled, appealing to the supreme judge of the world for the rectitude of our intentions, do, in the name, and by authority of the good people of these colonies, solemnly publish and declare, That these United Colonies are, and of Right ought to be Free and Independent States; that they are Absolved from all Allegiance to the British Crown, and that all political connection between them and the State of Great Britain, is and ought to be totally dissolved; and that as Free and Independent States, they have full Power to levy War, conclude Peace, contract Alliances, establish Commerce, and to do all other Acts and Things which Independent States may of right do. And for the support of this Declaration, with a firm reliance on the protection of divine Providence, we mutually pledge to each other our Lives, our Fortunes and our sacred Honor.

The 56 signatures on the Declaration appear in the positions indicated:

Column 1
Georgia
Button Gwinnett
Lyman Hall
George Walton

Column 2
North Carolina
William Hooper
Joseph Hewes
John Penn

South Carolina
Edward Rutledge
Thomas Heyward, Jr.
Thomas Lynch, Jr.
Arthur Middleton

Column 3
Massachusetts
John Hancock

Maryland
Samuel Chase
William Paca
Thomas Stone
Charles Carroll of Carrollton

Virginia
George Wythe
Richard Henry Lee

Thomas Jefferson
Benjamin Harrison
Thomas Nelson, Jr.
Francis Lightfoot Lee
Carter Braxton

Column 4
Pennsylvania
Robert Morris
Benjamin Rush
Benjamin Franklin
John Morton
George Clymer
James Smith
George Taylor
James Wilson
George Ross

Delaware
Caesar Rodney
George Read
Thomas McKean

Column 5
New York
William Floyd
Philip Livingston
Francis Lewis
Lewis Morris

New Jersey
Richard Stockton
John Witherspoon
Francis Hopkinson
John Hart
Abraham Clark

Column 6
New Hampshire
Josiah Bartlett
William Whipple

Massachusetts
Samuel Adams
John Adams
Robert Treat Paine
Elbridge Gerry

Rhode Island
Stephen Hopkins
William Ellery

Connecticut
Roger Sherman
Samuel Huntington
William Williams
Oliver Wolcott

New Hampshire

Matthew Thornton

The Articles of Confederation [1]

Ratified March 1, 1781

Preamble

To all to whom these Presents shall come, we the undersigned Delegates of the States affixed to our Names send greeting.

Whereas the Delegates of the United States of America in Congress assembled did on the fifteenth day of November in the Year of our Lord One Thousand Seven Hundred and Seventy seven, and in the Second Year of the Independence of America, agree to certain articles of Confederation and perpetual Union between the States of New Hampshire, Massachusetts-bay, Rhode Island and Providence Plantations, Connecticut, New York, New Jersey, Pennsylvania, Delaware, Maryland, Virginia, North Carolina, South Carolina and Georgia, in the words following, viz:

Articles of Confederation and perpetual Union between the States of New Hampshire, Massachusetts-bay, Rhode Island and Providence Plantations, Connecticut, New York, New Jersey, Pennsylvania, Delaware, Maryland, Virginia, North Carolina, South Carolina and Georgia.

Article I

The Stile of this Confederacy shall be "The United States of America."

Article II

Each state retains its sovereignty, freedom, and independence, and every Power, Jurisdiction, and right, which is not by this confederation expressly delegated to the United States, in Congress assembled.

Article III

The said States hereby severally enter into a firm league of friendship with each other, for their common defense, the security of their liberties, and their mutual and general welfare, binding themselves to assist each other, against all force offered to, or attacks made upon them, or any of them, on account of religion, sovereignty, trade, or any other pretense whatever.

Article IV

The better to secure and perpetuate mutual friendship and intercourse among the people of the different States in this union, the free inhabitants of each of these States, paupers, vagabonds, and fugitives from justice excepted, shall be entitled to all privileges and immunities of free citizens in the several States; and the people of each State shall have free ingress and regress to and from any other State, and shall enjoy therein all the privileges of trade and commerce, subject to the same duties, impositions, and restrictions as the inhabitants thereof respectively, provided that such restrictions shall not extend so far as to prevent the removal of property imported into any State, to any other State, of which the owner is an inhabitant; provided also that no imposition, duties or restriction shall be laid by any State, on the property of the united States, or either of them.

If any person guilty of, or charged with, treason, felony, or other high misdemeanor in any State, shall flee from justice, and be found in any of the united States, he shall, upon demand of the Governor or executive power of the State from which he fled, be delivered up and removed to the State having jurisdiction of his offense.

Full faith and credit shall be given in each of these States to the records, acts, and judicial proceedings of the courts and magistrates of every other State.

Article V

For the most convenient management of the general interests of the united States, delegates shall be annually appointed in such manner as the legislatures of each State shall direct, to meet in Congress on the first Monday in November, in every year, with a power reserved to each State to recall its delegates, or any of them, at any time within the year, and to send others in their stead for the remainder of the year.

No State shall be represented in Congress by less than two, nor more than seven members; and no person shall be capable of being a delegate for more than three years in any term of six years; nor shall any person, being a delegate, be capable of holding any office under the united States, for which he, or another for his benefit, receives any salary, fees or emolument of any kind.

Each State shall maintain its own delegates in a meeting of the States, and while they act as members of the committee of the States.

In determining questions in the united States, in Congress assembled, each State shall have one vote.

Freedom of speech and debate in Congress shall not be impeached or questioned in any court or place out of Congress, and the members of Congress shall be protected in their persons from arrests or imprisonments, during the time of their going to and from, and attendance on Congress, except for treason, felony, or breach of the peace.

Article VI

No State, without the consent of the united States in Congress assembled, shall send any embassy to, or receive any embassy from, or enter into any conference, agreement, alliance or treaty with any King, Prince or State; nor shall any person holding any office of profit or trust under the united States, or any of them, accept any present, emolument, office or title of any kind whatever from any King, Prince or foreign State; nor shall the United States in congress assembled, or any of them, grant any title of nobility.

No two or more States shall enter into any treaty, confederation or alliance whatever between them, without the consent of the united States in congress assembled, specifying accurately the purposes for which the same is to be entered into, and how long it shall continue.

No State shall lay any imposts or duties, which may interfere with any stipulations in treaties, entered into by the united States in congress assembled, with any King, Prince or State, in pursuance of any treaties already proposed by congress, to the courts of France and Spain.

No vessel of war shall be kept up in time of peace by any State, except such number only, as shall be deemed necessary by the united States in congress assembled, for the defense of such State, or its trade; nor shall any body of forces be kept up by any State in time of peace, except such number only, as in the judgement of the united States, in congress assembled, shall be deemed requisite to garrison the forts necessary for the defense of such State; but every State shall always keep up a well-regulated and disciplined militia, sufficiently armed and accoutered, and shall provide and constantly have ready for use, in public stores, a due number of field pieces and tents, and a proper quantity of arms, ammunition and camp equipage.

No State shall engage in any war without the consent of the united States in congress assembled, unless such State be actually invaded by enemies, or shall have received certain advice of a resolution being formed by some nation of Indians to invade such State, and the danger is so imminent as not to admit of a delay till the united States in congress assembled can be consulted; nor shall any State grant commissions to any ships or vessels of war, nor letters of marque or reprisal, except it be after a declaration of war by the united States in congress assembled, and then only against the kingdom or State and the subjects thereof, against which war has been so declared, and under such regulations as shall be established by the united States in congress assembled, unless such State be infested by pirates, in which case vessels of war may be fitted out for that occasion, and kept so long as the danger shall continue, or until the united States in congress assembled shall determine otherwise.

Article VII

When land forces are raised by any State for the common defense, all officers of or under the rank of colonel, shall be appointed by the legislature of each State respectively, by whom such forces shall be raised, or in such manner as such State shall direct, and all vacancies shall be filled up by the State which first made the appointment.

Article VIII

All charges of war, and all other expenses that shall be incurred for the common defense or general welfare, and allowed by the united States in congress assembled, shall be defrayed out of a common treasury, which shall be supplied by the several States in proportion to the value of all land within each State, granted or surveyed for any person, as such land and the buildings and improvements thereon shall be estimated according to such mode as the united States in congress assembled, shall from time to time direct and appoint.

The taxes for paying that proportion shall be laid and levied by the authority and direction of the legislatures of the several States within the time agreed upon by the united States in congress assembled.

Article IX

The united States in congress assembled, shall have the sole and exclusive right and power of determining on peace and war, except in the cases mentioned in the sixth article—of sending and receiving ambassadors— entering into treaties and alliances, provided that no treaty of commerce shall be made whereby the legislative power of the respective States shall be restrained from imposing such imposts and duties on foreigners, as their own people are subjected to, or from prohibiting the exportation or importation of any species of goods or commodities whatsoever—of establishing rules for deciding in all cases, what captures on land or water shall be legal, and in what manner prizes taken by land or naval forces in the service of the United States shall be divided or appropriated—of granting letters of marque and reprisal in times of peace—appointing courts for the trial of piracies and felonies committed on the high seas and establishing courts for receiving and determining finally appeals in all cases of captures, provided that no member of Congress shall be appointed a judge of any of the said courts.

The United States in Congress assembled shall also be the last resort on appeal in all disputes and differences now subsisting or that hereafter may arise between two or more States concerning boundary, jurisdiction or any other causes whatever; which authority shall always be exercised in the manner following. Whenever the legislative or executive authority or lawful agent of any State in controversy with another shall present a petition to Congress stating the matter in question and praying for a hearing, notice thereof shall be given by order of Congress to the legislative or executive authority of the other State in controversy, and a day assigned for the appearance of the parties by their lawful agents, who shall then be directed to appoint by joint consent, commissioners or judges to constitute a court for hearing and determining the matter in question: but if they cannot agree, Congress shall name three persons out of each of the United States, and from the list of such persons each party shall alternately strike out one, the petitioners beginning, until the number shall be reduced to thirteen; and from that number not less than seven, nor more than nine names as Congress shall direct, shall in the presence of Congress be drawn out by lot, and the persons whose names shall be so drawn or any five of them, shall be commissioners or judges, to hear and finally determine the controversy, so always as a major part of the judges who shall hear the cause shall agree in the determination: and if either party shall neglect to attend at the day appointed, without showing reasons, which Congress shall judge sufficient, or being present shall refuse to strike, the Congress shall proceed to nominate three persons out of each State, and the secretary of Congress shall strike in behalf of such party absent or refusing; and the judgement and sentence of the court to be appointed, in the manner before prescribed, shall be final and conclusive; and if any of the parties shall refuse to submit to the authority of such court, or to appear or defend their claim or cause, the court shall nevertheless proceed to pronounce sentence, or judgement, which shall in like manner be final and decisive, the judgement or sentence and other proceedings being in either case transmitted to Congress, and lodged among the acts of Congress for the security of the parties concerned: provided that every commissioner, before he sits in judgement, shall take an oath to be administered by one of the judges of the supreme or superior court of the State, where the cause shall be tried, 'well and truly to hear and determine the matter in question, according to the best of his judgement, without favor, affection or hope of reward': provided also, that no State shall be deprived of territory for the benefit of the United States.

All controversies concerning the private right of soil claimed under different grants of two or more States, whose jurisdictions as they may respect such lands, and the States which passed such grants are adjusted, the said grants or either of them being at the same time claimed to have originated antecedent to such settlement of jurisdiction, shall on the petition of either party to the Congress of the United States, be finally determined as near as may be in the same manner as is before prescribed for deciding disputes respecting territorial jurisdiction between different States.

The United States in Congress assembled shall also have the sole and exclusive right and power of regulating the alloy and value of coin struck by their own authority, or by that of the respective States—fixing the standards of weights and measures throughout the United States—regulating the trade and managing all affairs with the Indians, not members of any of the States, provided that the legislative right of any State within its own limits be not infringed or violated—establishing or regulating post offices from one State to another, throughout all the United States, and exacting such postage on the papers passing through the same as may be requisite to defray the expenses of the said office—appointing all officers of the land forces, in the service of the United States, excepting regimental officers—appointing all the officers of the naval forces, and commissioning all officers whatever in the service of the United States—making rules for the government and regulation of the said land and naval forces, and directing their operations.

The United States in Congress assembled shall have authority to appoint a committee, to sit in the recess of Congress, to be denominated 'A Committee of the States', and to consist of one delegate from each

State; and to appoint such other committees and civil officers as may be necessary for managing the general affairs of the United States under their direction—to appoint one of their members to preside, provided that no person be allowed to serve in the office of president more than one year in any term of three years; to ascertain the necessary sums of money to be raised for the service of the United States, and to appropriate and apply the same for defraying the public expenses—to borrow money, or emit bills on the credit of the United States, transmitting every half-year to the respective States an account of the sums of money so borrowed or emitted—to build and equip a navy—to agree upon the number of land forces, and to make requisitions from each State for its quota, in proportion to the number of white inhabitants in such State; which requisition shall be binding, and thereupon the legislature of each State shall appoint the regimental officers, raise the men and cloath, arm and equip them in a solid- like manner, at the expense of the United States; and the officers and men so cloathed, armed and equipped shall march to the place appointed, and within the time agreed on by the United States in Congress assembled. But if the United States in Congress assembled shall, on consideration of circumstances judge proper that any State should not raise men, or should raise a smaller number of men than the quota thereof, such extra number shall be raised, officered, cloathed, armed and equipped in the same manner as the quota of each State, unless the legislature of such State shall judge that such extra number cannot be safely spread out in the same, in which case they shall raise, officer, cloath, arm and equip as many of such extra number as they judge can be safely spared. And the officers and men so cloathed, armed, and equipped, shall march to the place appointed, and within the time agreed on by the united States in congress assembled.

The united States in congress assembled shall never engage in a war, nor grant letters of marque or reprisal in time of peace, nor enter into any treaties or alliances, nor coin money, nor regulate the value thereof, nor ascertain the sums and expenses necessary for the defense and welfare of the United States, or any of them, nor emit bills, nor borrow money on the credit of the united States, nor appropriate money, nor agree upon the number of vessels of war, to be built or purchased, or the number of land or sea forces to be raised, nor appoint a commander in chief of the army or navy, unless nine States assent to the same: nor shall a question on any other point, except for adjourning from day to day be determined, unless by the votes of the majority of the united States in congress assembled.

The congress of the united States shall have power to adjourn to any time within the year, and to any place within the united States, so that no period of adjournment be for a longer duration than the space of six months, and shall publish the journal of their proceedings monthly, except such parts thereof relating to treaties, alliances or military operations, as in their judgement require secrecy; and the yeas and nays of the delegates of each State on any question shall be entered on the journal, when it is desired by any delegates of a State, or any of them, at his or their request shall be furnished with a transcript of the said journal, except such parts as are above excepted, to lay before the legislatures of the several States.

Article X

The committee of the States, or any nine of them, shall be authorized to execute, in the recess of congress, such of the powers of congress as the united States in congress assembled, by the consent of the nine States, shall from time to time think expedient to vest them with; provided that no power be delegated to the said Committee, for the exercise of which, by the articles of confederation, the voice of nine States in the Congress of the United States assembled be requisite.

Article XI

Canada acceding to this confederation, and adjoining in the measures of the united States, shall be admitted into, and entitled to all the advantages of this union; but no other colony shall be admitted into the same, unless such admission be agreed to by nine States.

Article XII

All bills of credit emitted, monies borrowed, and debts contracted by, or under the authority of congress, before the assembling of the united States, in pursuance of the present confederation, shall be deemed and considered as a charge against the United States, for payment and satisfaction whereof the said united States, and the public faith are hereby solemnly pledged.

Article XIII

Every State shall abide by the determination of the united States in congress assembled, on all questions which by this confederation are submitted to them. And the Articles of this confederation shall be inviolably observed by every State, and the union shall be perpetual; nor shall any alteration at any time hereafter be made in any of them; unless such alteration be agreed to in a congress of the united States, and be afterwards confirmed by the legislatures of every State.

And Whereas it hath pleased the Great Governor of the World to incline the hearts of the legislatures we respectively represent in Congress, to approve of, and to authorize us to ratify the said articles of confederation and perpetual union. Know Ye that we the undersigned delegates, by virtue of the power and authority to us given for that purpose, do by these presents, in the name and in behalf of our respective constituents, fully and entirely ratify and confirm each and every of the said articles of confederation and perpetual union, and all and singular the matters and things therein contained: And we do further solemnly plight and engage the faith of our respective constituents, that they shall abide by the determinations of the united States in congress assembled, on all questions, which by the said confederation are submitted to them. And that the articles thereof shall be inviolably observed by the States we respectively represent, and that the union shall be perpetual.

In Witness whereof we have hereunto set our hands in Congress. Done at Philadelphia in the State of Pennsylvania the ninth Day of July in the Year of our Lord one thousand seven Hundred and Seventy-eight, and in the Third Year of the independence of America.

On the part and behalf of the State of New Hampshire:
Josiah Bartlett
John Wentworth Junr. August 8th 1778

On the part and behalf of the State of Massachusetts Bay:
John Hancock
Samuel Adams
Elbridge Gerry
Francis Dana
James Lovell
Samuel Holten

On the part and behalf of the State of Rhode Island and Providence Plantations:
William Ellery
Henry Marchant
John Collins

On the part and behalf of the State of Connecticut:
Roger Sherman
Samuel Huntington
Oliver Wolcott
Titus Hosmer
Andrew Adams

On the Part and behalf of the State of New York:
James Duane
Francis Lewis
Wm Duer
Gouv Morris

On the Part and in behalf of the State of New Jersey, November 26, 1778.
Jno Witherspoon
Nath. Scudder

On the part and behalf of the State of Pennsylvania:
Robt Morris
Daniel Roberdeau
John Bayard Smith
William Clingan
Joseph Reed 22nd July 1778

On the part and behalf of the State of Delaware:

Tho Mckean February 12, 1779
John Dickinson May 5th 1779
Nicholas Van Dyke

On the part and behalf of the State of Maryland:
John Hanson March 1 1781
Daniel Carroll

On the part and behalf of the State of Virginia:
Richard Henry Lee
John Banister
Thomas Adams
Jno Harvie
Francis Lightfoot Lee

On the part and behalf of the State of No Carolina:
John Penn July 21st 1778
Corns Harnett
Jno Williams

On the part and behalf of the State of South Carolina:
Henry Laurens
William Henry Drayton
Jno Mathews
Richd Hutson
Thos Heyward Junr

On the part and behalf of the State of Georgia:
Jno Walton 24th July 1778
Edwd Telfair
Edwd Langworthy

The Constitution of the United States[1]

Ratified June 21, 1788

Preamble

We the People of the United States, in Order to form a more perfect Union, establish Justice, insure domestic Tranquility, provide for the common defence, promote the general Welfare, and secure the Blessings of Liberty to ourselves and our Posterity, do ordain and establish this Constitution for the United States of America.

Article I—The Legislative Branch

Section 1—The Legislature

All legislative Powers herein granted shall be vested in a Congress of the United States, which shall consist of a Senate and House of Representatives.

Section 2—The House

The House of Representatives shall be composed of Members chosen every second Year by the People of the several States, and the Electors in each State shall have the Qualifications requisite for Electors of the most numerous Branch of the State Legislature.

No Person shall be a Representative who shall not have attained to the Age of twenty five Years, and been seven Years a Citizen of the United States, and who shall not, when elected, be an Inhabitant of that State in which he shall be chosen.

Representatives and direct Taxes shall be apportioned among the several States which may be included within this Union, according to their respective Numbers, which shall be determined by adding to the whole Number of free Persons, including those bound to Service for a Term of Years, and excluding Indians not taxed, three fifths of all other Persons. (The preceding italicized sentence was modified by the 14th Amendment, section 2.) The actual Enumeration shall be made within three Years after the first Meeting of the Congress of the United States, and within every subsequent Term of ten Years, in such Manner as they shall by Law direct. The Number of Representatives shall not exceed one for every thirty Thousand, but each State shall have at Least one Representative; and until such enumeration shall be made, the State of New Hampshire shall be entitled to chuse three, Massachusetts eight, Rhode-Island and Providence Plantations one, Connecticut five, New-York six, New Jersey four, Pennsylvania eight, Delaware one, Maryland six, Virginia ten, North Carolina five, South Carolina five, and Georgia three.

When vacancies happen in the Representation from any State, the Executive Authority thereof shall issue Writs of Election to fill such Vacancies.

The House of Representatives shall chuse their Speaker and other Officers; and shall have the sole Power of Impeachment.

Section 3—The Senate

The Senate of the United States shall be composed of two Senators from each State, *chosen by the Legislature thereof* for six Years; and each

Senator shall have one Vote. (The underlined portion of the preceding sentence was superseded by the 17th Amendment, section 1.)

Immediately after they shall be assembled in Consequence of the first Election, they shall be divided as equally as may be into three Classes. The Seats of the Senators of the first Class shall be vacated at the Expiration of the second Year, of the second Class at the Expiration of the fourth Year, and of the third Class at the Expiration of the sixth Year, so that one third may be chosen every second Year; *and if Vacancies happen by Resignation, or otherwise, during the Recess of the Legislature of any State, the Executive thereof may make temporary Appointments until the next Meeting of the Legislature, which shall then fill such Vacancies.* (The preceding italicized sentence was superseded by the 17th Amendment, section 2.)

No Person shall be a Senator who shall not have attained to the Age of thirty Years, and been nine Years a Citizen of the United States, and who shall not, when elected, be an Inhabitant of that State for which he shall be chosen.

The Vice President of the United States shall be President of the Senate, but shall have no Vote, unless they be equally divided.

The Senate shall chuse their other Officers, and also a President pro tempore, in the Absence of the Vice President, or when he shall exercise the Office of President of the United States.

The Senate shall have the sole Power to try all Impeachments. When sitting for that Purpose, they shall be on Oath or Affirmation. When the President of the United States is tried, the Chief Justice shall preside: And no Person shall be convicted without the Concurrence of two thirds of the Members present.

Judgment in Cases of Impeachment shall not extend further than to removal from Office, and disqualification to hold and enjoy any Office of honor, Trust or Profit under the United States: but the Party convicted shall nevertheless be liable and subject to Indictment, Trial, Judgment and Punishment, according to Law.

Section 4—Elections and Assembly

The Times, Places, and Manner of holding Elections for Senators and Representatives, shall be prescribed in each State by the Legislature thereof; but the Congress may at any time by Law make or alter such Regulations, except as to the Places of chusing Senators.

The Congress shall assemble at least once in every Year, and such Meeting shall *be on the first Monday in December*, unless they shall by Law appoint a different Day.

(The italicized portion of the preceding sentence was superseded by the 20th Amendment, section 2.)

Section 5—Membership, Rules, Journals, and Adjournment

Each House shall be the Judge of the Elections, Returns and Qualifications of its own Members, and a Majority of each shall constitute a Quorum to do Business; but a smaller number may adjourn from day to day, and may be authorized to compel the Attendance of absent Members, in such Manner, and under such Penalties as each House may provide.

Each House may determine the Rules of its Proceedings, punish its Members for disorderly Behavior, and, with the Concurrence of two-thirds, expel a Member.

Each House shall keep a Journal of its Proceedings, and from time to time publish the same, excepting such Parts as may in their Judgment require Secrecy; and the Yeas and Nays of the Members of either House on any question shall, at the Desire of one fifth of those Present, be entered on the Journal.

Neither House, during the Session of Congress, shall, without the Consent of the other, adjourn for more than three days, nor to any other Place than that in which the two Houses shall be sitting.

Section 6—Compensation

The Senators and Representatives shall receive a Compensation for their Services, to be ascertained by Law, and paid out of the Treasury of the United States. (The preceding italicized sentence was modified by the 27th Amendment.) They shall in all Cases, except Treason, Felony and Breach of the Peace, be privileged from Arrest during their Attendance at the Session of their respective Houses, and in going to and returning from the same; and for any Speech or Debate in either House, they shall not be questioned in any other Place.

No Senator or Representative shall, during the Time for which he was elected, be appointed to any civil Office under the Authority of the United States, which shall have been created, or the Emoluments whereof shall have been encreased during such time; and no Person holding any Office under the United States, shall be a Member of either House during his Continuance in Office.

Section 7—Revenue Bills, Legislative Process, and Presidential Veto

All Bills for raising Revenue shall originate in the House of Representatives; but the Senate may propose or concur with Amendments as on other Bills.

Every Bill which shall have passed the House of Representatives and the Senate, shall, before it become a Law, be presented to the President of the United States: If he approve he shall sign it, but if not he shall return it, with his Objections to that House in which it shall have originated, who shall enter the Objections at large on their Journal, and proceed to reconsider it. If after such Reconsideration two thirds of that House shall agree to pass the Bill, it shall be sent, together with the Objections, to the other House, by which it shall likewise be reconsidered, and if approved by two thirds of that House, it shall become a Law. But in all such Cases the Votes of both Houses shall be determined by yeas and Nays, and the Names of the Persons voting for and against the Bill shall be entered on the Journal of each House respectively. If any Bill shall not be returned by the President within ten Days (Sundays excepted) after it shall have been presented to him, the Same shall be a Law, in like Manner as if he had signed it, unless the Congress by their Adjournment prevent its Return, in which Case it shall not be a Law.

Every Order, Resolution, or Vote to which the Concurrence of the Senate and House of Representatives may be necessary (except on a question of Adjournment) shall be presented to the President of the United States; and before the Same shall take Effect, shall be approved by him, or being disapproved by him, shall be repassed by two thirds of the Senate and House of Representatives, according to the Rules and Limitations prescribed in the Case of a Bill.

Section 8—Powers of Congress

The Congress shall have Power To lay and collect Taxes, Duties, Imposts and Excises, to pay the Debts and provide for the common Defence and general Welfare of the United States; but all Duties, Imposts and Excises shall be uniform throughout the United States;

To borrow Money on the credit of the United States;

To regulate Commerce with foreign Nations, and among the several States, and with the Indian Tribes;

To establish an uniform Rule of Naturalization, and uniform Laws on the subject of Bankruptcies throughout the United States;

To coin Money, regulate the Value thereof, and of foreign Coin, and fix the Standard of Weights and Measures;

To provide for the Punishment of counterfeiting the Securities and current Coin of the United States;

To establish Post Offices and post Roads;

To promote the Progress of Science and useful Arts, by securing for limited Times to Authors and Inventors the exclusive Right to their respective Writings and Discoveries;

To constitute Tribunals inferior to the supreme Court;

To define and punish Piracies and Felonies committed on the high Seas, and Offences against the Law of Nations;

To declare War, grant Letters of Marque and Reprisal, and make Rules concerning Captures on Land and Water;

To raise and support Armies, but no Appropriation of Money to that Use shall be for a longer Term than two Years;

To provide and maintain a Navy;

To make Rules for the Government and Regulation of the land and naval Forces;

To provide for calling forth the Militia to execute the Laws of the Union, suppress Insurrections and repel Invasions;

To provide for organizing, arming, and disciplining, the Militia, and for governing such Part of them as may be employed in the Service of the United States, reserving to the States respectively, the Appointment of the Officers, and the Authority of training the Militia according to the discipline prescribed by Congress;

To exercise exclusive Legislation in all Cases whatsoever, over such District (not exceeding ten Miles square) as may, by Cession of particular States, and the Acceptance of Congress, become the Seat of the Government of the United States, and to exercise like Authority over all Places purchased by the Consent of the Legislature of the State in which the Same shall be, for the Erection of Forts, Magazines, Arsenals, dock-Yards, and other needful Buildings.

To make all Laws which shall be necessary and proper for carrying into Execution the foregoing Powers, and all other Powers vested by this Constitution in the Government of the United States, or in any Department or Officer thereof.

Section 9—Limits on Congress

The Migration or Importation of such Persons as any of the States now existing shall think proper to admit, shall not be prohibited by the Congress prior to the Year one thousand eight hundred and eight, but a Tax or duty may be imposed on such Importation, not exceeding ten dollars for each Person.

The Privilege of the Writ of Habeas Corpus shall not be suspended, unless when in Cases of Rebellion or Invasion the public Safety may require it.

No Bill of Attainder or ex post facto Law shall be passed.

No Capitation, or other direct, Tax shall be laid, unless in Proportion to the Census or enumeration herein before directed to be taken. (The preceding italicized sentence was clarified by the 16th Amendment.)

No Tax or Duty shall be laid on Articles exported from any State.

No Preference shall be given by any Regulation of Commerce or Revenue to the Ports of one State over those of another; nor shall Vessels bound to, or from, one State, be obliged to enter, clear, or pay Duties in another.

No Money shall be drawn from the Treasury, but in Consequence of Appropriations made by Law; and a regular Statement and Account of the Receipts and Expenditures of all public Money shall be published from time to time.

No Title of Nobility shall be granted by the United States: And no Person holding any Office of Profit or Trust under them, shall, without the Consent of the Congress, accept of any present, Emolument, Office, or Title, of any kind whatever, from any King, Prince, or foreign State.

Section 10—Powers Prohibited of States

No State shall enter into any Treaty, Alliance, or Confederation; grant Letters of Marque and Reprisal; coin Money; emit Bills of Credit; make any Thing but gold and silver Coin a Tender in Payment of Debts; pass any Bill of Attainder, ex post facto Law, or Law impairing the Obligation of Contracts, or grant any Title of Nobility.

No State shall, without the Consent of the Congress, lay any Imposts or Duties on Imports or Exports, except what may be absolutely necessary for executing it's inspection Laws: and the net Produce of all Duties and Imposts, laid by any State on Imports or Exports, shall be for the Use of the Treasury of the United States; and all such Laws shall be subject to the Revision and Controul of the Congress.

No State shall, without the Consent of Congress, lay any Duty of Tonnage, keep Troops, or Ships of War in time of Peace, enter into any Agreement or Compact with another State, or with a foreign Power, or engage in War, unless actually invaded, or in such imminent Danger as will not admit of delay.

Article II—The Executive Branch

Section 1—The President

The executive Power shall be vested in a President of the United States of America. He shall hold his Office during the Term of four Years, and, together with the Vice President, chosen for the same Term, be elected, as follows:

Each State shall appoint, in such Manner as the Legislature thereof may direct, a Number of Electors, equal to the whole Number of Senators and Representatives to which the State may be entitled in the Congress: but no Senator or Representative, or Person holding an Office of Trust or Profit under the United States, shall be appointed an Elector.

The Electors shall meet in their respective States, and vote by Ballot for two Persons, of whom one at least shall not be an Inhabitant of the same State with themselves. And they shall make a List of all the Persons voted for, and of the Number of Votes for each; which List they shall sign and certify, and transmit sealed to the Seat of the Government of the United States, directed to the President of the Senate. The President of the Senate shall, in the Presence of the Senate and House of Representatives, open all the Certificates, and the Votes shall then be counted. The Person having the greatest Number of Votes shall be the President, if such Number be a Majority of the whole Number of Electors appointed; and if there be more than one who have such Majority, and have an equal Number of Votes, then the House of Representatives shall immediately chuse by Ballot one of them for President; and if no Person have a Majority, then from the five highest on the List the said House shall in like Manner chuse the President. But in chusing the President, the Votes shall be taken by States, the Representation from each State having one Vote; A quorum for this purpose shall consist of a Member or Members from two thirds of the States, and a Majority of all the States shall be necessary to a Choice. In every Case, after the Choice of the President, the Person having the greatest Number of Votes of the Electors shall be the Vice President. But if there should remain two or more who have equal Votes, the Senate shall chuse from them by Ballot the Vice President. (The preceding italicized clause was superseded by the 12th Amendment.)

The Congress may determine the Time of chusing the Electors, and the Day on which they shall give their Votes; which Day shall be the same throughout the United States.

No Person except a natural born Citizen, or a Citizen of the United States, at the time of the Adoption of this Constitution, shall be eligible to the Office of President; neither shall any Person be eligible to that Office who shall not have attained to the Age of thirty five Years, and been fourteen Years a Resident within the United States.

In Case of the Removal of the President from Office, or of his Death, Resignation, or Inability to discharge the Powers and Duties of the said

Office, the Same shall devolve on the Vice President, and the Congress may by Law provide for the Case of Removal, Death, Resignation or Inability, both of the President and Vice President, declaring what Officer shall then act as President, and such Officer shall act accordingly, until the Disability be removed, or a President shall be elected. (The preceding italicized clause was modified by the 20th and 25th Amendments.)

The President shall, at stated Times, receive for his Services, a Compensation, which shall neither be increased nor diminished during the Period for which he shall have been elected, and he shall not receive within that Period any other Emolument from the United States, or any of them.

Before he enter on the Execution of his Office, he shall take the following Oath or Affirmation:—"I do solemnly swear (or affirm) that I will faithfully execute the Office of President of the United States, and will to the best of my Ability, preserve, protect and defend the Constitution of the United States."

Section 2—Civilian Power Over Military, Cabinet, Pardons, and Appointments

The President shall be Commander in Chief of the Army and Navy of the United States, and of the Militia of the several States, when called into the actual Service of the United States; he may require the Opinion, in writing, of the principal Officer in each of the executive Departments, upon any Subject relating to the Duties of their respective Offices, and he shall have Power to grant Reprieves and Pardons for Offences against the United States, except in Cases of Impeachment.

He shall have Power, by and with the Advice and Consent of the Senate, to make Treaties, provided two thirds of the Senators present concur; and he shall nominate, and by and with the Advice and Consent of the Senate, shall appoint Ambassadors, other public Ministers and Consuls, Judges of the supreme Court, and all other Officers of the United States, whose Appointments are not herein otherwise provided for, and which shall be established by Law: but the Congress may by Law vest the Appointment of such inferior Officers, as they think proper, in the President alone, in the Courts of Law, or in the Heads of Departments.

The President shall have Power to fill up all Vacancies that may happen during the Recess of the Senate, by granting Commissions which shall expire at the End of their next Session.

Section 3—State of the Union and Convening Congress

He shall from time to time give to the Congress Information of the State of the Union, and recommend to their Consideration such Measures as he shall judge necessary and expedient; he may, on extraordinary Occasions, convene both Houses, or either of them, and in Case of Disagreement between them, with Respect to the Time of Adjournment, he may adjourn them to such Time as he shall think proper; he shall receive Ambassadors and other public Ministers; he shall take Care that the Laws be faithfully executed, and shall Commission all the Officers of the United States.

Section 4—Disqualification

The President, Vice President and all civil Officers of the United States, shall be removed from Office on Impeachment for, and Conviction of, Treason, Bribery, or other high Crimes and Misdemeanors.

Article III—The Judicial Branch

Section 1—Judicial Powers

The judicial Power of the United States shall be vested in one supreme Court, and in such inferior Courts as the Congress may from time to time ordain and establish. The Judges, both of the supreme and inferior Courts, shall hold their Offices during good Behaviour, and shall, at stated Times, receive for their Services a Compensation, which shall not be diminished during their Continuance in Office.

Section 2—Jury Trials and Original Jurisdiction

The judicial Power shall extend to all Cases, in Law and Equity, arising under this Constitution, the Laws of the United States, and Treaties made, or which shall be made, under their Authority;—to all Cases affecting Ambassadors, other public Ministers and Consuls;—to all Cases of admiralty and maritime Jurisdiction;—to Controversies to which the United States shall be a Party;—to Controversies between two or more States;—between a State and Citizens of another State,—*between Citizens of different States,*—between Citizens of the same State claiming Lands under Grants of different States, and between a State, or the Citizens thereof, and foreign States, Citizens or Subjects. (The preceding italicized text was modified by the 11th Amendment.)

In all Cases affecting Ambassadors, other public Ministers and Consuls, and those in which a State shall be Party, the supreme Court shall have original Jurisdiction. In all the other Cases before mentioned, the supreme Court shall have appellate Jurisdiction, both as to Law and Fact, with such Exceptions, and under such Regulations as the Congress shall make.

The Trial of all Crimes, except in Cases of Impeachment, shall be by Jury; and such Trial shall be held in the State where the said Crimes shall have been committed; but when not committed within any State, the Trial shall be at such Place or Places as the Congress may by Law have directed.

Section 3—Treason

Treason against the United States, shall consist only in levying War against them, or in adhering to their Enemies, giving them Aid and Comfort. No Person shall be convicted of Treason unless on the Testimony of two Witnesses to the same overt Act, or on Confession in open Court.

The Congress shall have Power to declare the Punishment of Treason, but no Attainder of Treason shall work Corruption of Blood, or Forfeiture except during the Life of the Person attainted.

Article IV—The States

Section 1—Each State to Honor All States

Full Faith and Credit shall be given in each State to the public Acts, Records, and judicial Proceedings of every other State. And the Congress may by general Laws prescribe the Manner in which such Acts, Records and Proceedings shall be proved, and the Effect thereof.

Section 2—State Citizens and Extradition

The Citizens of each State shall be entitled to all Privileges and Immunities of Citizens in the several States.

A Person charged in any State with Treason, Felony, or other Crime, who shall flee from Justice, and be found in another State, shall on Demand of the executive Authority of the State from which he fled, be delivered up, to be removed to the State having Jurisdiction of the Crime.

No Person held to Service or Labour in one State, under the Laws thereof, escaping into another, shall, in Consequence of any Law or Regulation therein, be discharged from such Service or Labour, but shall be delivered up on Claim of the Party to whom such Service or Labour may be due. (The preceding italicized clause was superseded by the 13th Amendment.)

Section 3—New States

New States may be admitted by the Congress into this Union; but no new State shall be formed or erected within the Jurisdiction of any other State; nor any State be formed by the Junction of two or more States, or Parts of States, without the Consent of the Legislatures of the States concerned as well as of the Congress.

The Congress shall have Power to dispose of and make all needful Rules and Regulations respecting the Territory or other Property belonging to the United States; and nothing in this Constitution shall be so construed as to Prejudice any Claims of the United States, or of any particular State.

Section 4—Republican Government

The United States shall guarantee to every State in this Union a Republican Form of Government, and shall protect each of them against Invasion; and on Application of the Legislature, or of the Executive (when the Legislature cannot be convened), against domestic Violence.

Article V—Amendment

The Congress, whenever two thirds of both Houses shall deem it necessary, shall propose Amendments to this Constitution, or, on the Application of the Legislatures of two thirds of the several States, shall call a Convention for proposing Amendments, which, in either Case, shall be valid to all Intents and Purposes, as Part of this Constitution, when ratified by the Legislatures of three fourths of the several States, or by Conventions in three fourths thereof, as the one or the other Mode of Ratification may be proposed by the Congress; Provided that no Amendment which may be made prior to the Year One thousand eight hundred and eight shall in any Manner affect the first and fourth Clauses in the Ninth Section of the first Article; and that no State, without its Consent, shall be deprived of its equal Suffrage in the Senate.

Article VI—Debts, Supremacy, and Oaths

All Debts contracted and Engagements entered into, before the Adoption of this Constitution, shall be as valid against the United States under this Constitution, as under the Confederation.

This Constitution, and the Laws of the United States which shall be made in Pursuance thereof; and all Treaties made, or which shall be made, under the Authority of the United States, shall be the supreme Law of the Land; and the Judges in every State shall be bound thereby, any Thing in the Constitution or Laws of any State to the Contrary notwithstanding.

The Senators and Representatives before mentioned, and the Members of the several State Legislatures, and all executive and judicial Officers, both of the United States and of the several States, shall be bound by Oath or Affirmation, to support this Constitution; but no religious Test shall ever be required as a Qualification to any Office or public Trust under the United States.

Article VII—Ratification

The Ratification of the Conventions of nine States, shall be sufficient for the Establishment of this Constitution between the States so ratifying the Same.

The Word, "the," being interlined between the seventh and eighth Lines of the first Page, the Word "Thirty" being partly written on an Erazure in the fifteenth Line of the first Page, The Words "is tried" being interlined between the thirty second and thirty third Lines of the first Page and the Word "the" being interlined between the forty third and forty fourth Lines of the second Page.

Attest William Jackson Secretary

Done in Convention by the Unanimous Consent of the States present the Seventeenth Day of September in the Year of our Lord one thousand seven hundred and Eighty seven and of the Independence of the United States of America the Twelfth In witness whereof We have hereunto subscribed our Names,

George Washington
President and deputy from Virginia

Delaware
George Read
Gunning Bedford Jr.
John Dickinson
Richard Bassett
Jacob Broom

Maryland
James McHenry
Daniel of St. Thomas Jenifer
Daniel Carroll

Virginia
John Blair

James Madison Jr.

North Carolina
William Blount
Richard Dobbs Spaight
Hugh Williamson

South Carolina
John Rutledge
Charles Cotesworth Pinckney
Charles Pinckney
Pierce Butler

Georgia
William Few
Abraham Baldwin

New Hampshire
John Langdon
Nicholas Gilman

Massachusetts
Nathaniel Gorham
Rufus King

Connecticut
William Samuel Johnson
Roger Sherman

New York
Alexander Hamilton

New Jersey
William Livingston
David Brearley
William Paterson
Jonathan Dayton

Pennsylvania
Benjamin Franklin

Thomas Mifflin
Robert Morris
George Clymer
Thomas FitzSimons
Jared Ingersoll
James Wilson
Gouverneur Morris

The Constitution is presented in its original format* including all misspellings and typographical errors. Understand that the Constitution was written in 1787, long before software spell checkers, the undo command, or simple text editing existed. The non-standard capitalization of words is done to most nouns and was a matter of style only and has no other significant meaning.

One of the most commonly perceived mistakes was the spelling of some of the words within the Constitution, such as the word *choose* as *chuse*. However, this was not an actual mistake and was the correct spelling used during that time period. Other examples exist as well, words that were written using the British manner of spelling, such as *defence*, *controul*, and *labour*. All of the words contained in the Bill of Rights, with the exception of the word *defence* in the Sixth Amendment, are spelled using the style we are accustomed to. These words were *Americanized* with the introduction of Webster's Dictionary, which changed their spelling permanently and provided us with the words we use today.

For a full listing of definitions please reference the glossary.

With the exception of the brief Article, Amendment, and Section descriptions.

The Bill of Rights [1]

The First Ten Amendments to the Constitution

Ratified December 15, 1791

Preamble

Congress of the United States begun and held at the City of New-York, on Wednesday the fourth of March, one thousand seven hundred and eighty nine.

The Conventions of a number of the States, having at the time of their adopting the Constitution, expressed a desire, in order to prevent misconstruction or abuse of its powers, that further declaratory and restrictive clauses should be added: And as extending the ground of public confidence in the Government, will best ensure the beneficent ends of its institution.

Resolved by the Senate and House of Representatives of the United States of America, in Congress assembled, two-thirds of both Houses concurring, that the following Articles be proposed to the Legislatures of the several States, as amendments to the Constitution of the United States, all, or any of which Articles, when ratified by three fourths of the said Legislatures, to be valid to all intents and purposes, as part of the said Constitution; viz.

Articles in addition to, and Amendment of the Constitution of the United States of America, proposed by Congress, and ratified by the Legislatures of the several States, pursuant to the fifth Article of the original Constitution.

Amendment I—Freedom of Religion, Speech, and Press

Congress shall make no law respecting an establishment of religion, or prohibiting the free exercise thereof; or abridging the freedom of speech, or of the press; or the right of the people peaceably to assemble, and to petition the Government for a redress of grievances.

Amendment II—The Right to Bear Arms

A well regulated Militia, being necessary to the security of a free State, the right of the people to keep and bear Arms, shall not be infringed.

Amendment III—Quartering of Soldiers

No Soldier shall, in time of peace be quartered in any house, without the consent of the Owner, nor in time of war, but in a manner to be prescribed by law.

Amendment IV—Search and Seizure

The right of the people to be secure in their persons, houses, papers, and effects, against unreasonable searches and seizures, shall not be violated, and no Warrants shall issue, but upon probable cause, supported by Oath or affirmation, and particularly describing the place to be searched, and the persons or things to be seized.

Amendment V—Trial and Punishment & Property Compensation

No person shall be held to answer for a capital, or otherwise infamous crime, unless on a presentment or indictment of a Grand Jury, except in cases arising in the land or naval forces, or in the Militia, when in actual service in time of War or public danger; nor shall any person be subject for the same offence to be twice put in jeopardy of life or limb; nor shall be compelled in any criminal case to be a witness against himself, nor be deprived of life, liberty, or property, without due process of law; nor shall private property be taken for public use, without just compensation.

Amendment VI—Right to Speedy Trial

In all criminal prosecutions, the accused shall enjoy the right to a speedy and public trial, by an impartial jury of the State and district wherein the crime shall have been committed, which district shall have been previously ascertained by law, and to be informed of the nature and cause of the accusation; to be confronted with the witnesses against him; to have compulsory process for obtaining witnesses in his favor, and to have the Assistance of Counsel for his defence.

Amendment VII—Trial by Jury

In Suits at common law, where the value in controversy shall exceed twenty dollars, the right of trial by jury shall be preserved, and no fact tried by a jury, shall be otherwise re-examined in any Court of the United States, than according to the rules of the common law.

Amendment VIII—Cruel and Unusual Punishment

Excessive bail shall not be required, nor excessive fines imposed, nor cruel and unusual punishments inflicted.

Amendment IX—Construction of the Constitution

The enumeration in the Constitution, of certain rights, shall not be construed to deny or disparage others retained by the people.

Amendment X—Power of the States and People

The powers not delegated to the United States by the Constitution, nor prohibited by it to the States, are reserved to the States respectively, or to the people.

The Remaining Seventeen Constitutional Amendments

Amendment XI—Judicial Limits, Ratified February 7, 1795

Note: Article III, section 2, of the Constitution was modified by amendment 11.

The Judicial power of the United States shall not be construed to extend to any suit in law or equity, commenced or prosecuted against one of the United States by Citizens of another State, or by Citizens or Subjects of any Foreign State.

Amendment XII—Selecting the President, Ratified June 15, 1804

Note: A portion of Article II, section 1 of the Constitution was superseded by the 12th amendment.

The Electors shall meet in their respective states and vote by ballot for President and Vice-President, one of whom, at least, shall not be an inhabitant of the same state with themselves; they shall name in their ballots the person voted for as President, and in distinct ballots the person voted for as Vice-President, and they shall make distinct lists of all persons voted for as President, and of all persons voted for as Vice-President, and of the number of votes for each, which lists they shall sign and certify, and transmit sealed to the seat of the government of the United States, directed to the President of the Senate; — the President of the Senate shall, in the presence of the Senate and House of Representatives, open all the certificates and the votes shall then be counted; — The person having the greatest number of votes for President, shall be the President, if such number be a majority of the whole number of Electors appointed; and if no person have such majority, then from the persons having the highest numbers not exceeding three on the list of those voted for as President, the House of Representatives shall choose immediately, by ballot, the President. But in choosing the President, the votes shall be taken by states, the representation from each state having one vote; a quorum for this purpose shall consist of a member or members from two-thirds of the states, and a majority of all the states shall be necessary to a choice. *And if the House of Representatives shall not choose a President whenever the right of choice shall devolve upon them, before the fourth day of March next following, then the Vice-President shall act as President, as in case of the death or other constitutional disability of the President.* (The preceding italicized text was superseded by section 3 of the 20th amendment.) The person having the greatest number of votes as Vice-President, shall be the Vice-President, if such number be a majority of the whole number of Electors appointed, and if no person have a majority, then from the two highest numbers on the list, the Senate shall choose the Vice-President; a quorum for the purpose shall consist of two-thirds of the whole number of Senators, and a majority of the whole number shall be necessary to a choice. But no person constitutionally ineligible to the office of President shall be eligible to that of Vice-President of the United States.

Amendment XIII—Slavery Abolished,
Ratified December 6, 1865

Note: A portion of Article IV, section 2, of the Constitution was superseded by the 13th amendment.

Section 1—Definition

Neither slavery nor involuntary servitude, except as a punishment for crime whereof the party shall have been duly convicted, shall exist within the United States, or any place subject to their jurisdiction.

Section 2—Congressional Enforcement

Congress shall have power to enforce this article by appropriate legislation.

Amendment XIV—Citizenship Rights, Ratified July 9, 1968

Note: Article I, section 2, of the Constitution was modified by section 2 of the 14th amendment.

Section 1—Naturalization

All persons born or naturalized in the United States, and subject to the jurisdiction thereof, are citizens of the United States and of the State wherein they reside. No State shall make or enforce any law, which shall abridge the privileges or immunities of citizens of the United States; nor shall any State deprive any person of life, liberty, or property, without due process of law; nor deny to any person within its jurisdiction the equal protection of the laws.

Section 2—State Representatives

Representatives shall be apportioned among the several States according to their respective numbers, counting the whole number of persons in each State, excluding Indians not taxed. But when the right to vote at any election for the choice of electors for President and Vice-President of the United States, Representatives in Congress, the Executive and Judicial officers of a State, or the members of the Legislature thereof, is denied to any of the male inhabitants of such State, *being twenty-one years of age,* (The preceding italicized text was Changed by section 1 of the 26th amendment.) and citizens of the United States, or in any way abridged, except for participation in rebellion, or other crime, the basis of representation therein shall be reduced in the proportion which the number of such male citizens shall bear to the whole number of male citizens twenty-one years of age in such State.

Section 3—Treason and Congress

No person shall be a Senator or Representative in Congress, or elector of President and Vice-President, or hold any office, civil or military, under the United States, or under any State, who, having previously taken an oath, as a member of Congress, or as an officer of the United States, or as a member of any State legislature, or as an executive or judicial officer of any State, to support the Constitution of the United States, shall have engaged in insurrection or rebellion against the same, or given aid or comfort to the enemies thereof. But Congress may by a vote of two-thirds of each House, remove such disability.

Section 4—Obligation of Debt

The validity of the public debt of the United States, authorized by law, including debts incurred for payment of pensions and bounties for services in suppressing insurrection or rebellion, shall not be questioned. But neither the United States nor any State shall assume or pay any debt or obligation incurred in aid of insurrection or rebellion against the United States, or any claim for the loss or emancipation of any slave; but all such debts, obligations and claims shall be held illegal and void.

Section 5—Congressional Enforcement

The Congress shall have the power to enforce, by appropriate legislation, the provisions of this article.

Amendment XV—Right to Vote, Ratified February 3, 1870

Section 1—Voter Rights

The right of citizens of the United States to vote shall not be denied or abridged by the United States or by any State on account of race, color, or previous condition of servitude—

Section 2—Congressional Enforcement

The Congress shall have the power to enforce this article by appropriate legislation.

Amendment XVI—Income Tax Clarified, Ratified February 3, 1913

Note: Article I, section 9, of the Constitution was modified by amendment 16.

The Congress shall have power to lay and collect taxes on incomes, from whatever source derived, without apportionment among the several States, and without regard to any census or enumeration.

Amendment XVII—Election of Senators, Ratified April 8, 1913

Note: Article I, section 3, of the Constitution was modified by the 17th amendment.

The Senate of the United States shall be composed of two Senators from each State, elected by the people thereof, for six years; and each Senator shall have one vote. The electors in each State shall have the qualifications requisite for electors of the most numerous branch of the State legislatures.

When vacancies happen in the representation of any State in the Senate, the executive authority of such State shall issue writs of election to fill such vacancies: Provided, That the legislature of any State may empower the executive thereof to make temporary appointments until the people fill the vacancies by election as the legislature may direct.

This amendment shall not be so construed as to affect the election or term of any Senator chosen before it becomes valid as part of the Constitution.

Amendment XVIII—Prohibition, Ratified January 16, 1919

Note: This amendment was repealed by the 21st amendment.

Section 1—Liquor Prohibited

After one year from the ratification of this article the manufacture, sale, or transportation of intoxicating liquors within, the importation thereof into, or the exportation thereof from the United States and all territory subject to the jurisdiction thereof for beverage purposes is hereby prohibited.

Section 2—Congressional Enforcement

The Congress and the several States shall have concurrent power to enforce this article by appropriate legislation.

Section 3—Inoperative Limit Defined

This article shall be inoperative unless it shall have been ratified as an amendment to the Constitution by the legislatures of the several States, as provided in the Constitution, within seven years from the date of the submission hereof to the States by the Congress.

Amendment XIX—Women's Suffrage, Ratified August 18, 1920

The right of citizens of the United States to vote shall not be denied or abridged by the United States or by any State on account of sex.

Congress shall have power to enforce this article by appropriate legislation.

Amendment XX—Presidential Terms, Ratified January 23, 1933

Note: Article I, section 4, of the Constitution was modified by section 2 of this amendment. In addition, a portion of the 12th amendment was superseded by section 3.

Section 1—Term Definition

The terms of the President and the Vice President shall end at noon on the 20th day of January, and the terms of Senators and Representatives at noon on the 3d day of January, of the years in which such terms would have ended if this article had not been ratified; and the terms of their successors shall then begin.

Section 2—Congressional Term

The Congress shall assemble at least once in every year, and such meeting shall begin at noon on the 3d day of January, unless they shall by law appoint a different day.

Section 3—Vice President

If, at the time fixed for the beginning of the term of the President, the President elect shall have died, the Vice President elect shall become President. If a President shall not have been chosen before the time fixed for the beginning of his term, or if the President elect shall have failed to qualify, then the Vice President elect shall act as President until a President shall have qualified; and the Congress may by law provide for the case wherein neither a President elect nor a Vice President shall have qualified, declaring who shall then act as President, or the manner in which one who is to act shall be selected, and such person shall act accordingly until a President or Vice President shall have qualified.

Section 4—Choice of President and Vice President

The Congress may by law provide for the case of the death of any of the persons from whom the House of Representatives may choose a President whenever the right of choice shall have devolved upon them, and for the case of the death of any of the persons from whom the Senate may choose a Vice President whenever the right of choice shall have devolved upon them.

Section 5—Date of Activation

Sections 1 and 2 shall take effect on the 15th day of October following the ratification of this article.

Section 6—Inoperative Limit Defined

This article shall be inoperative unless it shall have been ratified as an amendment to the Constitution by the legislatures of three-fourths of the several States within seven years from the date of its submission.

Amendment XXI—Repeal of Prohibition, Ratified December 5, 1933

Section 1—Amendment 18 Repealed

The eighteenth article of amendment to the Constitution of the United States is hereby repealed.

Section 2—Transportation of Liquor

The transportation or importation into any State, Territory, or Possession of the United States for delivery or use therein of intoxicating liquors, in violation of the laws thereof, is hereby prohibited.

Section 3—Inoperative Limit Defined

This article shall be inoperative unless it shall have been ratified as an amendment to the Constitution by conventions in the several States, as provided in the Constitution, within seven years from the date of the submission hereof to the States by the Congress.

Amendment XXII—Term Limits, Ratified February 27, 1951

Section 1—Term Limit Defined

No person shall be elected to the office of the President more than twice, and no person who has held the office of President, or acted as President, for more than two years of a term to which some other person was elected President shall be elected to the office of President more than once. But this Article shall not apply to any person holding the office of President when this Article was proposed by Congress, and shall not prevent any person who may be holding the office of President, or acting as President, during the term within which this Article becomes operative from holding the office of President or acting as President during the remainder of such term.

Section 2—Inoperative Limit Defined

This article shall be inoperative unless it shall have been ratified as an amendment to the Constitution by the legislatures of three-fourths of the several States within seven years from the date of its submission to the States by the Congress.

Amendment XXIII—District of Columbia, Ratified March 29, 1961

Section 1—Presidential Vote for DC

The District constituting the seat of Government of the United States shall appoint in such manner as Congress may direct:

A number of electors of President and Vice President equal to the whole number of Senators and Representatives in Congress to which the District would be entitled if it were a State, but in no event more than the least populous State; they shall be in addition to those appointed by the States, but they shall be considered, for the purposes of the election of President and Vice President, to be electors appointed by a State; and they shall meet in the District and perform such duties as provided by the twelfth article of amendment.

Section 2—Congressional Enforcement

The Congress shall have power to enforce this article by appropriate legislation.

Amendment XXIV—Poll Tax Barred, Ratified January 23, 1964

Section 1—Denial of Vote by Tax Prohibited

The right of citizens of the United States to vote in any primary or other election for President or Vice President, for electors for President or Vice President, or for Senator or Representative in Congress, shall not be denied or abridged by the United States or any State by reason of failure to pay poll tax or other tax.

Section 2—Congressional Enforcement

The Congress shall have power to enforce this article by appropriate legislation.

Amendment XXV—Succession, Ratified February 10, 1967

Note: Article II, section 1, of the Constitution was affected by the 25th amendment.

Section 1—Succession Defined

In case of the removal of the President from office or of his death or resignation, the Vice President shall become President.

Section 2—Nomination of Vice President

Whenever there is a vacancy in the office of the Vice President, the President shall nominate a Vice President who shall take office upon confirmation by a majority vote of both Houses of Congress.

Section 3—Presidential Declaration

Whenever the President transmits to the President pro tempore of the Senate and the Speaker of the House of Representatives his written declaration that he is unable to discharge the powers and duties of his office, and until he transmits to them a written declaration to the contrary, such powers and duties shall be discharged by the Vice President as Acting President.

Section 4—Vice Presidential Powers

Whenever the Vice President and a majority of either the principal officers of the executive departments or of such other body as

Congress may by law provide, transmit to the President pro tempore of the Senate and the Speaker of the House of Representatives their written declaration that the President is unable to discharge the powers and duties of his office, the Vice President shall immediately assume the powers and duties of the office as Acting President.

Thereafter, when the President transmits to the President pro tempore of the Senate and the Speaker of the House of Representatives his written declaration that no inability exists, he shall resume the powers and duties of his office unless the Vice President and a majority of either the principal officers of the executive department or of such other body as Congress may by law provide, transmit within four days to the President pro tempore of the Senate and the Speaker of the House of Representatives their written declaration that the President is unable to discharge the powers and duties of his office. Thereupon Congress shall decide the issue, assembling within forty-eight hours for that purpose if not in session. If the Congress, within twenty-one days after receipt of the latter written declaration, or, if Congress is not in session, within twenty-one days after Congress is required to assemble, determines by two-thirds vote of both Houses that the President is unable to discharge the powers and duties of his office, the Vice President shall continue to discharge the same as Acting President; otherwise, the President shall resume the powers and duties of his office.

Amendment XXVI—Voting Age, Ratified July 1, 1971

Note: Amendment 14, section 2, of the Constitution was modified by section 1 of the 26th amendment.

Section 1—Age of Eligibility

The right of citizens of the United States, who are eighteen years of age or older, to vote shall not be denied or abridged by the United States or by any State on account of age.

Section 2—Congressional Enforcement

The Congress shall have power to enforce this article by appropriate legislation.

Amendment XXVII—Congressional Pay, Ratified May 7, 1992

No law, varying the compensation for the services of the Senators and Representatives, shall take effect, until an election of representatives shall have intervened.

Glossary

Accounts Receivable Tax—Accounts receivables are subject to taxation under some state laws, which vary by state. Accounts receivable not arising from the normal course of trade or business are taxable under this law, while accounts receivable that arise from, or are issued in connection with, a business' normal trade or business activity are exempt. [1]

Ad valorem tax—a Latin term meaning "based on value," which applies to property taxes based on a percentage of the county's assessment of the property's value [1]

Adjourn—verb: to suspend indefinitely or until a later stated time.

Adjournment—noun: the act of adjourning. [2]

Appellate—adj.: of, relating to, or recognizing appeals; specifically: having the power to review the judgment of another tribunal <an appellate court> [2]

Apportion—verb: to divide and share out according to a plan; especially: to make a proportionate division or distribution of

Apportionment—noun: the act or result of apportioning [2]

Attainder—noun: extinction of the civil rights and capacities of a person upon sentence of death or outlawry usually after a conviction of treason [2]

Building Permit Tax—The building permit application and review process ensures that the plans for construction comply with the local area's land use and construction standards. Specific building code issues include appropriate zoning, structural integrity, proper exiting, fire resistance, sanitation and other health concerns, tapping into water and sewer lines, the extension of electrical service, industrial waste review for commercial buildings etc. [1]

Capital Gains Tax—A capital gain tax is assessed on profits realized from the sale of a capital asset. For example, stock. A capital gain is assessed on the difference between cost basis of an asset and its fair market value. [1]

Commercial Drivers License Tax—People tend to associate a commercial license, or commercial driver's license (CDL), with driving an eighteen-wheeler or a school bus, but in many states, a commercial license is required for a variety of different reasons. Plus, some employers require a commercial license even if you aren't transporting passengers or driving an unusually large vehicle. [1]

Cigarette Tax—Cigarettes are taxed at the corporate, federal, state, and local levels. The cigarette manufacturer pays taxes assessed at the corporate level, including corporate income taxes, property taxes, payroll taxes, etc. Then there are the taxes paid by the wholesalers, the retailers, the warehouses, and the taxes embodied in the products the manufacturer uses to make the cigarettes. [1]

Concur—verb: 1: to act together to a common end or single effect. 2a : approve b : to express agreement [II]

Concurrence—noun: agreement or union in action.

Corporate Income Tax—Corporations may be taxed at both the federal and state levels. Federal tax laws establish a tax rate and tax forms specifically applicable to for corporate income. [1]

Court Fines—A fine is an amount of money that the court has ordered to be paid as a penalty. Fines may be ordered in a variety of civil cases, such as traffic citations or drunk and disorderly citations. Fines can include court costs and other fees. A judge may order a fine as the whole or part of a sentence. Fines can be ordered for a wide range of offenses. [1]

Dog License Tax—Dog licensing is governed by state and local laws, which vary by jurisdiction. Licensing helps the recovery of lost or stray animals and helps protect the public from rabies, since licensed dogs must have proof of vaccination. [I]

Due process—In the Magna Carta, due process is referred to as "law of the land" and "legal judgment of peers." In the context of the United States it refers to how and why laws are enforced. It applies to all persons, citizen or alien, as well as to corporations. [III]

Emolument—noun: the returns arising from office or employment usually in the form of compensation or perquisites. [II]

Enumerate—verb: to ascertain the number of [II]

Estate Tax—Estate tax is imposed on the transfer of property based upon the net value of a decedent's estate. Congress has approved a schedule that increases the amount an individual can leave to heirs tax-free to $1.5 million in 2004 and eventually to $3.5 million in 2009. In 2010, it will supposedly be repealed altogether. [I]

Excise—noun: an internal tax levied on the manufacture, sale, or consumption of a commodity [II]

Excise Taxes—A type of ad valorem tax that is imposed at the time of a purchase or sale transaction (sales tax or value added tax (VAT)) or in connection with importation across a political border (tariffs). [I]

Ex post facto—adverb: after the fact [II]

Federal Income Tax—The Sixteenth Amendment to the U.S. Constitution empowered Congress to tax "incomes, from whatever source derived, without apportionment among the several States, and without regard to any census or enumeration." The Internal Revenue Code is now embodied as Title 26 of the United States Code (26 U.S.C.) and was enacted following ratification of the Sixteenth Amendment. [I]

Federal Unemployment Tax—The Federal Unemployment Tax Act (FUTA), with state unemployment systems, provides for payments of unemployment compensation to workers who have lost their jobs. Most employers pay both a federal and a state unemployment tax. Only the employer pays FUTA tax; it is not deducted from the employee's wages. [I]

Fishing License Tax—States are entrusted with the protection of fish and wildlife within its borders. In order to preserve its fish population, many states require fishing licenses to be purchased by residents and certain others, unless exempt. Different licenses maybe issued for freshwater and saltwater fishing. [I]

Food License Tax—State and local laws, which vary by jurisdiction, govern the licensing of certain food vendors and establishments. A food establishment license is typically required in almost all instances where food is commercially handled or served to the general public. [1]

Framers—Delegates to the federal convention that took part in framing or drafting the proposed Constitution of the United States. [VI]

Fuel Permit Tax—Fuel permit laws are governed by state laws, which vary by state. Generally, you must have a fuel permit or license to operate certain vehicles in the state and if you operate the above vehicles on a public highway in state without a required permit or license, you may be subject to fines and penalties, and your vehicle could be impounded. [1]

Gasoline Tax—A gasoline tax is a sales tax imposed on the sale of gasoline. In the United States the funds are dedicated or hypothecated to be used for transportation or roads purposes so that the gas tax is considered by many to be a user fee. [1]

Gross domestic product—The total market value of all final goods and services produced in a country in a given year, equal to total consumer, investment, and government spending, plus the value of exports, minus the value of imports. [VII]

Habeas corpus—noun: any of several common-law writs issued to bring a party before a court or judge [II]

Hunting License Tax—States are entrusted with the protection of fish and wildlife within its borders. In order to preserve its wildlife population many states require hunting licenses to be purchased by residents, non-residents, and certain others, unless exempt. Different licenses maybe issued for various purposes. A hunting license may not be needed to hunt furbearing animals if the hunter possesses a trapper's license. [1]

Impeachment—noun: a: to bring an accusation against; b: to charge with a crime or misdemeanor; specifically, to charge (a public official) before a competent tribunal with misconduct in office; c: to remove from office especially for misconduct [II]

Impost—noun: something imposed or levied [II]

Infringe—verb: to encroach upon in a way that violates law or the rights of another [II]

Inheritance Tax—In some states, an inheritance tax may apply to gifts received from a decedent. The tax is based upon a person's (beneficiary's) right to receive money or property, which was owned by the decedent at the date of death. [1]

Inventory Tax IRS Interest Charges—Some state laws, which vary by state, require that certain inventory, such as that of motor vehicles, boats and trailers, mobile homes, and heavy equipment, be appraised and taxed.[1]

IRS Penalties—The Internal Revenue Service is authorized to assess penalties for various tax violations, including—among others—late filing, late filing due to fraud, late payments, negligence or disregard of IRS tax rules and IRS tax regulations, substantial understatements of income tax owed, and fraud.[1]

Jurisdiction—noun: 1: the power, right, or authority to interpret and apply the law; 2: a: the authority of a sovereign power to govern or legislate; b: the power or right to exercise authority: control; 3: the limits or territory within which authority may be exercised [II]

Liquor Tax—The distribution of liquor is a state enterprise under the auspices of some state liquor authorities. This tax may be imposed upon computed on the actual price paid by the consumer, as well as the first sale of liquor being subject to the sales and use tax at the time of purchase. Other states impose a flat rate on a certain volume of liquor.[1]

Local Income Tax—A local income tax rate is relative to where you live. The local income tax is calculated as a percentage of taxable income. In some states, the rate is flat—a single tax rate for all income levels. Many other states have progressively higher rates as taxpayers' income levels rise. In some areas, only individuals and not corporations pay local income taxes.[1]

Luxury Taxes—A levy on articles that are considered expensive, nonessential items.[1]

Marriage License Tax—Marriage license laws are governed by state and local laws, which vary by jurisdiction. Some areas require a waiting period, residency, blood testing, and other requirements. Some states prohibit certain people from getting a marriage license, such as cousins and persons of the same sex.[1]

Mead—Mead (also called honey wine) is an alcoholic beverage that is produced by fermenting a solution of honey and water. It may also be produced by fermenting a solution of water and honey with grain mash; the mash is strained off immediately after fermentation. [IV]

Medicare Tax—A tax used to provide medical benefits for certain individuals when they reach age sixty-five. Known as FICA taxes, these are withheld from an employee's wages.[1]

Metheglin—A mead that also contains spices (such as: cloves, cinnamon, or nutmeg), or herbs (such as: oregano, hops, or even lavender or chamomile), is called a metheglin. [IV]

Ordain—verb: to establish or order by appointment, decree, or law [II]

Personal Property Tax—Personal property tax means an ad valorem tax, which is imposed on an annual basis in respect of personal property. [I]

Pro tempore—adverb: for the time being [II]

Property Tax—Property tax is a tax on the ownership of property. It is a tax assessed on all property or on all property of a certain class located within a certain territory in proportion to its value, the obligation to pay which is absolute and is not based upon any voluntary action of the person assessed. Property tax is levied on things tangible or intangible, as distinguished from a tax on a right to use or transfer things, or on the proceeds of a business in which the use of things is essential. [I]

Potash—noun: potassium carbonate especially from wood ashes [II]

Quarter—verb: to provide with lodging or shelter [II]

Real Property Tax—Real property tax is a tax based on the value of the property. Real property taxes are governed by state laws, which vary by state. Appraisals which are the basis for property values can generally be appealed according to local rules. [I]

Redress—transitive verb: a (1) to set right: remedy; (2) to make up for: compensate, b: to remove the cause of (a grievance or complaint), c : to exact reparation for [II]

Reprisal—noun: the act or practice in international law of resorting to force short of war in retaliation for damage or loss suffered [II]

Republic—noun: a (1) a government having a chief of state who is not a monarch and who in modern times is usually a president; (2) a political unit (as a nation) having such a form of government, b (1) a government in which supreme power resides in a body of citizens entitled to vote and is exercised by elected officers and representatives responsible to them and governing according to law, (2) a political unit (as a nation) having such a form of government, c: a usually specified republican government of a political unit [II]

Road, Tunnel, and Bridge Toll Tax—A toll road or turnpike is a road on which a toll authority collects a fee for use. Similarly there are toll bridges and toll tunnels. [I]

Road Use Tax—Road use tax law is governed by state laws, which vary by state. These funds are primarily used for the construction and maintenance of highways. [1]

Sales Taxes—A tax collected on retail sales as provided under state laws, which vary by state. For purposes of collecting sales tax, a sale includes installment and credit sales and the exchange of properties as well as the sale thereof for money. [1]

School Tax—School tax laws very by state and local area. School districts typically collect taxes through payment of local residents' property taxes. [1]

Septic Permit Tax—Local laws, which vary by area, govern septic permit requirements. As more people move into rural areas, the need for proper sewage disposal becomes increasingly important in order to protect the health of the public, of the environment, and of our drinking water supplies. The permit process assures that septic systems are designed, installed and operated according to current codes. [1]

Service Charge Taxes—Service charges are extra levies on services of various providers. Service charges may be added to a basic real estate tax for services, such as: garbage disposal, leaf pickup, and water or sewer service. [1]

Social Security Tax—Social security is designed as a safety net national insurance system to protect individuals from financial distress caused by unforeseen catastrophes. In the United States, the social security program was created in 1935 (42 U.S.C. 301 et seq.) to provide old age, survivors, and disability insurance benefits to workers and their families. Unlike welfare, social security benefits are paid to an individual or his or her family at least in part on the basis of that person's employment record and prior contributions to the system. The program is administered by the Social Security Administration (SSA) and since 1965 it has included health insurance benefits under the Medicare program. While social security benefits under the act are most often associated with old age, survivors, and disability insurance, in its broadest sense, they also include federally funded welfare programs and unemployment compensation. [1]

State Income Tax—The majority of states tax the income of its residents. Some states tax only dividend and interest income. Such authority is provided in the state's constitution, which authorizes the taxation of incomes, and the rates of such taxation may be either uniform or graduated, and may be applied to such incomes and with such exemptions as may be provided by law.[I]

State Unemployment Tax (SUTA)—State unemployment taxes are paid by the employer and are not deducted from the employee's wages in almost all states. These taxes are in addition to any federal unemployment taxes owed.[I]

Stump—verb: to travel over (a region) making political speeches or supporting a cause [II]

Suffrage—noun: the right of voting: franchise; also: the exercise of such right [II]

Telephone Federal Excise Tax—In 1898, Congress passed a 3 percent excise tax on telephone calls to raise the funding necessary to fight the Spanish-American War. At the time the tax was imposed, only 2,000 phone lines were operational in America. Today, over 90 percent of American households have telephone service.[I]

Telephone Federal Universal Service Fee Tax—Since May of 1997 the Federal Communications Commission (FCC) requires telecommunication carriers to pay into the universal service fund. This helps provide affordable phone service and gives schools, libraries, and rural health care providers access to the Internet. Telecommunication carriers are required by the FCC to pay a percentage of their revenues for state-to-state and international services into the Universal Service Fund.[I]

Telephone Minimum Usage Surcharge Tax—Telephone minimum usage surcharges are charged by some telephone companies and vary by company. The usage minimum surcharge is based on usage and is not a monthly fee. If you spend less than the minimum in a given month in qualifying, your account will be charged the difference between what you use and the minimum.[I]

Traffic Fines—The total amount of a traffic fine is made up of amounts required to be paid by state laws as well as county and city ordinances, which vary by jurisdiction. There are three levels of severity of traffic violations: infractions, misdemeanors, and felonies.[I]

Trailer Registration Tax—A trailer may be subject to registration in order to legally tow it on public roads. Trailer registration requirements are regulated by each state and local government. Some states require annual renewal and registration fees often vary by weight of the trailer.[I]

Treason—noun: the offense of attempting by overt acts to overthrow the government of the state to which the offender owes allegiance or to kill or personally injure the sovereign or the sovereign's family [II]

Underemployed—adjective: 1. Employed only part-time when one needs and desires full-time employment. 2. Inadequately employed, especially employed at a low-paying job that requires less skill or training than one possesses. [VIII]

Usurp—transitive verb: to seize and hold (as office, place, or powers) in possession by force or without right <usurp a throne> [II]

Utility Taxes—A utility tax is a tax on public service businesses, including businesses that engage in transportation, communications, and the supply of energy, natural gas, and water. The tax may exist in lieu of a business and occupation (B&O) tax. Such taxes are governed by state laws, which vary by state. In some instances, a portion, however, provides financial assistance to local governments for maintenance of public works facilities. [I]

Vehicle License Registration Tax—Vehicle license registration is governed by state laws, which vary by state. Motor vehicle registration and titling in a state is typically done in the individual's county of residence. New residents often have a grace period in which to apply for registration in the new state. Some states require that your vehicle must first pass a vehicle safety inspection and an inspection of the vehicle identification number. [I]

Vehicle Sales Tax—Vehicle sales tax laws are governed by state and local laws, which vary by jurisdiction. Typically, the sales tax is paid in the county where the purchaser resides and is due prior to first registration of a vehicle and within a certain number of days from the date of purchase. [I]

Victualing house—noun: a house where provision is made for strangers to eat. [V]

Watercraft Registration Tax— Boat registration laws are governed by state laws, which vary by state. Applications for vessel registration and title certificates are usually filed by the vessel owner with the county tax collector's office in the county where the vessel is located or in the county where the vessel owner resides. A bill of sale with proof of the date of purchase is often required, as many states require the watercraft to be registered within a certain time after purchase. [I]

Welfare—noun: the state of doing well especially in respect to good fortune, happiness, well-being, or prosperity [II]

Well Permit Tax—Water well permits are governed by state and local laws, which vary by jurisdiction. The process of obtaining a water well permit involves primarily identifying potential sources of contamination and then maintaining separation distances to protect the water quality. Well permits are required to assure construction consistent with regulations for the safeguarding of persons and property from hazards arising from unsanitary and unhealthy drinking water and to assure an adequate supply of water. [I]

Workers Compensation Tax—Workers' compensation laws are designed to ensure payment by employers for some part of the cost of injuries, or in some cases of occupational diseases, received by employees in the course of their work. State workers' compensation tax laws vary by state. Some states have a quarterly workers compensation tax, although most states let employers purchase workers compensation insurance from private insurance companies. [I]

Bibliography

Chapter I: A Brief History

[I] HistoryCentral.com. (n.d.). French and Indian War 1754-1763. Retrieved March 26, 2011 from http://www.historycentral.com/revolt/French.html

[II] Ohio History Central. (n.d.). Fort Duquesne. Retrieved March 26, 2011 from http://www.ohiohistorycentral.org/entry.php?rec=705

[III] HistoryCentral.com. (n.d.). British Actions After the French Indian War. Retrieved April 2, 2011 from http://www.historycentral.com/revolt/sugart.html

[IV] USHistory.org. (n.d.). The Quartering Act of 1765. Retrieved March 28, 2011 from http://www.ushistory.org/declaration/related/quartering.htm

[V] HistoryCentral.com. (n.d.). Stamp Tax Imposed. Retrieved March 28, 2011 from http://www.historycentral.com/revolt/stamptax.html

[VI] USHistory.org. (n.d.). The Sons of Liberty. Retrieved March 29, 2011 from http://www.ushistory.org/declaration/related/sons.htm

[VII] Stamp Act. (n.d.). Colonial America, 1765. Retrieved March 29, 2011 from http://www.u-s-history.com/pages/h642.html

[VIII] Wikipedia.org. (n.d.). Townshend Acts. Retrieved March 29, 2011 from http://en.wikipedia.org/wiki/Townshend_Acts

[IX] Revolutionary War and Beyond. (n.d.). Samuel Adams Facts. Retrieved March 30, 2011 from http://www.revolutionary-war-and-beyond.com/samuel-adams-facts.html

[X] Matthew Spalding. (March 31, 2010). Intolerable Acts and Tea Parties. Retrieved April 2, 2011 from http://www.ocpathink.org/articles/832

[XI] Wikipedia.org. (n.d.). First Continental Congress. Retrieved April 2, 2011 from http://en.wikipedia.org/wiki/First_Continental_Congress

[XII] Paul Revere Heritage Project. (n.d.). One if by Land Two if by Sea. Retrieved April 4, 2011 from http://www.paul-revere-heritage.com/one-if-by-land-two-if-by-sea.html

[XIII] USHistory.org. (n.d.). Concord. Retrieved April 5, 2011 from http://www.ushistory.org/us/11c.asp

[XIV] The Charters of Freedom. (n.d.). Declaration of Independence. Retrieved April 8, 2011 from http://www.archives.gov/exhibits/charters/declaration.html

[XV] HistoryCentral.com. (n.d.). Valley Forge-Winter 1777-1778. Retrieved April 6, 2011 from http://www.historycentral.com/revolt/valleyforge.html

[XVI] Archiving Early America. (n.d.). The Articles of Confederation and Perpetual Union. Retrieved April 8, 2011 from http://www.earlyamerica.com/earlyamerica/milestones/articles/

[XVII] Charters of Freedom. (n.d.). Constitution of the United States. Retrieved April 11, 2011 from http://www.archives.gov/exhibits/charters/constitution.html

[XVIII] United States Senate. (n.d.). 1787-1800. Retrieved April 11, 2011 from http://www.senate.gov/artandhistory/history/minute/The_Significance_of_March_4.htm

[XIX] Joseph Ellis, Encyclopedia Britannica. (Feb. 18, 2007). The U.S. Founding Fathers: Who Were These Guys? Retrieved April 6, 2011 from http://www.britannica.com/blogs/2007/02/the-us-founding-fathers-who-were-these-guys/

[XX] Wikipedia.org. (n.d.). Founding Fathers of the United States. Retrieved April 6, 2011 from http://en.wikipedia.org/wiki/Founding_Fathers_of_the_United_ States

XXI Revolutionary War and Beyond. (n.d.). John Adams Quotes. Retrieved April 13, 2011 from http://www.revolutionary-war-and-beyond.com/john-adams-quotes-4.html

XXII American History Central. (n.d.). Benjamin Franklin, (1706-1790). Retrieved April 16, 2011 from http://www.americanhistorycentral.com/entry.php? rec=469&view=main

XXIII Brandywine Battlefield Historic Site. (n.d.). Alexander Hamilton. Retrieved April 16, 2011 from http://www.ushistory.org/brandywine/special/art08.htm

XXIV Whitehouse.gov. (n.d.). Thomas Jefferson. Retrieved April 18, 2011 from http://www.whitehouse.gov/about/presidents /thomasjefferson

XXV Wikipedia.org. (n.d.). Thomas Jefferson, Democracy. Retrieved April 18, 2011 from http://en.wikipedia.org/wiki/Thomas_Jefferson.

XXVI Monticello.org. (n.d.). Famous Quotations. Retrieved April 23, 2011 from http://www.monticello.org/site/jefferson/natural-progress-things-quotation

XXVII Whitehouse.gov. (n.d.). James Madison. Retrieved April 23, 2011 from http://www.whitehouse.gov/about/presidents/jamesmadison

XXVIII Wikipedia.org. (n.d.). James Madison. Retrieved April 23, 2011 from http://en.wikipedia.org/wiki/James_Madison

XXIX Gordon S. Wood. (2006). Is There a "James Madison Problem"? Retrieved April 23, 2011 from http://oll.libertyfund.org/?option=com_staticxt&staticfile=show.php%3Ftitle=1727&chapter=81746&layout=html&Itemid=27

XXX Whitehouse.gov. (n.d.). George Washington. Retrieved April 23, 2011 from http://www.whitehouse.gov/about/presidents/georgewashington

XXXI Peace Through Wealthl. (n.d.). Best Presidents. Retrieved April 23, 2011 from http://peacethroughwealth.com/best-presidents/

Chapter II: Freedom of Speech and the Press

I Robert Barnes. (March 2, 2011). Supreme Court rules First Amendment protects church's right to picket funerals. Retrieved June 11, 2011 from http://www.washingtonpost.com/politics/supreme-court-rules-first-amendment-protects-churchs-right-to-picket-funerals/2011/03/02/ABDzbrM_story.html

[II] Alex Dominguez. (Nov 2, 2007). Jury awards father $11 million in damages for church's protest at son's military funeral. Retrieved June 11, 2011 from http://www.nctimes.com/news/local/military/article_602fcf9b-487f-59eb-afa9-7da9506b8db5.html

[III] Dan Lamothe. (April 5, 2010). Snyder-Phelps fight has many twists, turns. Retrieved June 11, 2011 from http://www.marinecorpstimes.com/news/2010/04/marine_scotus_040510w/

[IV] Tracy Loew. (n.d.). States look to guarantee civility at military funerals. Retrieved June 11, 2011 from http://www.usatoday.com/news/nation/ 2011-06-02-military-funerals-freedom-of-speech-protests_n.htm

[V] Freedom Forum. (n.d.). What is the Fighting Words Doctrine? Retrieved June 14, 2011 from http://www.freedomforum.org/templates/document.asp?documentID=13718

[VI] US Supreme Court Center. (n.d.). SceCK V. UNITED STATES, 249 U. S. 47 (1919). Retrieved June 14, 2011 from http://supreme.justia.com/us/249/47/case.html

[VII] America.gov Archive. (June 23, 2008). Freedom of the Press. Retrieved June 15, 2011 from http://www.america.gov/st/democracyhr-english/2008/June/20080630215145eaifas0.6333842.html

[VIII] Ed Morrissey. (Jan. 14, 2011). GOP ready to cut off NPR? Retrieved June 18, 2011 from http://hotair.com/archives/2011/01/14/gop-ready-to-cut-off-npr/

[IX] Tom Watkins. (Oct. 22, 2010). NPR head says analyst was dropped for repeatedly crossing into opinion. Retrieved June 18, 2011 from http://www.cnn.com/2010/SHOWBIZ/10/21/npr.analyst.fired/index.html?hpt=T2

[X] Nile Gardiner, Ph.D. and James Phillips. (June 4, 2010). The Gaza Flotilla Incident: U.N. Inquiry Will Be an Anti-Israel Farce. Retrieved June 18, 2011 from http://www.heritage.org/research/reports/2010/06/the-gaza-flotilla-incident-un-inquiry-will-be-an-anti-israel-farce

[XI] FoxNews.com. (Oct. 21, 2010). A Brief History of NPR's Intolerance and Imbalance. Retrieved June 18, 2011 from http://www.foxnews.com/politics/2010/10/21/brief-history-nprs-intolerance-imbalance/

[XII] Huma Khan and Z. Byron Wolf. (March 9, 2011). NPR CEO Vivian Schiller Resigns After Hidden Camera Sting Snares Top Fundraiser.

Retrieved June 18, 2011 from http://abcnews.go.com/Politics/npr-ceo-vivian-schiller-resigns-james-okeefe-orchestrated/story?id=13092007

[XIII] CNN.com. (Dec. 26, 2010). 2010: No Ordinary Year. Retrieved Dec. 29, 2010 from http://www.cnn.com/video/#/video/us/2010/12/28/pn.big.10.of.2010. hln?hpt=T2

[XIV] David S. Hilzenrath, Washington Post Staff Writer. (Dec. 28, 2010). 2010 worst year for bank failures since 1992. Retrieved Dec. 30, 2010 from http://www.washingtonpost.com/wp-dyn/content/article/2010/12/28/AR2010122803649.html

[XV] Impact Segment. (Feb. 21, 2011). O'Reilly Factor. FOX News Channel.

[XVI] Chris Wallace. (June 19, 2011). Exclusive: Jon Stewart on 'Fox News Sunday'. Retrieved June 21, 2011 from http://video.foxnews.com/v/1007046245001/exclusive-jon-stewart-on-fox-news-Sunday

[XVII] Bill O'Reilly. (June 20, 2011). The Presidential Election and the Media. Retrieved June 21, 2011 from http://www.foxnews.com/on-air/oreilly/index.html#/v/1009801582001/the-presidential-election-and-the-media/?playlist_id=86923

[XVIII] Gallup. (Sept. 29, 2010). Distrust in U.S. Media Edges Up to Record High. Retrieved June 18, 2011 from http://www.gallup.com/poll/143267/Distrust-Media-Edges-Record-High.aspx

[XIX] Don Irvine. (May 20, 2011). Poll: Fox Most Trusted Political News Source. Retrieved June 20, 2011 from http://www.aim.org/don-irvine-blog/poll-fox-most-trusted-political-news-source/

[XX] Donald Rieck. (Dec. 2, 2008). OBAMA'S COVERAGE WAS HISTORIC TOO. Retrieved June 20, 2011 from http://www.cmpa.com/media_room_press_12_2_08.htm

[XXI] John Brandon. (Feb. 8, 2011). Is Bulletstorm the Worst Video Game in the World? Retrieved July 9, 2011 from http://www.foxnews.com/scitech/2011/02/08/bulletstorm-worst-game-kids/

[XXII] RicardoT, Gamespot.com Member. (Feb. 8, 2011). Is FOX News the worst news outlet in the world? Retrieved July 8, 2011 from http://www.gamespot.com/users/RicardoT/show_blog_entry.php?topic_id=m-100-25907144&om_act=convert&om_clk=picks&tag=picks%3Btitle%3B9#generic_comments

[XXIII] Lindsay Powers. (May 31, 2011). Hollywood Accused of

Rampant Liberal Bias in New Book. Retrieved June 22, 2011 from http://www.hollywoodreporter.com/news/hollywood-accused-rampant-liberal-bias-193304

XXIV Examiner Staff Writer. (Aug. 27, 2010). Obama, Democrats got 88 percent of 2008 contributions by TV network execs, writers, reporters UPDATED! Retrieved July 8, 2011 from http://washingtonexaminer.com/blogs/beltway-confidential/obama-democrats-got-88-percent-2008-contributions-tv-network-execs-writers

XXV Robert Seidman. (June 21, 2011). Updated: Cable News Ratings for Monday, June 20, 2011. Retrieved Sept. 21, 2011 from http://tvbythenumbers.zap2it.com/2011/06/21/cable-news-ratings-for-monday-june-20-2011/96203/

Chapter III: The Right to Bear Arms

I U.S. Constitution Online. (n.d.). Constitutional Topic: The Second Amendment. Retrieved May 11, 2011 from http://www.usconstitution.net/consttop_2nd.html

II The Avalon Project–Documents in Law, History and Diplomacy. (n.d.). Constitution of Pennsylvania–September 28, 1776. Retrieved May 14, 2011 from http://avalon.law.yale.edu/18th_century/pa08.asp

III Quotes Museum. (n.d.). Patrick Henry. Retrieved May 14, 2011 from http://www.quotes-museum.com/quote/40613

IV Founders Quotes. (n.d.). Noah Webster. Retrieved May 14, 2011 from http://www.Foundersquotes.com/Noah_Webster/before-a-standing-army-can-rule-the-people-must-be-disarmed/

V The Federalist No. 46. (n.d.). The Influence of the State and Federal Governments Compared. Retrieved May 31, 2011 from http://www.constitution.org/fed/federa46.htm

VI Sam R. Cummings. (April 7, 1999). UNITED STATES OF AMERICA v. TIMOTHY JOE EMERSON. Retrieved May 14, 2011 from http://law2.umkc.edu/faculty/projects/ftrials/conlaw/emerson.html

VII Justia.com, U.S. Supreme Court Center. (n.d.). PRESSER V. ILLINOIS, 116 U. S. 252 (1886). Retrieved May 21, 2011 from http://supreme.justia.com/us/116/252/case.html

VIII Justia.com, U.S. Supreme Court Center. (n.d.). ROBERTSON V.

BALDWIN, 165 U. S. 275 (1897). Retrieved May 21, 2011 from http://supreme.justia.com/us/165/275/case.html

[IX] Justia.com, U.S. Supreme Court Center. (n.d.). UNITED STATES V. MILLER, 307 U. S. 174 (1939). Retrieved May 21, 2011 from http://supreme.justia.com/us/307/174/case.html

[X] NRA-ILA.org. (n.d.). The Case For Reforming The District of Columbia`s Gun Laws. Retrieved May 21, 2011 from http://www.nraila.org/Issues/ FactSheets/Read.aspx?ID=72

[XI] U.S. Constitution Online. (n.d.). Constitutional Topic: The Second Amendment. Retrieved May 21, 2011 from http://www.usconstitution.net/consttop_2nd.html

[XII] Shannon Bream. (Jan. 10, 2011). Arizona Rampage Reignites Gun Control Debate in D.C.. Retrieved May 21, 2011 from http://www.foxnews.com/politics/2011/01/10/arizona-rampage-reignites-gun-control-debate-dc/

[XIII] John Lott. (June 28, 2010). Court's Gun Decision An Important Win for Americans Who Want to Defend Themselves. Retrieved May 24, 2011 from http://www.foxnews.com/opinion/2010/06/28/john-lott-supreme-court-guns-ban-washington-chicago-daley-kagan-sotomayor/

[XIV] Mike Bauman. (Dec. 15, 2010). City with strictest gun control laws has most officers killed by gunfire. Retrieved May 25, 2011 from http://www.greeleygazette.com/press/?p=7101

[XV] Piers Morgan Tonight. (May 18, 2011). Ted Nugent on guns and Obama. Retrieved May 31, 2011 from http://www.cnn.com/video/#/video/showbiz/2011/05/18/piers.ted.nugent.obama.cnn?hpt=Mid

[XVI] Alan L. Lund. (n.d.). Gun Control really does work! Retrieved May 25, 2011 from http://www.kc3.com/editorial/gun_control_works.htm

[XVII] Lott, J. (May 24, 1010). More Guns, Less Crime: Third Edition, Understanding Crime and Gun Control Laws. University Of Chicago Pressk.

[XVIII] Larry Bell. (June 7, 2011). U.N. Agreement Should Have All Gun Owners Up In Arms. Retrieved June 7, 2011 from http://blogs.forbes.com/larrybell/2011/06/07/u-n-agreement-should-have-all-gun-owners-up-in-arms/

[XIX] Brady Campaign to Prevent Gun Violence. (n.d.). History of the Brady Campaign. Retrieved May 29, 2011 from http://www.bradycampaign.org/about/history

[XX] Fox Nation. (May 25, 2011). Obama: We're Working on Gun Control

'Under the Radar'. Retrieved May 29, 2011 from http://nation.foxnews.com/guns/2011/05/25/obama-were-working-gun-control-under-radar

XXI Sam Stein. (March 23, 2011). Obama Looking For Ways Around Congress On Gun Policy. Retrieved May 29, 2011 from http://www.huffingtonpost.com/2011/03/15/obama-gun-laws-congress_n_836138.html

XXII Ed Morrissey. (May 25, 2011). Obama: We're working on gun control "under the radar". Retrieved May 29, 2011 from http://hotair.com/archives/2011/05/25/obama-were-working-on-gun-control-under-the-radar/

Chapter IV: Your *Right* to Healthcare

I Medicare. (Jan. 2011). What is Medicare? Retrieved Jan. 25, 2011 from http://ssa.gov/pubs/10043.html#part2

II Medicaid. (n.d.). Description. Retrieved Jan. 26, 2011 from http://www.surgeryencyclopedia.com/La-Pa/Medicaid.html

III Jim Kouri, Examiner.com. (July 23, 2009). $Billions in Medicare/Medicaid lost to fraud, abuse. Retrieved Jan. 29, 2011 from http://www.examiner.com/law-enforcement-in-national/billions-medicare-medicaid-lost-to-fraud-abuse

IV 60 Minutes. (Oct. 25, 2009). Medicare Fraud: A $60 Billion Crime. Retrieved Jan. 29, 2011 from http://www.cbsnews.com/stories/2009/10/23/60minutes/main5414390.shtml

V Media Health Leaders. (Jan. 25, 2011). Medicare Fraud Recovery Totaled $4B in 2010. Retrieved Jan. 26, 2011 from http://www.healthleadersmedia.com/content/FIN-261710/Medicare-Fraud-Recovery-Totaled-4B-in-2010##

VI Center on Budget and Policy Priorities. (April 14, 2010). Policy Basics: Where Do Our Federal Tax Dollars Go? Retrieved Jan. 26, 2011 from http://www.cbpp.org/cms/index.cfm?fa=view&id=1258

VII Rasmussen Reports. (Jan. 3, 2011). Health Care Law. Retrieved Jan. 8, 2011 from http://www.rasmussenreports.com/public_content/politics/current_events/health care/health_care_law

VIII FoxNews.com. (Jan. 18, 2011). Health Law Looks Shaky. Retrieved Jan. 25, 2011 from http://www.foxnews.com/politics/2011/01/18/heath-law-looks-shaky-abortion-fight-renewed-china-wont-blink/

^{IX} Republican Ways & Means Committee. (April 14, 2010). Democrats Have Increased Taxes by $670 Billion and Counting…. Retrieved Sept. 21, 2011 from http://republicans.waysandmeans.house.gov/UploadedFiles/DemTaxIncreases1.pdf

^X Kevin Hassett, Bloomberg Columnist. (Aug. 1, 2010). Obamacare Only Looks Worse Upon Further Review: Kevin Hassett. Retrieved Jan. 31, 2011 from http://www.bloomberg.com/news/2010-08-02/obamacare-only-looks-worse-upon-further-review-kevin-hassett.html

^{XI} Paul Bedard. (Feb.15, 2011). Health care Reform Law Requires New IRS Army Of 1,054. Retrieved Feb. 16, 2011 from http://www.usnews.com/news/blogs/washington-whispers/2011/02/15/healthcare-reform-law-requires-new-irs-army-of-1054

^{XII} KaiserEdu.org. (March. 2010). U.S. Health Care Costs. Retrieved Jan. 31, 2011 from http://www.kaiseredu.org/Issue-Modules/US-Health-Care-Costs/Background-Brief.aspx

^{XIII} Ricardo Alonso-Zaldivar, Associated Press. (Nov. 4, 2010). Citing health overhaul, AARP hikes employee costs. Retrieved Jan. 29, 2011 from http://news.yahoo.com/s/ap/20101104/ap_on_bi_ge/us_aarp_health_plan

^{XIV} Duke Helfand, Los Angeles Times. (Jan. 5, 2011). Blue Shield of California rate increase prompts criticism. Retrieved Jan. 29, 2011 from http://latimesblogs.latimes.com/money_co/2011/01/rate-increase-by-blue-shield-of-california-prompts-criticism.html

^{XV} A CBO Study. (Dec. 2006). Consumer Directed Healthplans: Potential Effects on Health Care Spending and Outcomes. Retrieved Jan. 31, 2011 from http://www.cbo.gov/ftpdocs/77xx/doc7700/12-21-HealthPlans.pdf

^{XVI} Philip Klein. (Jan. 7, 2011). BREAKING: CBO Says Repealing ObamaCare Would Reduce Net Spending by $540 Billion. Retrieved Jan. 31, 2011 from http://spectator.org/blog/2011/01/07/breaking-cbo-says-repealing-ob

^{XVII} U.S. Department of Health & Human Services. (Dec. 3, 2010). Approved Applications for Waiver of the Annual Limits Requirements of the PHS Act Section 2711. Retrieved Jan. 8, 2011 from http://www.hhs.gov/ociio/regulations/approved_applications_for_waiver.html

^{XVIII} Matthew Boyle–The Daily Caller. (May 17, 2011). Gov. Sarah Palin on Pelosi district's Obamacare waivers: 'Seriously, this is corrupt'.

Retrieved May. 17, 2011 from http://dailycaller.com/2011/05/17/ gov-sarah-palin-on-pelosi-districts-obamacare-waivers-seriously-this-is- corrupt/

XIX Sheldon Richman. (Aug. 1995). The Commerce Clause: Route to Omnipotent Government. Retrieved Feb. 5, 2011 from http://www.fff. org/freedom/0895g.asp

XX Tony Messenger. (Aug. 4, 2010). Prop C passes overwhelmingly. Retrieved Feb. 7, 2011 from http://www.stltoday.com/news/local/govt- and-politics/article_c847dc7c-564c-5c70-8d90-dfd25ae6de56.html

XXI Ballot Pedia. (July 30, 2010). Florida Health Care Freedom, Amendment 9 (2010). Retrieved Feb. 7, 2011 from http://ballotpedia. org/wiki/index.php/Florida_Health_Care_Freedom,_Amendment_9_ (2010)

XXII Associated Press. (Sept. 13, 2010). 20 States Prepare for Day in Court Against Health Care Law. Retrieved Feb. 12, 2011 from http:// www.foxnews.com/politics/2010/09/13/states-prepare-day-court-health- care-law/

XXIII Case 3:10CV188-HEH. (Dec 13, 2010). IN THE UNITED STATES DISTRICT COURT FOR THE EASTERN DISTRICT OF VIRGINIA. Retrieved Sept. 21, 2011 from http://www.justice.gov/health care/docs/cucinelli-v-sebelius-memo-opinion-summary-judgment.pdf

XXIV Kaiser Health News. (Jan 31, 2011). Text: Judge Vinson's Decision On Health Law. Retrieved Sept. 21, 2011 from http://www. kaiserhealthnews.org/Stories/2011/January/31/Florida-Judge-Rules- Health-Law-Unconstitutional-Text.aspx

XXV Sarah Lyall, New York Times. (July 24, 2010). Britain Plans to Decentralize Health Care. Retrieved Feb. 12, 2011 from http://www. nytimes.com/2010/07/25/world/europe/25britain.html?_r=3&hp

XXVI Sally C. Pipes, Save Your Rights. (Jan 1, 2011). Has Massachusetts Experience Put ObamaCare On A Path To Repeal? Retrieved Feb. 12, 2011 from http://www.saveyourrights.com/health care-reform/ massachusetts-healthcare-model-a-microcosm-of-obamacare-is-an- exorbitant-and-abject-failure/

XXVII The O'Reilly Factor. (May 24, 2010). Segment on Mitt Romney's Presidential Bid and Overcoming Romney Care, Episode 348, Fox News Channel.

XXVIII Speaker.gov. (Nov 4, 2009). Republicans' Common-Sense

Reforms Will LOweR HEALTH CARE COSTS. Retrieved Feb. 12, 2011 from http://www.speaker.gov/UploadedFiles/Summary_of_Republican_Alternative_Health_Care_plan_Updated_11-04-09.pdf

[xxix] Justinian Lane. (March 1, 2004). What Is Tort Reform – And Why Is It Bad For The Public? Retrieved Feb. 14, 2011 from http://www.justinian.us/2004/03/what-is-tort-reform-and-why-is-it-bad-for-the-public.html

[xxx] NCPA.org. (n.d.). Interstate Competition in the Individual Health Insurance Marketplace. Retrieved Feb. 14, 2011 from http://www.ncpa.org/healthcare/interstate-competition-in-the-individual-health-insurance-marketplace

Chapter V: Taxes and Government Waste

[i] Supreme Court Justice Paterson in Hylton v US. (3 US 171 [1796]). Direct Tax Apportionment clause. Retrieved Dec. 6, 2010 from http://www.usconstitution.net/glossary.html#APPORTIONMENT

[ii] Finding Dulcinea. (June 1, 2010). On This Day: Congress Passes Act Creating First Income Tax. Retrieved June 11, 2011 from http://www.findingdulcinea.com/news/on-this-day/July-August-08/On-this-Day—Congress-Enacts-First-Income-Tax.html

[iii] Merriam Webster. (n.d.). Definition of extortion. Retrieved Dec. 7, 2010 from http://www.merriam-webster.com/dictionary/extortion

[iv] Jason Morgan. (April 22, 2009), How Much Do You Really Pay in Taxes? Retrieved Dec. 7, 2010 from http://www.babeled.com/2009/04/22/how-much-do-you-really-pay-in-taxes/

[v] Bureau of Labor Statistics. (Nov. 2010). Table A-1 Employment status of the civilian population by sex and age. Retrieved Dec. 8, 2010 from http://www.bls.gov/news.release/empsit.t01.htm

[vi] US Debt Clock.org. (n.d.). Retrieved Dec. 8, 2010 from http://www.usdebtclock.org

[vii] U.S. Census Bureau. (2000). U.S. & World Population Clocks. Retrieved Dec. 8, 2010 from http://www.census.gov/main/www/popclock.html

[viii] John Stossel. (Oct. 7, 2010). Description of CBO Graphs during a discussion on Stossel's show, Episode 36, Fox Business Network.

[IX] WordIQ.com. (n.d.). Taxation in the United States – Definition. Retrieved Dec. 18, 2010 from http://www.wordiq.com/definition/Taxation_in_the_United_States

[X] Matt Cover, CNS News. (Sept. 13, 2010). Feds Spent $800,000 of Economic Stimulus on African Genital-Washing Program. Retrieved Jan. 3, 2011 from http://cnsnews.com/news/article/75198

[XI] Brian Riedl, The Heritage Foundation. (June 1, 2010). Federal Spending by the Numbers 2010. Retrieved Jan. 29, 2011 from http://www.heritage.org/research/reports/2010/06/federal-spending-by-the-numbers-2010

[XII] Jeff Mason, Red White Blue News. (Sept. 21, 2010). US taxpayers to give UN $50 million for stoves. Retrieved Jan. 3, 2011 from http://redwhitebluenews.com/?p=2562

[XIII] Ernie, Smith, AOL News. (July 21, 2010). Congress' Food Tab: $604,000 for Bottled Water, $152 at Quiznos. Retrieved Jan. 3, 2011 from http://www.aolnews.com/2010/07/21/congress-food-tab-604-000-for-bottled-water-152-at-quiznos/

[XIV] Fox News. (Aug. 19, 2010). Obama's Fundraising Spree Costs Taxpayers $2M, Analyst Estimates. Retrieved Jan. 3, 2011 from http://www.foxnews.com/politics/2010/08/19/obamas-fundraising-spree-costs-taxpayers-m-analyst-says/

[XV] Associated Press. (Dec. 30, 2010). Audit Finds CDC Misplaced $8M in Equipment. Retrieved Jan. 4, 2011 from http://www.foxnews.com/politics/2010/12/30/audit-finds-cdc-misplaced-m-equipment/

[XVI] John Cook. (Nov. 12, 2010). White House Staffers Got a Bigger Raise Than You Did Last Year. Retrieved Jan. 4, 2011 from http://gawker.com/5687778/white-house-staffers-got-a-bigger-raise-than-you-did-last-year

[XVII] Kim Gamel, The Daily Caller. (Aug. 29, 2010). AP IMPACT: US wasted billions in rebuilding Iraq. Retrieved Jan. 3, 2011 from http://dailycaller.com/2010/08/29/ap-impact-us-wasted-billions-in-rebuilding-iraq/

[XVIII] Clynton Namuo. (Nov. 4, 2010). UNH scientists to study cow burps … and more. Retrieved Jan. 4, 2011 from http://www.unionleader.com/article.aspx?headline=UNH+scientists+to+study+cow+burps+.+.+.+and+more&articleId=c43c3680-3551-47ed-be8a-0b5b87880d6e

[XIX] Stephen Ohlemacher, Associated Press. (Oct. 7, 2010). 72,000 stimulus payments went to dead people. Retrieved Jan. 3, 2011 from http://news.yahoo.com/s/ap/20101007/ap_on_go_ca_st_pe/us_stimulus_checks_dead_people

[XX] The Wasington Examiner. (Dec. 1, 2010). The Daily Outrage: More on why our economy is going extinct. Retrieved Jan. 4, 2011 from http://washingtonexaminer.com/opinion/daily-outrage/2010/12/daily-outrage-more-why-our-economy-going-extinct

[XXI] Joshua Rhett Miller. (Nov. 12, 2010). DOJ Gave Millions to Illegal Immigrant 'Sanctuaries,' Report Finds. Retrieved Jan. 4, 2011 from http://www.foxnews.com//us/2010/11/12/doj-gave-millions-sanctuary-communities-report-finds/

[XXII] Rachel Stevens, Federal News Radio. (July 27, 2010). SIGIR: Defense can't account for $8.7 billion. Retrieved Jan. 3, 2011 from http://www.federalnewsradio.com/?sid=2012362&nid=35

[XXIII] Ed Barnes. (Oct. 22, 2010). Up to $1 Billion in U.S. Aid Winds Up In Taliban Coffers. Retrieved Jan. 4, 2011 from http://www.foxnews.com/politics/2010/10/27/aid-winds-taliban-coffers/

[XXIV] Jonathan Karl, Matthew Jaffe and Gregory Simmons, Good Morning America. (Aug. 3, 2010). Stimulus Slammed: Republican Senators Release Report Alleging Waste. Retrieved Jan. 3, 2011 from http://abcnews.go.com/GMA/summer-recovery-slammed-stimulus-waste-report-released/story?id=11309090

[XXV] Merriam Webster. (n.d.). Definition of earmark. Retrieved Jan. 11, 2011 from http://www.merriam-webster.com/dictionary/earmark

[XXVI] Wikipedia. (n.d.). Definition of pork barrel. Retrieved Jan. 11, 2011 from http://en.wikipedia.org/wiki/Pork_barrel

[XXVII] Center on Budget and Policy Priorities. (April 14, 2010). Policy Basics: Where Do Our Federal Tax Dollars Go? Retrieved Dec. 14, 2010 from http://www.cbpp.org/cms/index.cfm?fa=view&id=1258

[XXVIII] FoxNews.com. (Jan. 27, 2011). Social Security Fund to Be Empty by 2037. Retrieved Jan. 29, 2011 from http://www.foxnews.com/politics/2011/01/27/social-security-fund/

Chapter VI: Government
Bailouts and Stimulus

[I] Richard Heinberg. (Jan. 31, 2011). Stimulus duds, bailout blanks. Retrieved Feb. 19, 2011 from http://www.energybulletin.net/stories/2011-01-31/stimulus-duds-bailout-blanks

[II] Srote, Robert. (Jan. 11, 2011). Wildfire – The Legislation that Ignited the Great Recession. St. Louis: Tate Publishing.

[III] Edmonds.com. (Oct. 28, 2009). Cash for Clunkers Results Finally In: Taxpayers Paid $24,000 per Vehicle Sold, Reports Edmunds.com. Retrieved March 12, 2011 from http://www.edmunds.com/about/press/cash-for-clunkers-results-finally-in-taxpayers-paid-24000-per-vehicle-sold-reports-edmundscom.html?articleid=159446&

[IV] David Goldman. (Nov. 16, 2009). CNNMoney.com's bailout tracker. Retrieved Feb. 23, 2011 from http://money.cnn.com/news/storysupplement/economy/bailouttracker/index.html

[V] Jim Powell. (Feb. 11, 2009). The 'Old' New Deal Still Isn't Paid For. Retrieved Feb. 28, 2011 from http://www.cato.org/pub_display.php?pub_id=9971

[VI] www.wikipedia.org. (n.d.). New Deal. Retrieved Feb. 26, 2011 from http://en.wikipedia.org/wiki/New_Deal

[VII] John Stossel. (July 23, 2011). Union Segment on Stossel. Fox News Channel.

[VIII] Barry Ritholtz, The Bailout Nation. (Nov. 25, 2008). Bailout costs more than Marshall Plan, Louisiana Purchase, moonshot, S&L bailout, Korean War, New Deal, Iraq war, Vietnam war, and NASA's lifetime budget — *combined*!. Retrieved Feb. 19, 2011 from http://boingboing.net/2008/11/25/bailout-costs-more-t.html

[IX] Citizen News. (Dec.3, 2010). Unemployment rate 9.8 percent, Worst stretch since World War II, 19 months above 9 percent. Retrieved Feb. 28, 2011 from http://citizenwells.com/2010/12/03/unemployment-rate-9-8-percent-december-3-2010-worst-stretch-since-world-war-ii-19-months-above-9-percent/

[X] Jonathan Karl, Matthew Jaffe and Gregory Simmons. (Aug. 3, 2010). Stimulus Slammed: Republican Senators Release Report Alleging Waste. Retrieved March 1, 2011 from http://abcnews.go.com/GMA/summer-recovery-slammed-stimulus-waste-report-released/story?id=11309090

[XI] Jia Lynn Yang, Neil Irwin and David S. Hilzenrath. (Dec. 2, 2010). Fed aid in financial crisis went beyond U.S. banks to industry, foreign firms. Retrieved March 1, 2011 from http://www.washingtonpost. com/wp-dyn/content/article/2010/12/01/AR2010120106870. html?sid=ST2010120106876

[XII] Byron York. (Dec. 19, 2010). Report: In Obama's Chicago, stimulus weatherization money buys shoddy work, widespread fraud. Retrieved March 1, 2011 from http://washingtonexaminer.com/blogs/beltway-confidential/report-obamas-chicago-stimulus-weatherization-money-buys-shoddy-work-wides

[XIII] Gregory Korte. (Dec. 6, 2010). $162 million in stimulus funds not disclosed. Retrieved March 1, 2011 from http://www.usatoday.com/news /washington/2010-10-06-stimulus06_ST_N.htm

[XIV] Yahoo News. (Feb. 27, 2011). Madoff to NY magazine: Government a Ponzi scheme. Retrieved Feb. 28, 2011 from http://finance.yahoo.com/ news/Madoff-to-NY-magazine-apf-2369562769.html?x=0&.v=2

[XV] Veronique de Rugy. (Feb. 4, 2011). The Mercatus Center, George Mason University. Retrieved March 5, 2011 from http://mercatus.org/ sites/default/files/publication/Stimulus%20Facts%207%20(for%20 web).xls

[XVI] William Lajeunesse. (Sept. 17, 2010). L.A.: $111M in Stimulus Saved Just 55 Jobs. Retrieved March 5, 2011 from http://www.foxnews. com/politics/2010/09/16/los-angeles-official-disappointed-city-used-stimulus-funds/

[XVII] Rick Santelli. (March 4, 2011). Santelli: 'Good' Jobs Report Has Dark Side. Retrieved March 9, 2011 from http://www.cnbc.com/ id/41911006

[XVIII] Brian McDowell. (Nov. 3, 2010). Stimulus Funds–Tracking the local dollars and jobs. West Newsmagazine, pp. 34-35.

[XIX] Staff Reporter, TheSun.co.uk. (Oct. 20, 2010). Osborne wields spending axe. Retrieved March 12, 2011 from http://www.thesun.co.uk/ sol/homepage/news/3189051/Chancellor-George-Osborne-wields-spending-axe.html

[XX] HM Treasury. (Nov. 22, 2010). Spending Review. Retrieved March 12, 2011 from http://www.hm-treasury.gov.uk/spend_index.htm

[XXI] U.S. Small Business Administration. (n.d.). How important are small businesses to the U.S. economy? Retrieved March 12, 2011 from http://www.sba.gov/advocacy/7495/8420

XXII Harvey Katz. (Jan. 13, 2011). The Real Unemployment Rate–January 13, 2011. Retrieved March 5, 2011 from http://www.valueline.com/Markets/Commentary.aspx?id=10133

XXIII Terence P. Jeffrey. (Dec. 27, 2010). 111th Congress Added More Debt Than First 100 Congresses Combined: $10,429 Per Person in U.S. Retrieved March 12, 2011 from http://www.cnsnews.com/news/article/111th-congress-added-more-debt-first-100

Chapter VII: A New Amendment

I Hamilton Abert Long. (n.d.). A Principle of The Traditional American Philosophy. Retrieved August 9, 2011 from http://www.lexrex.com/enlightened/AmericanIdeal/yardstick/pr5.html

II James Madison. (n.d.). Memorial and Remonstrance Against Religious Assessments. Retrieved August 16, 2011 from http://religiousfreedom.lib.virginia.edu/sacred/madison_m&r_1785.html

III Stossel. (Jan. 13, 2011). Will Washington Change segment. Fox Business Channel.

IV J. D. Heyes. (Aug. 10, 2011). U.S. debt crisis worsens as borrowing tops 100 percent of GDP. Retrieved August 16, 2011 from http://www.naturalnews.com/033274_debt_crisis_borrowing_money.html

V David Logan. (Aug. 19, 2011). Warren Buffett's Taxing the Rich Won't Solve Deficit, Says Tax Foundation. Retrieved August 21, 2011 from http://www.cnsnews.com/news/article/warren-buffett-s-tax-solution-won-t-solv

VI Stossel. (Jan. 29, 2011). State of the Union episode. Fox Business Channel.

VII Benjamin H. Friedman and Christopher Preble. (Nov. 2010). A Plan to Cut Military Spending. Retrieved August 18, 2011 from http://www.downsizing government.org/defense/cut_military_spending

VIII Amanda Carey. (Jan. 31, 2011). Republican lawmakers begin assault on Fannie Mae and Freddie Mac. Retrieved August 26, 2011 from http://dailycaller.com/2011/01/31/republican-lawmakers-begin-assault-on-fannie-mae-and-freddie-mac/

IX Jake Tapper. (March 25, 2011). General Electric Paid No Federal

Taxes in 2010. Retrieved June 19, 2011 from http://abcnews.go.com/Politics/general-electric-paid-federal-taxes-2010/story?id=13224558

[X] Fred Barnes. (Jan. 21, 2011). Jeffrey Immelt, Obama's Pet CEO. Retrieved June 19, 2011 from http://www.weeklystandard.com/blogs/jeffrey-immelt-obama-s-pet-ceo_536837.html

[XI] Stuart Varney. (April 25, 2011). The O'Reilly Factor. Fox News Channel.

[XII] Veronique Derugy & Nick Gillespie. (Feb. 17, 2011). Stossel. Fox Business Channel.

[XIII] John Stossel. (April 14, 2011). Stossel. Fox Business Channel.

[XIV] Illinois Policy Institute. (Aug. 19, 2011). Policy Chart: Illinois Loses Most Jobs in the Nation. Retrieved August 24, 2011 from http://www.illinoispolicy.org/news/article.asp?ArticleSource=4362

[XV] Stossel. (March 17, 2011). Government Redundancy. Fox Business Channel.

[XVI] Center on Budget and Policy Priorities. (April 14, 2010). Policy Basics: Where Do Our Federal Tax Dollars Go? Retrieved Dec. 14, 2010 from http://www.cbpp.org/cms/index.cfm?fa=view&id=1258

[XVII] Conservative Home. (March 23, 2011). Stossel talks welfare reform on Fox. Retrieved April 6, 2011 from http://www.foxnews.com/on-air/your-world-cavuto/index.html

[XVIII] The O'Reilly Factor. (April 5, 2011). Stossel talks welfare reform with Bill O'Reilly. Retrieved April 9, 2011 from http://www6.lexisnexis.com/publisher/EndUser?Action=UserDisplayFullDocument&orgId=574&topicId=100007424&docId=l:1393060052&start=4

Glossary

[I] USLegal.com. (n.d.). Definitions of various types of taxes. Retrieved Dec. 15, 2010 from http://definitions.uslegal.com/

[II] Merriam Webster. (n.d.). Definitions. Retrieved Dec. 7, 2010 from http://www.merriam-webster.com/dictionary/

[III] U.S. Constitution Online. (n.d.). Constitutional Topic: Due Process. Retrieved Jan. 8, 2011 from http://www.usconstitution.net/consttop_duep.html

[IV] Wikipedia.org. (n.d.). Mead. Retrieved March 28, 2011 from http://en.wikipedia.org/wiki/Mead

[V] 1828 Webster's Dictionary. (n.d.). 1828 Definition. Retrieved March 28, 2011 from http://www.1828-dictionary.com/d/word/victualing-house

[VI] Wikipedia.org. (n.d.). Founding Fathers of the United States. Retrieved April 20, 2011 from http://en.wikipedia.org/wiki/Founding_Fathers_of_the_ United_States

[VII] InvestorWords.com. (n.d.). GDP. Retrieved August 17, 2011 from http://www.investorwords.com/2153/GDP.html

[VIII] thefreedictionary.com. (n.d.). underemployed. Retrieved September 25, 2011 from http://www.thefreedictionary.com/underemployed